Interrogating Belonging for Young People in Schools

Christine Halse
Editor

Interrogating Belonging for Young People in Schools

palgrave
macmillan

Editor
Christine Halse
The Education University of Hong Kong
Hong Kong, China

ISBN 978-3-319-75216-7   ISBN 978-3-319-75217-4   (eBook)
https://doi.org/10.1007/978-3-319-75217-4

Library of Congress Control Number: 2018936142

Cover illustration: Brain light / Alamy Stock Photo

Printed on acid-free paper

This Palgrave Macmillan imprint is published by the registered company Springer International Publishing AG part of Springer Nature.
The registered company address is: Gewerbestrasse 11, 6330 Cham, Switzerland

For the young people who are our world's future

Preface

This book had an unusual genesis. It is a tale worth recounting because it serves as a message—even a moral—to those academics and researchers who feel alone, isolated and crave for an intellectual space, place and community where they feel they can belong. The book's genesis is also unusual because it was a pleasurable, positive consequence of Australia's research assessment exercise known as 'Excellence in Research' (ERA)—that intensive, periodic, bureaucratic exercise in research accountability and governmentality that haunts academics and universities around the globe.

Reflecting on the publications submitted for ERA, it seemed self-evident that the School of Education at Deakin University had a group of highly-talented scholars doing cutting-edge research on issues of gender and sexuality, race, intercultural relations and multicultural education, as well as citizenship and class. Many worked with post-structural theory but would describe their research field as falling in the gamut of education sociology. However, they largely worked independently and in isolation, publishing in different journals and attending different conferences. Many were only vaguely aware of the work done by their colleagues or the potential intellectual connections and intersections in their research interests and scholarship.

These conditions gave birth to a collaborative reading and writing group called the 'Critical Studies of Young People Research Group'.

We comprised 12 academics. Overwhelming, our group comprised women at the beginning or middle of their careers, with a couple of exceptions.

We set up our group by agreeing on some 'ground rules'. First, we set ourselves a common theoretical goal, namely to interrogate the concept of belonging and its salience to our research interests. Second, we set up a *modus operandi*. We would read and critique various theories of belonging, relate these to our respective research in education, and to develop ways for collaborative writing—a new experience for many—about belonging for young people in schools. We also undertook to fulfil these ambitions by meeting for two hours, face-to-face, every month for 12 months. This was a significant commitment because we all worked on different campuses, the furthest of which were 270 km apart. But the benefits of face-to-face meetings, colleagues agreed, outweighed the burden of travelling between 1.5 and 4 hours (one way). We swapped the meeting location occasionally to share around the travelling and, in hindsight, we might have done better in sharing the burden more equably.

I expected attendance to fall off quickly as the weight of the travel and busy-ness of teaching, marking and academic administration swamped us. To the contrary, the diligence of the Critical Studies of Young People Research Group surprised us all. Our monthly meetings became the event we all looked forward to and only extraordinary circumstances, such as the birth of a child, caused us to miss meetings or fail to complete the readings we took turns setting and leading in discussions. What's more, our meetings soon morphed into half or full day events. It was just too easy to continue once we started talking and writing. And our initial 12-month commitment stretched out to nearly 20 months until one of us moved universities and the group's composition was altered by internal, structural changes with the university.

Until this time, and despite the busy-ness of academic life, we treated our research as we did our teaching: preparing, turning up and completing our follow-up tasks and writing. The regular meeting of our group gave us the space and place where we felt comfortable, 'at home' and where we belonged. These meetings also gave us permission: to stop; to think, talk and engage with colleagues; and bring these activities together in our writing.

We also adopted a process for collaborative writing that was new to many in our group. We grouped ourselves according to the theoretical aspect of belonging we were interested in writing about, and revisited data from our *prior* individual research projects to identify extracts or elements that aligned with our theoretical concerns. We shared these with our writing team, selected the body of data that ignited our imaginations and, in some cases, reworked the data into an extended vignette. Chapters 1 and 15 are illustrations. Each team collectively analysed the vignette, drilling down into the theoretical insights the empirical data generated. We then allocated the task of writing up the analysis across team members and collaboratively read, reviewed and revised the multiple iterations.

We all felt the silent pressure of not letting our team down. This was productive pressure and we each worked hard to ensure we kept our respective commitments and obligations. I will not speak for others in the group but, at a personal level, it was one of the most collegial, engaging and authentic experiences of collaborative work that I have ever experienced.

There were two concrete products from our collective endeavours. The first was an international symposium on 'Interrogating belonging of young people'. The symposium was standing room only and had a waitlist, testifying to the interest in belonging generated among education researchers. Second, the publication of this edited collection. From the larger group of authors who presented at the symposium were drawn most of those whose chapters appear this collection. All these chapters are extensive revisions of the symposium papers, reshaped in the light of the ideas and thinking that emerged during the symposium and subsequent peer review. And some contributors have been added.

The commonality across the contributions to this collection is that authors bring theories of belonging from disciplines beyond the field of education *into dialogue* with empirical data. In particular, they focus on the tangible, material and desired ways young people experience, enact and understand belonging through their interactions with peers, teachers and practices in schools. Schools are critical sites in the construction of belonging and nonbelonging in young people's lives. Schools and schooling give young people the opportunities for the social interactions and educational experiences that create their present *and* open up possibilities for their futures. At the same time, schools are social institutions of the nation-state. Their purpose is to socialise and structure individuals into the values and practices that serve the interests of the social majority and nation state and, in doing so, risk reinforcing the marginalisation of those who do not meet normative expectations.

Bearing in mind these complexities, this book addresses three overarching questions:

1. How is 'belonging' understood, enacted and experienced among diverse young people in schools?
2. What pedagogies and practices do teachers and schools deploy that impact on young people's experience of youth and schools as places of 'belonging'?
3. How might belonging and non-belonging in schools be theorised in the light of these analyses?

Attending to these questions, each chapter examines a facet of belonging in the lives of young people. It is a collection that is directly relevant to academics and students of education, sociology of education, and related other disciplines. Its chapters will also provide new insights for teachers, school, and schooling. Each chapter engages with one or more central themes in education and the sociology of education including race, class, citizenship and national identity, gender and sexuality, curriculum, pedagogy and practices in schools. Each chapter, however, focuses unselfconsciously on the micro-detail and effects of belonging in the daily lives of young people across primary and secondary schools. In doing so, the authors variously address the spaces and places, flows, emotions and relationships to different peoples, objects, social structures and contexts through which belonging is constructed, enacted, experienced. These close, detailed analyses expose the diverse ways belonging is created, enacted and manifested, and how quickly and covertly belonging (and non-belonging) is done and undone.

Each section in the book concludes with a reflective commentary by an internationally renowned scholar. These commentaries engage with the ideas and arguments in the preceding chapters, relate them to the commentator's own work, and raise provocative political questions about the intersections of belonging, schooling and the everyday of young people's lives. Collectively, the chapters not only extend empirical analysis, thinking and theorising about belonging in new directions but construct a new grammar of belonging for education as a discipline and a field.

Hong Kong, China   Christine Halse

Acknowledgements

This book would not be possible without the contributions of many people. First and foremost, thanks is due to the collegiality, collaboration and sense of belonging generated by the 'Critical Studies of Young People Research Group', at Deakin University, Australia. The members of this group were Rosalyn Black, Claire Charles, Emma Charlton, Leanne Coll, Lyn Harrison, Catherine Hartung, Chris Hickey, Amanda Mooney, Debbie Ollis, and Emma Rowe. Thanks is also due to the Faculty of Arts and Education at Deakin, which provided funding to support the group's endeavours and the production of this book, and the on-going support of Deakin Strategic Centre for 'Research in Educational Impact' (REDI), particularly through its Director, Professor Julianne Moss. Sincere thanks also to the other authors who contributed to the collection, with particular thanks to the eminent scholars who found the time in their busy schedules to prepare provocative discussion essays. The production of any book also involves many heroes who work silently behind the scenes. In this instance, I was fortunate to have help from Holly Sellers who proofread the pre-production manuscript, Juliet Ritchers who prepared the index, Sarah Debelle who provided critical feedback on the cover graphics for the cover (with apologies if all her dreams could not be realised) and Eleanor Christie and her team from Palgrave Macmillan who patiently supported the project throughout. As often happens, one person stands out from the crowd. This book would not have been possible without the support of my friend, the wonderful Diana Langmead. It was Diana's fabulous organisational skills, talent for graciously but firmly getting authors to stay (mostly) on task and on time, her responsiveness to shifting deadlines, the delicious snacks she thoughtfully brought to all meetings, her enviable optimism and seemingly unending patience. For these contributions, I will forever be indebted.

Contents

Notes on Contributors

Peter Bansel (Western Sydney University, Australia), Senior Lecturer, is a member of Sexualities and Gender Research (SaGR) at the School of Social Sciences and Psychology. His interdisciplinary research focuses on the sociopolitical practices through which identities are formed, embodied and lived. This work focuses specifically on socially marginalised groups of young people and the impacts of this marginalisation on their health and well-being.

Aspa Baroutsis (The Queensland University of Technology, Australia) is a research fellow whose work explores socially just educational approaches for young people, with a methods focus on student voice and media constructions of schooling.

Rosalyn Black (Deakin University, Australia), Senior Lecturer of Education, researches young people's experience of citizenship in socially unequal contexts. She is co-author of *Rethinking Youth Citizenship after the Age of Entitlement* (forthcoming) and *Rethinking Digital Life: Young People's Perspectives on Safety, Risk, Inclusion and Citizenship* (Palgrave Macmillan, forthcoming).

Claire Charles (Deakin University, Australia), Senior Lecturer in Education Studies, researches how contemporary educational contexts prepare young people to engage with diversity and social justice issues in an era characterised by individualisation. She is author of *Elite Girls' Schooling, Social Class and Sexualised Popular Culture* (2014).

Emma Charlton (Deakin University, Australia) researches young people in relation to gender, sexuality and place, and how the differences attributed to these identity markers constitute ways of being in educational spaces.

Leanne Coll (Deakin University, Australia) lectures in Health & Physical Education and her research with young people centres on the conditions of possibility for transformational learning related to gender and sexualities in schooling.

Barbara Comber (University of South Australia) is a research professor in the School of Education. Her research interests include early career teachers, critical literacy, place-conscious pedagogies and social justice.

Hernan Cuervo (The University of Melbourne, Australia) is a senior researcher in the Youth Research Centre and lecturer and Associate Dean (Diversity & Inclusion) in the Graduate School of Education. His research interests are youth studies, rural education, inequality and theory of justice. His latest book is *Understanding Social Justice in Rural Education* (Palgrave Macmillan, 2016).

Mauro Giardiello (University of Roma Tre, Italy) is Professor of Sociology of Education in the Department of Educational Sciences. He researches youth culture and public space, social cohesion and generativity, and marginality. His latest book is *Marginality & Modernity* (2016).

Christine Halse (The Education University of Hong Kong, Hong Kong) is Chair Professor of Intercultural Education and Associate Dean (Research). Her research focuses on the sociology of race, identity and intercultural relations in educational contexts. She is editor of *Asia Literate Schooling in the Asian Century* (2015/2018) and *Responsibility and Responsibilisation* (2018; with Catherine Hartung and Jan Wright).

Lyn Harrison (Deakin University, Australia) is Honorary Associate Professor in Education whose research concerns young people, gender, sexuality education and the construction of 'risk'.

Chris Hickey (Deakin University, Australia) is a professor and Chair Academic Board. His research focuses on the relationship between young people, identity, social cohesion and exclusion, particularly in relation to gender in sport and physical education.

Adam Howard (Colby College, Maine, USA) is professor of Education and Director of Education with numerous articles and papers on social class issues in education, with a particular focus on privilege and elite education. His latest (co-authored) book is *Negotiating Privilege and Identity in Educational Contexts* (2014).

Kerry J. Kennedy (The Education University of Hong Kong), professor in the Department of Curriculum and Instruction and senior research fellow in the Centre for Governance and Citizenship, researches in civics and citizenship education and its cultural, social and political contexts. His most recent co-edited book is *Young People and Active Citizenship in Post-Soviet Times – A Challenge for Citizenship Education* (2018).

Tiffany Jones (La Trobe University, Australia) is an Australian Research Council DECRA Fellow, associate professor in the Australian Research Centre in Sex, Health and Society (ARCSHS) and a UNESCO advisor on LGBIQ issues. Her research focuses on issues affecting LGBTIQ young people, bullying and student well-being in education and health policy. She is author of *Policy and Gay, Lesbian, Bisexual, Transgender and Intersex Students* (2015).

Peter Kelly (RMIT University, Australia) professor at and Deputy Head of School for Research and Innovation, his most recent book is an edited collection entitled *A Critical Youth Studies for the 21st Century* (2015; with A. Kamp).

Julie McLeod (University of Melbourne, Australia) is Professor (Curriculum, Equity and Social Change) in the Melbourne Graduate School of Education, and Pro-Vice Chancellor (Research Capability). Her research in the history and sociology of education encompasses curriculum, youth, gender and feminist studies. Her most recent books are edited collections entitled *Rethinking Youth Wellbeing: Critical Perspectives* (Springer, 2015; with K. Wright) and *The Promise of the New: Genealogies of Educational Reform* (2015).

Martin Mills (Institute of Education, University College London) is a professor at and Director of the Centre for Research on Teachers and Teaching. He researches social justice in education, alternative schooling, gender and education, school reform and new pedagogies. He recently co-authored *Re-engaging Young People in Education: Learning from Alternative Schools* (2014).

Amanda Mooney (Deakin University, Australia) is Senior Lecturer in Health and Physical Education. She uses qualitative research methods to explore how cultural and societal factors, particularly gender, shape identities, practices and pedagogies in physical education, health and sport.

Hoa Nguyen (Colby College, USA) is an undergraduate student and research assistant to Professor Adam Howard. He is studying economics and mathematics, concentrating on financial markets.

Debbie Ollis (Deakin University, Australia), Associate Professor in Education, teaches and researches young people, gender and sexuality education with a particular focus on respectful relationships and gender-based violence.

Kitty te Riele (University of Tasmania, Australia) is Deputy Director (Research) of the Peter Underwood Centre. Her research focus is on youth studies in education, particularly policies and practices to engage marginalised young people. Her most recent book is *Interrogating Conceptions of 'Vulnerable Youth' in Theory, Policy and Practice* (2015; co-edited with R. Gorur).

Jessica Walton (Deakin University, Australia) is an Australian Research Council DECRA Fellow. Her current research examines transnational adoption, experiences of embodied identity and belonging, and children's interethnic relations in South Korea and Australia.

Bronwyn E. Wood (Victoria University of Wellington, New Zealand) has researched and published in the areas of youth citizenship participation, geographies of youth and citizenship education. Her work has been published widely, including in *Emotion, Space and Society*, *Children's Geographies*, *Political Geography* and the *British Journal of Sociology of Education*.

Annette Woods (Queensland University of Technology, Australia) is a professor in the School of Early Childhood and Inclusive Education in the Faculty of Education. Her research interests include literacy, pedagogy, school reform and social justice.

List of Figures

List of Tables

1

Theories and Theorising of Belonging

Christine Halse

Introduction

This collection of essays and commentaries appears at a critical moment in history. It is an era marked by increasing transnational mobility and interconnectedness and the largest flow of refugees and migrants fleeing war, persecution and poverty in search of a safer, better life in recorded history. Around the globe, it is also an era of resurgent conservatism, nationalism and nativism, increasing physical, social and political attacks on racial, ethnic, cultural and religious minorities, and growing social and economic disparities within and between societies.

Deeply entangled in these historical conditions are profound questions about what belonging—and not belonging—means, how it is enacted and experienced, and its effects on and implications for individuals, groups and societies. Some of these questions are: what criteria are deployed to

C. Halse (✉)
The Education University of Hong Kong, Hong Kong, China
e-mail: chalse@eduhk.hk

© The Author(s) 2018
C. Halse (ed.), *Interrogating Belonging for Young People in Schools*,
https://doi.org/10.1007/978-3-319-75217-4_1

mark particular individuals and groups as belonging or not belonging? Who has the authority and power to decide who is entitled and not entitled to 'belong'? What technologies, strategies, processes and social institutions are mobilised to enforce inclusion and exclusion? What privileges does belonging confer? How do the material, bodily and affective consequences of belonging/not belonging manifest themselves? What is lost or gained when individuals or groups are positioned as belonging/not belonging to the social majority? What are the personal, educational, social, political, economic and ethical implications for individuals and societies?

The contributors to this collection address such questions. They do so by bringing theories about belonging from disciplines *beyond* the field of education *into dialogue* with empirical data about the tangible, material and desired ways that young people experience, enact and understand belonging through their interactions with peers, teachers, schools and schooling practices. While attending to broader social and educational themes, each chapter offers a nuanced, micro-level analysis of the operation and experience of belonging and the haunting alternative of not belonging for young people, schools and schooling. These detailed analyses reveal the complexity of belonging as a theory, practice and mode of being, and its contemporary salience for young people and education.

The Concept of Belonging

Belonging has been described as 'still a rather new theoretical term' (Youkhana 2015, p. 12). Yet 'questions of belonging and the politics of belonging constitute some of the most difficult issues that are confronting all of us these days' as a new arena of political and cultural contestation (Yuval-Davis 2011, p. 1). For these reasons, the processes, practices and theories of belonging have become a subject of interest and interrogation across multiple disciplines. These include but are not limited to political science and social policy (e.g., Börner 2013; Yuval-Davis 2011; Yuval-Davis et al. 2006), gender studies (e.g., Cervantes-Carson and Rumens 2007), studies of religion (e.g., Day 2011), race relations (e.g., Garbutt 2011), sociology (e.g., Savage et al. 2005), migration studies (e.g., Singh and Babacan 2010; Steiner et al. 2013), social geography (e.g., Antonsich 2010; Taylor 2009; Wright 2015); psychology and adolescent health (Bernat and Resnick 2009; Resnick et al. 1997; Walton and Carr 2012); philosophy and cultural studies (e.g., Probyn 1996), and youth studies (e.g., Bauer et al. 2012; White and Wyn 2013).

In contrast, significantly less attention has been paid to how belonging operates and might be theorised in the field of education. Of course, there are important exceptions. A sizable body of research in educational psychology and learning theory demonstrates that young people both need and benefit from a sense of belonging in schools (e.g., Osterman 2000). The concept of belonging is also central to citizenship education (e.g., Carson 2006; Gill and Howard 2009), refugees in schools (e.g., Arnot et al. 2009; Arnot and Swartz 2012; Pinson et al. 2010), teaching minority populations (e.g., Maher 2014; Matthews 2008), international education (e.g., Fail et al. 2004) and social justice in education (Hayes and Skattebol 2015). Debra Hayes and Jen Skattebol (2015) show, for example, how the emotional attachments of disadvantaged youth to family and friends constructs a politics of belonging that is manifest in resistance to conventional schooling. However, the social justice practices of an alternative school that attends to these specific ways of belonging gives students a second chance at education that can address their social disadvantage.

Nevertheless, belonging is a broad concept that has been described as vaguely defined (see Crowley 1999) and under-theorised (see Anthias 2006; Antonsich 2010; Mee and Wright 2009). In scholarly convention, the term is used as encompassing all its grammatical variations, operating as a noun and a verb depending on its context. Thus, belonging can mean 'to belong' (v) or to possess or own something; it can also mean 'belongingness' (n), denoting that one belongs to and is a member of a particular social group, solidarity, collectivity or organisation.

What belonging involves, however, is not straightforward in a world of increasing racial, religious, ethnic, cultural and language diversity in schools, cities, societies and nations; growing digital connectedness that distributes values, ideas, practices and cultures across diverse local, national and transnational groups; and accelerating global interconnectedness of economies, businesses, education policy and systems. Each of these conditions constructs new social solidarities and fields of social interaction that find expression in the lives of individuals and their connectedness and belonging to specific social groups, collectivities and solidarities and particular places, spaces and times.

In his critique of liberal cosmopolitanism, Craig Calhoun (2003) argues that belonging or connectedness to particular social solidarities is intrinsic to the social world and central to the constitution of daily human life:

> …it is impossible not to belong to social groups, relations, or culture … real people … are necessarily situated in particular webs of belonging [and] people are implicated in social actions which they are not entirely free to choose…. Moreover, when the limits of belonging to specific webs of relationships are transcended, this is not into a freedom from relationships but into a different organization of relationships [that creates] a patchwork of new connections. (Calhoun 2003, pp. 536–537)

Because the belonging that arises through connectedness is an active social process of everyday life, it is necessarily always relational. This means it is produced through the co-constitutive interaction of individuals with other people, things, institutions and specific socio-cultural contexts. It is this intersection between the self and the social—how individuals belong—that works to 'define and configure what it means to belong (and not belong)' (Wright 2015, p. 393).

The dynamics and experiences of belonging also have social and political effects. They structure individuals and societies by feeding into the operation of social institutions, such as families, religions and governments. They assert hegemonic and counter-hegemonic symbolic and social practices including languages, values, and cultural practices. Belonging and belongingness can also create social cohesion. They coalesce individuals into social alignments based on shared commonalities, such as race, class, gender, sexuality, citizenship and national affiliation. These same processes of belonging can lead to the formation of new social solidarities and social fields of interaction that can open up possibilities for positive social change. They can also entrench old, or create new, differences and inequalities between social groups, places and spaces. It is in these ways that the operation and experience of belonging shapes the present lives of young people and their social, economic, political and moral futures.

Theories of Belonging

Given the complexity, disciplinary differences and profound implications of belonging, the following section discusses some of the key ideas and theories entangled in the concept of belonging that have shaped the contributions to this collection.

A useful starting point is to consider the concept of belonging in terms of one's attachment to particular social groups, social solidarities or social collectivities, all of which are terms with similar meanings deployed by different authors (cf. Calhoun 2003; Yuval-Davis 2006a). Like all members of society, young people participate in multiple social solidarities. Social solidarities are not immutable, unchanging entities defined by a single place, space, community or geographic location. They are groupings formed on the basis of shared values, attitudes and cultures, of emotional attachments to specific places, spaces, people, animals and material things, or by participating in specific flows of ideas, cultures and social practices. Calhoun (2003, pp. 547–548) provides examples that illustrate the very different ways in which social solidarities can be organised:

1. mutual interdependence in exchange, ranging from simple, concrete exchanges between individuals to the operation of large macro-level systems, such as the "economy";
2. sharing a common culture, such as speaking the same language, having the same referents or participating in the same habitual arguments;
3. membership of culturally defined categories, such as nation, class, gender, race, clan, etc.;
4. networks that join individuals in relationships, either directly where members are known to each other or indirectly where there is no direct personal interaction, as in the operation of a large bureaucracy or organization;
5. public communication, for example that knits and mobilizes diverse groups of strangers into a common identity and undertaking, such as opposing a war; and the

6. operation of material power, for example when individuals are conquered, enslaved or evicted from traditional landholdings and forced to form new relationships and collective self-understandings that shape their lives and relations together.

Belonging can operate on multiple scales, ranging from the home (e.g., Walsh 2006), to the nation state (e.g., Ho 2009; Westwood and Phizacklea 2000), through to transnational networks or global communities (e.g., Bromley 2000; Beck 2003). Thus, young people can be attached or belong to a seemingly endless number of social groups, solidarities and structures. These include their immediate family and peer group, social institutions such as school or church, and transnational and global networks constructed by, for example, social media and the globalisation of consumer cultures, sports and on-line games.

There is also a seemingly endless range of modes or ways of belonging to any particular place, space or social group. These differ according to the type of relationship, social solidarity or context in which individuals are positioned. For example, one mode of belonging is concrete and public. It consists of a formal relationship that is overtly recognised by others and/or affirmed or created by law. Examples might include being a recognised member of a formally constituted family or a citizen of a nation-state. A different mode of belonging involves the emotions. It expresses itself as a sense attachment or a feeling that one 'fits in' and belongs. Examples of this might include experiencing an emotional connection to a family, peer-group, or particular place or space, such as the family home, physical landscape, or nation.

Consequently, young people are not constrained by a single social solidarity characterised by a single set of hegemonic values, beliefs and practices. Rather, they are enmeshed in multiple, changing and often deterritorialised relationships and social solidarities. Their modes and ways of belonging are diverse and can vary according to the particular social group or solidarity.

Belonging to a particular social solidarity, however, does not condemn one to a perpetual, unchanging and unchangeable identity or destiny. By both circumstance and choice, individuals slip in and out of a sense, and identity, of belonging to particular places or social solidarities. This can sometimes occur with a frequency, speed and subtlety that is barely detectable until it is subjected to close scrutiny. It is through such mechanisms and processes that a subject position and identity of belonging or not belonging is conferred on individuals and either taken up, scorned or resisted.

It is such complexities that make belonging and its operation a tricky phenomenon to pin down. Yet, in everyday life, belonging tends to be naturalised, unspoken and unrecognised. It is only when it is subjected to scrutiny—which the authors in this collection do—or when it is threatened in some way that belonging and belongingness becomes noticed and a matter of contestation and politics. Nira Yuval-Davis (2004, 2006a, b, 2007, 2010, 2011), writing from the perspective of a political theorist, is one of the most influential scholars of belonging. She points out that

> [b]elonging is not just about membership, rights, and duties.... Nor can it be reduced to identities and identifications, which are about individual and collective narratives of self and other, presentation and labeling, myths of origin and destiny. Belonging is a deep emotional need of people. (2004, p. 215)

Yuval-Davis' work focuses on understanding and differentiating between *how* people belong and the *politics of belonging* that arise when different social groups interact. Belonging involves an emotional or ontological attachment of feeling 'at home' and in a 'safe space' even when these feelings are not warm and positive (2011, p. 10). She proposes that understanding how people belong entails three levels of analysis. The first level involves examining the social location of the individual. A social location might be, for example, one's age group, kinship group, profession, gender, race, class, nationality or citizenship status. Not all social locations exercise equal status, influence and/or power. Rather, social locations tend to be positioned hierarchically on different power axes. This gives them greater or lesser status and power depending on the particular social context, social solidarity or historical moment in which the individual is situated (Yuval-Davis 2006a, pp. 199–200). For example, in racialised contexts, a social location as 'white' has more social, economic and political clout (power) than being 'coloured' or 'black'; in a business or organisation, a social location as the 'boss' carries more influence and control (power) than being a 'junior administrator'; in a school, a 'teacher' has more status and authority (power) than a 'student'; within a nation, a 'citizen' has greater social and political rights (power) than a 'refugee'.

However, particular social locations, such as gender, sexuality, race, class or national identity, often overlap, meaning that an individual can occupy multiple social locations simultaneously, for example as a black, working class woman, or a wealthy, elderly, white male. The intersection of social locations often mediates their respective power and influence. Thus, reflecting the emergence of intersectionality as a key theoretical framework in feminist scholarship (e.g., Cooper 2004; Davis 2008; Gregoriou 2013; McCall 2005), Yuval-Davis (2006b, 2007) argues that it is necessary to adopt an intersectional approach by examining how an individual's different social locations interact, the shifting, interconnected dynamics of relations in social life, and the effects and implications of these interactions.

The second level for analysing belonging focuses on how individuals identify with and are attached to particular social solidarities or social collectivities. Identifications and attachments are performative because they come into being through repeated processes of 'doing' them. This means that individuals reiterate specific attitudes, values, behaviour and social practices that link them to particular social solidarities and socio-cultural spaces and, through this process, both construct and communicate a particular identity narrative that affirms her/his identifications and attachments (Yuval-Davis 2011). The strategies and processes individuals use to construct and communicate their individual identity narrative includes what they say, how they behave and their embodiment in specific sets of practices and ways of being in the world (see Fortier 2000). It also includes the stories that individuals tell about themselves that reveal the sort of person they are or are not (Martin 1995; Yuval-Davis 2006a). Identity, however, is always an iterative construction. It is

[b]oth reflective and constitutive. It is not individual or collective, but involves both in and in-between perpetual state of becoming in which processes of identity construction, authorization and contestation take place. (Yuval-Davis 2010, p. 271)

Nor do identity narratives merely bring particular individual identities and relationships into being. Directly or indirectly, they also reveal the characteristics of the social collective and context to which an individual is attached and what this belonging involves and means for the individual.

Identity narratives, however, are not rational, realist representations of a 'true' self. They are always a partial, incomplete, performance based on past and present experiences, conditions and the socio-cultural context. As I discuss in relation to written auto/biographical narratives (Halse 2006), individuals cannot artlessly retrieve truthful memories and their original meanings from the past. Nor can they depict the totality of their original lived experience or understandings. Rather, the identity narratives individuals construct and the attachments and identifications they form are always based on 'partial and selective' understandings that are 'colored by attitudes, beliefs and values; reconfigured by experience; and fashioned by language' (ibid., p. 97).

For these reasons, identity narratives reflect who individuals *believe* they are but also who they *desire* to be. That is, their emotional investments in belonging and being attached to particular places, spaces, objects and social solidarities, and the identity they attribute to or desire for these. It is this syncretic process that Elspeth Probyn (1996) captures in describing identity as a process of perpetual transition and varying degrees of attachment: 'individuals and groups are caught within wanting to belong, wanting to become, a process that is fueled by getting rather than positing of identity as a stable state' (Probyn 1996, p. 19).

The third level for understanding and analysing belonging is that it always involves ethical and political values and the different ways these 'are assessed and valued by the self and others' and 'in many different ways by people with similar social locations' who 'identify themselves as belonging to the same community or group' (Yuval-Davis 2011, p. 18). It is in this arena of ethical and political values that attitudes, beliefs, ideologies and discourses come into play and work to pressure, shape and create the conditions of possibility that determine how particular identities, categories and boundaries are articulated and drawn.

According to Yuval-Davis (2011, p. 18), there is always contestation about belonging and this moves us into the politics of belonging.

The politics of belonging arise from the existence of clear social collectivities and social, cultural and geographic boundaries; how membership, entitlements and status affect different groups; and the tensions, disagreement, battles and contestations that arise between people of different social locations, identifications and attachments, and ethical and political values (Yuval-Davis 2011). Thus, the politics of belonging are not merely about who belongs and does not belong but about the discursive processes that make belonging possible and able to be performed and experienced. As Yuval-Davis (2011, p. 19) reminds us, politics involves the exercise of actual and symbolic power. The politics of belonging therefore always involves both physical and symbolic boundaries that separate individuals in the world, maintain and reproduce these boundaries, and are open to contestation, challenge and resistance (Yuval-Davis 2011, p. 20).

The entanglement of belonging with boundary maintenance is obvious when we think about national belonging. The nation state is constructed by physical, geographic borders, institutionalised through in its political, legal, health, economic and educational systems, and by the ethics and values articulated through these institutions and in the public sphere. In combination, these discursive forces work to define who belongs (and is entitled to belong) and who does not belong in the nation state; who is a citizen or holds different levels of immigrant status; who is familial or a stranger; and who is an insider or an outsider.

In real life, however, belonging is rarely as categorical. For example, one can be native-born and a citizen of a nation but wear clothes that testify to a different cultural, religious or ethnic affiliation and that can signify, or be interpreted as signifying, strangerhood and otherness to the social majority. Nevertheless, when hegemony prevails and belongingness is mobilised to create the identities of social collectives or to construct social, cultural, institutional and territorial boundaries and rights that include some and exclude others, the politics of belonging can transform itself into a 'regime of belonging' (Pfaff-Czarnecka 2011).

Moving beyond the narrow politics of belonging configured in terms of the nation state, Ash Amin in his book *Land of Strangers* (2012) examines the new social collectivities that he calls the 'societies of strangers' that have emerged in a world of increasing economic interdependence and accelerating exchange of diverse ideas, skills and peoples.

He asks how do these bridge the gap between singularity and plurality to hold together? Amin (2012) uses the metaphor of the hub-and-spoke to represent the position of the individual in this new world. For him, the individual is the hub who is constantly accumulating and navigating a variety of attachments to different spokes through different people, objects, networks and repeated, reciprocal, bodily practices. For Amin, these attachments occur in multiple everyday sites, including the micro publics of active encounters such as at schools, workplaces and youth clubs where membership involves regular, invested participation in shared projects. He describes these attachments as 'dispersed affiliations' (2012, p. 13), and they are akin to the diverse, mutable and sometimes contradictory forms of social solidarity that Susanna Hall calls 'densely acquired networks of familiarity' (2012, p. 48) or that Calhoun describes as the overlapping and jostling pluralism of a 'web of relations' (2003, p. 536).

Antonsich (2010) presents a different position. Writing from the perspective of a geographer, he is critical of what he sees as an over-emphasis on belonging as attachment to the social collective and the over-looking the emotional and spatial connectedness to places and spaces. A sense of belonging, he proposes, arises from an individual's attachment to a familiar locality, territory, geographic place or symbolic space that gives one a feeling of being 'attached to and rooted' and where one feels comfortable, secure and at home (Antonsich 2010, p. 647). He describes this personal, intimate and existential sense of self and place attachment as a relationship of 'place-belongingness'. Drawing on the literature, he argues that five factors contribute to a relationship of 'place-belongingness': (i) autobiographical factors such as the personal history, experiences, relationships and memories that attach an individual to a particular place; (ii) relational factors or 'the personal and social ties that enrich the life of an individual' attached to a given place, such as friends and family members; (iii) cultural factors such as language, religion and cultural traditions and practices that evoke the 'warm sensation' of community and being among people who are like oneself; (iv) economic factors because these help create 'a safe and stable material condition for the individual and his/her family'; and (v) legal factors that affirm you are safe and belong, such as citizenship status or a residency permit (Antonsich 2010, pp. 647–648). Place-belongingness produces connectedness but it can also be 'a discursive resource which constructs, plans, justifies, or resists forms of socio-spatial inclusion/inclusion' and, in this way, creates disconnections and boundaries (ibid., p. 645). In contrast to other theories and theorists, Antonsich (2010) argues that the absence of a sense of place-belongingness does not mean one experiences separation or exclusion. This is not to confuse the effects of place-belongingness with those of a politics of belonging. Rather, he argues, the consequence of an absence of place-belongingness is affective and experienced as a sense of loneliness, isolation, alienation, and displacement.

Eva Youkhana (2015) extends this theorising about place and space further. She proposes that conceptions of the social solidarity or social collective are essentialised because they comprehend belonging only in terms of social, political and territorial boundaries and demarcations. In other words, a sort of geo-determinism that imagines space as a biophysical container. To the contrary, she proposes, the concept of belonging ought to be anchored in its colloquial meaning of 'a circumstance connected with a person or thing ... [that] comes into being between people and things, and between people and people' (Youkhana 2015, p. 16). These connections are fluid—'a rhizomatic and chaotic network' (ibid., p. 16) of material conditions and attachment to multiple, heterogeneous actors. Viewed in this way, belonging is 'a socio-material resource that arises by means of multiple situated appropriation processes and that describes multiple attachments that can be social, imagined, and sensual material in nature' (ibid., p.16).

Youkhana's (2015) conceptualisation raises a challenging question. If belonging and belongingness comes into being through these multiple threads and knots of connections, how can we comprehend their intersectional entanglement without unravelling them in ways that reassert their singularity and the problematic politics of boundary-making? The strategy, Youkhana (2015) proposes, is to use space as an analytical category or tool because space is a concept that cuts across all established social locations such as race, class, gender and life stages. This involves focusing on the flows of values, ideas, artefacts, material culture, social practices, infrastructures, personal relationships and connections *across* social locations and the constant appropriating and remaking of space by multiple, heterogeneous actors involved in the production of belonging (ibid., p. 11). Such an analytical approach involves examining belonging not just in terms of the complex relations of individuals with other people but directs our gaze to the importance of *things* and to the material semiotics of social relations. Thus, belonging is elucidated *through* the circulating objects, artefacts, and the changing social, political and cultural landscapes that mirror [and possibly construct?] material conditions and power relations and are reiterated in everyday practices, rituals and regimes of belonging (ibid., p. 16). Drawing on Lefebvre (2006), de Certeau (1980) and Joas (1994), Youkhana (2015) argues that focusing on the *movement of the material* enables us to see 'the creative poetic acts within everyday practices and how they transgress dominant ideologies, political practices, and the politics of social boundary making' (Youkhana 2015, p. 11).

Sarah Wright (2015) approaches the question of belonging from the critical perspective of a scholar working in the field of cultural geography. Wright (2015) argues that belonging is a complex term that has different meanings for different people. Rather than shutting down these multiple meanings and uses, we ought to acknowledge them by thinking about belonging as an emotion and attending to its textures. In other words, we ought to consider how belonging is felt, used, practised and lived.

> Seldom are questions asked to explore what belonging feels like; how it works as an emotional attachment and the significance for the emotionality of belonging. Belonging tends to have it taken for granted emotional nature that is seldom explored. (Wood and Waite 2011, p. 201 cited in Wright 2015, p. 397)

Acknowledging that relationships and circumstances are connected, multiple and in flux, Wright argues for examining 'how belonging is constituted by and through emotional attachments' and 'to consider the work that belonging-as-emotion does in creating subjectivities, collectivities and places' (Wright 2015, pp. 392–393). This involves, she argues, examining the processes of attunement and attachment, and how these are 'actively created by both human and more-than human agents, including animals, places, emotions, and flows' (ibid., p. 392).

Emotions have effects that can transform the lives of individuals and groups. Shared emotions connect people to objects and places and shared sentiments bring people together to create social solidarities, groups and collectivities. It is belonging-as-an-emotion or how we feel about others in our social group—feelings such as patriotism, fraternity or faith—that aligns us to the collective and brings the collective into being (Ahmed 2004, p. 27). It is this coming together in emotionally connected, relational ways that defines what it means to belong. Conversely, this sense and state of belonging is only made possible through the collective coming together of emotions (Wright 2015, p. 393).

Of course, the emotions that bring belonging into being can be positive, affirming feeling towards others in one's social collective *and/or* negative, destructive emotions (such as loathing, intolerance and racism) toward those strangers or outsiders who do not belong to one's collective. For these reasons, I agree that emotions play an important part in constructing belonging and social collectivities. But emotions-as-belonging can have risky, even dire, effects because emotions can circle back on themselves in ways that reinforce and entrench boundaries, contestation and the politics of belonging.

Psychology has a well-established record of research and scholarship into the character and effects of belonging and the connectedness of individuals to particular social groups, particularly in relation to school-aged young people, pedagogy and learning (see Beck and Malley 1998). In psychology, belonging and the imperative to belong and be connected is recognised as *so* important that it is described as a fundamental human need, drive and desire akin to the need for food and water (Baumeister and Leary 1995). Psychologists consider belonging/connectedness as important because *how* one belongs has significant effects and implications for the sort of life an individual is able to lead and leads. Research indicates that there is a strong, positive relationship between students' sense of belonging in schools and their participation and achievement (e.g., Cemalcilar 2010; Gibson et al. 2004; Osterman 2000) and their enjoyment of school (Furrer and Skinner 2003; Goodenow 1993). The nature and extent of students belonging or connectedness to family, peers, schools and community are also associated with differences in young people's cognitive processes, emotional behaviour, health and well-being

(Baumeister and Leary 1995). High levels of belonging/connectedness contribute to positive emotions, such as happiness, contentment and calm (Osterman 2000, p. 327) and are widely regarded one of the 'key determinants of health and well-being' (Bernat and Resnick 2009, p. 376). A strong sense of belonging is also significantly associated with lower rates of emotional distress, suicidality, violence, substance abuse and sexual activity (Resnick et al. 1997), as well as positive educational outcomes, including the development of psychological processes necessary for success in school such as positive academic attitudes and motivation, social and personal attitudes, high levels of engagement and participation, and academic achievement (Osterman 2000, p. 327). On the other hand, 'lack of belongingness often leads to negative emotions, including depression, anxiety, grief and loneliness, and 'is a primary cause' of mental and physical illnesses, and behavioural problems ranging from traffic accidents to criminality and suicide (Baumeister and Leary 1995, p. 511. Also Osterman 2000, p. 327).

Summary

The complexities of belonging make its processes and effects particularly salient and significant in the lives of school-aged young people at a time when dynamics of belonging can have significant implications for their present *and* future lives. This is because how young people experience belonging shapes their subjectivity, sense of self, social location and identity. It also defines and perpetually redefines their relationships with peers, family members and wider society. A positionality of belonging also mediates how young people engage with the practices and pedagogies of schools and schooling; whether they experience schools and schooling as positive sites of inclusion and accomplishment or as uncomfortable spheres of loneliness, exclusion and failure. How young people experience belonging shapes how they interact with other social institutions, such as family, school, religion, the legal system and police and judiciary, and the character and extent of their participation in different local, national and transnational groups and communities.

Yet, we need to be wary of valourising or being reductive about belonging. Not all forms of belonging are personally beneficial, socially sanctioned or a 'good' thing. Belonging to a gang of criminals or terrorists, for example, may give young people formal membership to a group and an emotional sense of attachment and 'being at home' but such belongings are socially undesirable as well as potentially damaging, personally and for society. Furthermore, belonging is always doubly constituted. Even when silent and unspoken, what describes the conditions of belonging and delimits its possibility is the ever-present spectre of oppositional Other—living a life as one who does not belong. Unbelonging can be imposed, for example when a government rejects a refugee's application for asylum, a religion ostracises a member of its flock, or a peer group shuns one of its members. Unbelonging can also be an act of individual or group agency, a conscious choice or deliberate resistance to the idea, position or experience of belonging. This would be the case, for example, when a young person deliberately rejects the beliefs and practices of racist, misogynist or homophobic group or consciously defies the rules and governmentality that are a condition for belonging in a school community (see Hayes and Skattebol 2015).

Regardless of the form it takes, the possibility of not belonging is a daunting, risky prospect. At the emotional level described by Antonsich (2010), not belonging threatens loneliness, isolation, alienation and displacement. In the political terms described by Yuval-Davis (2006a, b, 2011), not belonging can mean being marginalised or excluded from one's desired social group, community or collectivity—physically or psychically banished outside the boundaries of one's group to be ignored and, ultimately, forgotten. Social psychologists point out that people's interpersonal relationships are deeply affected by their membership or lack of membership of particular groups and their position within these groups. The need and desire of individuals to belong is universal and its roots lie in the dual fears of inferiorisation and exclusion (Lewin 1948; Billig 1976; Tajfel 1982). Yet, regardless of its processes and modality, it is the 'doubleness' of belonging—its Janus-like identity—that holds us captive. It is this that makes belonging *so* sweet and desirable and unbelonging *so* very scary and unsettling.

Overview of Contributions

Theories of belonging do not capture the lived experience of belonging: what it means and ways it is understood, how it is constructed and bought into being, how it is enacted and performed, its affects and effects for individuals, groups and societies, and how belonging is undermined and undone. It is for these reasons that Yuval-Davis (2011) stresses the imperative for 'case studies' that elucidate belonging. Each chapter in this collection offers such a focused study, honing in on the minutiae and sometimes seemingly mundane in young people's lives, connecting these with broader contextual conditions and exposing the complex processes of belonging in its making and unmaking among young people in schools.

The collection begins with Part I: 'Gender, Sexuality and Belonging'. The opening chapter is written by Emma Charlton, Leanne Coll, Lyn Harrison and Debbie Ollis. These scholars combine Louisa Allen's (2011, 2013) insights into the unofficial sites and ways that constellations of sex, gender and sexuality (Youdell 2005, 2010) stick in spaces and places in schools with Sarah Wright (2015) attention to the 'more than human', the constitutive process of belonging between 'people and things and processes and places' (Wright 2015, p. 393). Drawing on empirical data, they show how the unexpected presence of a jumping mat in a middle-class, middle-school, co-ed drama class leads the teacher to devise an impromptu, incidental activity that exposes the embodied nature of belonging in the classroom's pedagogical space. Their analysis reveals how the material (gendered uniforms, a jumping mat) combine in a specific, incidental pedagogical moment to reinforce and perpetuate normative stereotypes of sex-gender-sexuality, and that work to constitute young people as students who belong/do not belong and successful/unsuccessful in that particular pedagogical moment.

In Chap. 3, Peter Bansel examines how young people form and perform sexual subjectivities and identities at school and through digital social media. Drawing on empirical data from the *Growing up Queer* (Robinson et al. 2013) study, he elucidates the desire and 'longing to belong' of queer young people and their search for the 'truth of one's self' in on-line spaces and at school. He draws out the 'cruel optimism' of desires that inhibit flourishing (Berlant 2011) and the burdens and responsibilities of non-normative bodies to fit in, be at home and belong in institutions like schools (Ahmed 2012). He details the competing, contradictory discourses across the spaces of social media and schools, the heteronormative identities embedded in the values, pedagogy, and curriculum of the everyday classroom, and how the latter limits the capacity of queer young people to openly become, be recognisable and belong and how this inequitably curbs their possibilities for establishing a viable and 'good' life.

Tiffany Jones (Chap. 4) responds to the ideas in the two previous chapters, relating them to own personal experiences around issues of sexuality and gender for belonging in educational spaces, and her recent research on belonging among lesbian, gay, bisexual, transgender and intersex (LGBTI) students. In her discussion, she contemplates the value of pedagogy and policy, activism and direct coverage, and online education sites for promoting the belonging and the wellbeing of LGBTI students and the extent to which such strategies can address the educational drop-out rates across these groups.

Part II: *Race, Class, Citizenship and Nation*, begins with Jessica Walton's discussion of the politics of belonging and emerging 'multiculturalism' in South Korea. Bringing together the insights of Yuval-Davis (2006a) and Aihwa Ong (1996) on racial relations, she examines the inter-ethnic relations of primary school children, their experiences of racialised difference in the forced togetherness of school, how children navigate feelings of contested belonging, and their experiences of socialisation, rejection and marginalisation. Going beyond multicultural education, cultural or linguistic assimilation and an imagined national Korean identity, this chapter argues for an affective understanding of belonging in a society grappling with the meaning of belonging in the face of increasing ethnic diversity, past and present nation-building, and intensifying globalisation.

In Chap. 6, Rosalyn Black, Claire Charles and I show that children and young people are active participants in the racialised politics of belonging (Yuval-Davis 2011) by examining how they construct asylum seekers arriving in Australia. For some students, the spectre of the asylum seeker summons up the racialised rhetoric of populist politicians and media of asylum seekers as strangers and a threat to the nation's values and institutions who do not meet their criteria as 'desirable' citizens. Others adopt an ethical, humanist stance. They argue that asylum seekers are ordinary people—'just like us'—who have experienced extraordinary suffering and warrant the nation's compassion and care. A third group struggles to circumvent the inclusion/exclusion binary but their strategy of 'containing the stranger' merely reasserts the logic and methods of Britain's invasion and colonisation of Indigenous Australia. These students support 'caring' for asylum seekers, but propose doing this in purpose-built model towns located in geographically remote, unoccupied lands (terra nullius) where the asylum seekers will be 'separated from us' but 'still live in Australia'. Even among young students, this chapter reveals, racial discourses lie close to the surface and are readily resurrected in the politics of belonging and the 'dirty work of boundary making' (Crowley 1999).

In Chap. 7, Adam Howard and Hoa Nguyen examine how the practices in an elite private school intersect with social class to reinforce bonds of privilege and to shape belonging into a collective, privileged identity that defines students by *who they are* rather than what they *have*. Drawing on an ethnographic study in an elite boarding school in Jordan, this chapter reveals the strategies and values that instill a sense and community of privileged belonging. Namely, that others are too different to relate to; success is achieved by working together; we are more alike than different; everyone's voice within the community matters; and that we are superior to others. The chapter reveals how these lessons of belonging give shape and meaning to students' self-understandings and work to produce and perpetuate elite privilege.

In Chap. 8, Bronwyn Wood and Rosalyn Black start from the premise that contemporary globalising processes have disrupted the traditional bonds between identity, citizenship and place, affecting how today's young people think and feel about themselves as citizens who act, influence and feel they belong within different spatial contexts. They offer a critical review of scholarship on national citizenship, noting that it often naturalizes belonging and presents socially produced relations as fixed, glossing over fissures, losses, absences and borders these create (Anthias 2006). They propose a more affective, geographically-responsive vocabulary of citizenship and the relationship between citizenship, place and belonging. This spatial, relational and affective framework for young people's citizenship would configure belonging as: (i) a feeling; (ii) in the context of others; and (iii) an experience within specific places. Such a theorisation, they propose, offers a more dynamic, expansive notion of citizenship and belonging that takes up the flexible social membership and spatial affiliations that are consistent with young people's lives as citizens today.

Part II concludes with a reflective response by Kerry Kennedy. He underlines the theme of social fragmentation and exclusion that pervades the preceding chapters. These are the 'multicultural' or 'multiethnic' children who yearn to be recognised as belonging to Korea but are repeatedly rejected because 'being Korean' is about appearance rather than values, language and commitments. Or the Australian students with no personal experience of asylum seekers but strong, constant views that signal the 'toxicity of Australia's social environment' on asylum seekers and the limited influence of liberal, multicultural attitudes, values and education in schools. Or about the ambitious agenda to move beyond the exclusionary character of national citizenship and the power associated with it. Or how an elite school fuels and protects privilege as a way of becoming, being and belonging to a collective class identity and destiny. For Kennedy, the complex social issues of fragmentation and exclusion are too important to be left to politicians and policy makers; academics need to speak out. Drawing on the lessons of political science, he argues that there is also a need to recognise the social role of civic regimes and the powerful influence of institutions on citizens' attitudes and values (Weldon 2006), and the role that human agency plays in supporting and resisting these pressures (Ng and Kennedy in press).

Part III turns specifically to the topic of *Places and Spaces of Belonging*. Drawing on their research in rural communities in Australia and Italy, Mauro Giardello and Hernan Cuervo show that belonging is not merely defined by place but by affective, cultural and relational practices that are sedimented over time through the daily rituals that structure social relations. Such reflexive, everyday practices, they argue, operate as social mechanisms. They shape the quality of young people's relationships and give meaning, value, identity and a sense of belonging to young people, even though they live in rural places and spaces characterised by uncertainty, social change and fragmentation.

In Chap. 11, Aspa Baroutis and Martin Mills attend to the sort of emotional exclusion young people in 'alternative' schools describe when speaking about their previous, mainstream schooling experiences. They show how the students' feelings of alienation, marginalisation and disengagement affected their capacity to learn and place them at risk of dropping out of schooling. From these accounts, Baroutis and Mills rework theories of space (Lefebvre 1991; Massey 1992; Soja 1996) to propose that four spaces of belonging are necessary to engage marginalised youth in schooling and enhance their ability to succeed: (i) an *educational space* that supports and guides students through meaningful learning experiences that they chose themselves; (ii) a *physical space*, often resembling a 'home', that offers a safe learning environment; (iii) a *social space* for convivial social interactions with peers and teachers; and (iv) *emotional spaces* that provide the sort of caring, accepting relationships young people associate with family.

In her discussion, Kitty te Riele (Chap. 12) extends the arguments presented in the preceding chapters. She proposes that belonging is multi-dimensional and multi-faceted but that a sense of belonging can have productive and counterproductive impacts for marginalised, disadvantaged young people. To address this, she proposes that attention to three facets of place and space is required. First, the *physical space* where the place-based approaches and the material configuration of classrooms impact on belonging. Second, the *pedagogical space* where the resources for belonging can keep learning environments small and draw on students' knowledges and interests. Finally, the *relational space* where care is practised, a sense of 'family' constructed and where students 'feel' they belong.

Pedagogy is the particular focus of Part IV, although pedagogical issues thread throughout all the chapters. Barbara Comber and Annette Woods provide a vivid, concrete illustration of how place and space can be resources to enable socially just, active participation and belonging of all children in the curriculum. Extending Doreen Massey's (2005) theory of belonging as a 'practicing place' (2005, p. 154), their chapter exposes the temporal and special specificities as well as the personal and political negotiations of primary school teacher in designing and enacting a curriculum and pedagogy for students to explore the different histories, places and ways of belonging in their neighborhood. Their chapter reveals how pedagogy creates a place and space for belonging in classrooms, transforms social relations and possibilities and enables students to learn and belong in ways that promise benefits and responsibilities for them a to participate in public, community, and economic life.

In Chap. 14, Amanda Mooney and Chris Hickey rework Antonsich's (2010) notion of 'place-belonging' into the dynamics of identity and belonging that arises for a teacher and students around a game of battle-ball in an all-boys Physical Education class. Their finely-tuned analysis reveals how belonging is embedded in the politics of institutional policies, pedagogic practices, gender and personal power relations and how the serendipitous conflation of these conditions can rapidly shift the boundaries and identities of belonging. In doing so, they reveal that belonging or not belonging—being in/out of place—are states that are not agentically sought or controlled but ones that can be 'done to you'. In this light, they propose that belonging and not belonging is best understood not as an encounter of oppositional forces but as a dynamic *process* involving subjective investments and desires.

In her discussion, Julie McLeod (Chap. 15) takes a critical perspective, teasing out the nuances of the preceding chapters but also noting the firm hold of belonging as a keyword in contemporary social and political discourse and education debates. She asks: what work does the word and concept of belonging 'do'? She then responds by examining the claims and practices of belonging in youth citizenship and student voice, drawing out the everyday, relational ways belonging (and its shadow of estrangement) arises from practice. In doing so, she argues that ethics, power and hospitality are central both to belonging as a political and analytical category and to making spaces, openings and orientations to belonging practical and possible, particularly within the interactions, inherited norms, expectations and dynamics of schooling.

In his *Afterword*, Peter Kelly (Chap. 16) presents an alternate view of the questions entangled in the concept of belonging. The chapters in this collection rework theories of belonging in/through the micro-politics of young people's lives as they are locate within broader historical, social and political conditions, such as gender, sexuality, race, class, educational and political institutions. Kelly advocates an even broader lens. Taking up recent debates and commentaries in the *Journal of Youth Studies*, he argues for viewing belonging through the lens of a political economy of youth. He proposes that this might involve looking beyond youth and young people to other economic, social and political actors and agendas, to the relationships, practices and structures that shape how young people make a life and to identifying what might be obscured, strange or even alien to these young people.

References

Ahmed, S. (2004). Collective feelings: Or, the impressions left by others. *Theory, Culture & Society, 21*, 25–42.

Ahmed, S. (2012). *On being included: Racism and diversity in institutional life.* Durham, NC: Duke University Press.

Allen, L. (2011). Picture this: Using photo-methods in research on sexualities and schooling. *Qualitative Research, 11*(5), 487–504.

Allen, L. (2013). Sexual assemblages: Mobile phones/young people/school. *Discourse: Studies in the Cultural Politics of Education, 36*(1), 1–13.

Amin, A. (2012). *Land of Strangers*. Cambridge: Polity.

Anthias, F. (2006). Belongings in a globalising and unequal world: Rethinking translocations. In N. Yuval-Davis, K. Kannabiran, & U. Vieten (Eds.), *The situated politics of belonging* (pp. 17–32). London: Sage.

Antonsich, M. (2010). Searching for belonging – An analytic framework. *Geography Compass, 4*(6), 644–659.

Arnot, M., & Swartz, S. (2012). Youth citizenship and the politics of belonging: Introducing contexts, voices, imaginaries. *Comparative Education, 48*(1), 1–10.

Arnot, M., Pinson, H., & Candappa, M. (2009). Compassion, caring and justice: Teachers' strategies to maintain moral integrity in the face of national hostility to the "non-citizen". *Educational Review, 61*(3), 249–264.

Bauer, S., Loomis, C., & Akkari, A. (2012). Intercultural immigrant youth identities in contexts of family, friends, and school. *Journal of Youth Studies, 16*(1), 54–69.

Baumeister, R., & Leary, M. (1995). The need to belong: Desire for interpersonal attachments as a fundamental human motivation. *Psychological Bulletin, 117*(3), 497–529.

Beck, U. (2003). The analysis of global inequality: From national to cosmopolitan perspective. In M. Kaldor, H. Anheier, & M. Glasius (Eds.), *Global civil society* (pp. 45–55). Oxford: Oxford University Press.

Beck, M., & Malley, J. (1998). A pedagogy of belonging. *Reclaiming Children and Youth, 7*(3), 133–137.

Berlant, L. (2011). *Cruel optimism.* Durham, NC: Duke University Press.

Bernat, D., & Resnick, M. (2009). Connectedness in the lives of adolescents. In R. Diclemente & R. Crosby (Eds.), *Adolescent health understanding and preventing risk behaviors* (pp. 375–389). San Fran, CA: Jossey-Bass.

Billig, M. (1976). *Social psychology and intergroup relations.* New York: Academic Press.

Börner, S. (2013). *Belonging, solidarity and expansion in social policy.* Basingstoke, Hampshire: Palgrave Macmillan.

Bromley, R. (2000). *Narratives for a new belonging.* Edinburgh: Edinburgh University Press.

Calhoun, C. (2003). Belonging in the cosmopolitan imaginary. *Ethnicities, 3*(4), 531–568.

Carson, T. R. (2006). The lonely citizen: Democracy, curriculum and the crisis of belonging. In G. H. Richardson & D. W. Blades (Eds.), *Troubling the canon of citzenship education* (pp. 25–30). New York: Peter Lang.

Cemalcilar, Z. (2010). Schools as socialisation contexts: Understanding the impact of school climate factors on students' sense of school belonging. *Applied Psychology, 59*(2), 243–272.

Certeau, M. D. (1980). *Kunst des Handelns.* Berlin, Germany: Merve Verlag.

Cervantes-Carson, A., & Rumens, N. (Eds.). (2007). *Sexual politics of desire and belonging.* Amsterdam and New York: Rodopi.

Cooper, D. (2004). *Challenging diversity: Rethinking equality and the value of difference.* Cambridge: Cambridge University Press.

Crowley, J. (1999). The politics of belonging: Some theoretical considerations. In A. Geddes & A. Favell (Eds.), *The politics of belonging: Migrants and minorities in contemporary Europe* (pp. 15–41). Aldershot: Ashgate.

Davis, K. (2008). Intersectionality as buzzword: A sociology of science perspective on what makes a feminist theory successful. *Feminist Theory, 9*(1), 67–85.

Day, A. (2011). *Believing in belonging: Belief and social identity in the modern world.* Oxford and New York: Oxford University Press.

Fail, F., Thompson, J., & Walker, G. (2004). Belonging, identity and third culture kids: Life histories of former international school students. *Journal of Research in International Education, 3*(3), 319–338.

Fortier, A.-M. (2000). *Migrant belongings: Memory, space, identities*. Oxford: Berg.

Furrer, C., & Skinner, E. (2003). Sense of relatedness as a factor in children's academic engagement and performance. *Journal of Educational Psychology*, 95(1), 148–162.

Garbutt, R. (2011). *The locals: Identity, place and belonging in Australia and beyond*. Oxford and New York: Peter Lang.

Gibson, M., Bejínez, L., Hidalgo, N., & Rolón, C. (2004). Belonging and school participation: Lessons from a migrant student club. In M. Gibson, P. Gándara, & J. Koyama (Eds.), *School connections: U.S. Mexican youth, peers, and school achievement* (pp. 129–149). New York: Teachers College Press.

Gill, J., & Howard, S. (2009). *Knowing our place: Children talking about power, identity and citizenship*. Camberwell, VIC: ACER Press.

Goodenow, C. (1993). The psychological sense of school membership among adolescents: Scale development and educational correlates. *Psychology in the Schools*, 30, 70–90.

Gregoriou, Z. (2013). Traversing new theoretical frames for intercultural education: Gender, intersectionality, performativity. *International Education Studies*, 6(3), 179–191.

Hall, S. (2012). *City, street and citizen: The measure of the ordinary*. London: Routledge.

Halse, C. (2006). Writing/reading a life: The rhetorical practice of autobiography. *Auto/Biography*, 14(2), 95–115.

Hayes, D., & Skattebol, J. (2015). Education and the politics of belonging: Attachments and actions. In J. Wyn & H. Cahill (Eds.), *Handbook of children and youth studies* (pp. 518–527). Netherlands: Springer.

Ho, E. (2009). Constituting citizenship through the emotions: Singaporean transmigrants in London. *Annals of the Association of American Geographers*, 99, 788–804.

Joas, H. (1994). Situation—Corporeality—Sociality: The fundamentals of a theory of creativity of action. In H. Joas (Ed.), *The creativity of action* (pp. 145–195). Chicago: University of Chicago Press.

Lefebvre, H. (1991). *The production of space*. (D. Nicholson-Smith, Trans.) Oxford: Blackwell.

Lefebvre, H. (2006). Die Produktion des Raums. In J. Dünne & S. Günzel (Eds.), *Raumtheorie. Grundla-gentexte aus Philosophie und Kulturwissenschaften* (pp. 330–342). Frankfurt am Main, Germany: Suhr-kamp Taschenbuch Verlag.

Lewin, K. (1948). *Resolving social conflicts: Selected papers and group dynamics.* New York: Harper & Row.

Maher, M. (2014). Asylum seeker and refugee children belonging, being and becoming: The early childhood educator's role. *Australasian Journal of Early Childhood, 39*(1), 22–29.

Martin, D. C. (1995). The choices of identity. *Social Identities, 1*(1), 5–16.

Massey, D. (1992). Politics and space/time. *New Left Review, 196,* 65–84.

Massey, D. (2005). *For space.* London: Sage.

Matthews, J. (2008). Schooling and settlement: Refugee education in Australia. *International Studies in Sociology of Education, 18*(1), 31–45.

McCall, L. (2005). The complexity of intersectionality. *Signs: Journal of Women in Culture and Society, 30*(3), 1771–1800.

Mee, K., & Wright, S. (2009). Geographies of belonging. *Environment and Planning A, 41*(4), 772–779.

Ng, H. Y., & Kennedy, K. (in press). Citizenship status and identity of ethnic minorities: Cases of Hong Kong Filipino youth. In J. Gube & F. Gao (Eds.), *Education, ethnicity and equity in the multilingual Asian context.* Singapore: Springer.

Ong, A. (1996). Cultural citizenship as subject-making: Immigrants negotiate racial and cultural boundaries in the United States. *Current Anthropology, 37*(5), 737–762.

Osterman, K. (2000). Students' need for belonging in the school community. *Review of Educational Research, 70*(3), 323–367.

Pfaff-Czarnecka, J. (2011). From 'identity' to 'belong-ing' in social research: Plurality, social boundaries, and the politics of the self. In S. Albiez, N. Castro, L. Jüssen, & E. Youkhana (Eds.), *Ethnicity, citizenship and belonging: Practices, theory and spatial dimensions* (pp. 197–218). Frankfurt am Main, Germany, and Madrid, Spain: Iberoamericana, Vervuert.

Pinson, H., Arnot, M., & Candappa, M. (2010). *Education, asylum and the non-citizen child: The politics of compassion and belonging.* Houndmills, Basingstoke, Hampshire, New York: Palgrave Macmillan.

Probyn, E. (1996). *Outside belongings.* New York and London: Routledge.

Resnick, M., Bearman, P. S., Blomberg, R. W., Bauman, K. D., Harris, K. M., Jones, J., Tabor, J., Bowring, T., Sitting, R. A., Shrew, M., Ireland, M., Behringer, L. H., & Andrew, J. R. (1997). Protecting adolescents from harm. *JAMA, 278*(10), 823–832.

Robinson, K., Bansel, P., Denson, N., Davies, C., & Ovendone, G. (2013). *Growing up queer: Issues facing young Australians who are gender variant and sexually diverse*. Retrieved June 19, 2017, from http://www.glhv.org.au/files/Growing_Up_Queer2014.pdf.

Savage, M., Longhurst, B., & Bagnall, G. (2005). *Globalization and belonging*. London: Sage.

Singh, S., & Babacan, A. (2010). *Migration, belonging and the nation state*. Newcastle upon Tyne: Cambridge Scholars Publishing.

Soja, E. W. (1996). *Thirdspace: Journeys to Los Angeles and other real-and-imagined places*. Cambridge, MA: Blackwell.

Steiner, N., Mason, R., & Hayes, A. (Eds.). (2013). *Migration and insecurity: Citizenship and social inclusion in a transnational era*. London: Routledge.

Tajfel, H. (1982). Social psychology of intergroup relations. *Annual Review of Psychology, 33*, 1–39.

Taylor, A. (2009). Belonging. In R. Kitchin & N. Thrift (Eds.), *International encyclopedia of human geography* (pp. 294–299). Amsterdam: Elsevier.

Walsh, K. (2006). 'Dad says I'm tied to a shooting star!' Grounding (research on) British expatriate belonging. *AREA, 38*(3), 268–278.

Walton, G. M., & Carr, P. B. (2012). Social belonging and the motivation and intellectual achievement of negatively stereotyped students. In M. Inzlicht & T. Schmader (Eds.), *Stereotype threat: Theory, process and application* (pp. 89–106). New York: Oxford University Press.

Weldon. (2006). The institutional context of tolerance for ethnic minorities: A comparative, multilevel analysis of Western Europe. *American Journal of Political Science, 50*(2), 331–349.

Westwood, S., & Phizacklea, A. (2000). *Trans-nationalism and the politics of belonging*. London: Routledge.

White, R. D., & Wyn, J. (2013). *Youth and society* (3rd ed.). South Melbourne, VIC: Oxford University Press.

Wright, S. (2015). More-than-human, emergent belongings: A weak theory approach. *Progress in Human Geography, 39*(4), 391–411.

Youdell, D. (2005). Sex-gender-sexuality: How sex, gender and sexuality constellations are constituted in secondary schools. *Gender and Education, 17*(3), 249–270.

Youdell, D. (2010). *School trouble: Identity, power and politics in education*. London: Routledge.

Youkhana, E. (2015). A conceptual shift in studies of belonging and the politics of belonging. *Social Inclusion, 3*(4), 10–24.

Yuval-Davis, N. (2004). Borders, boundaries and the politics of belonging. In S. May, T. Modood, & J. Squires (Eds.), *Ethnicity, nationalism and minority rights* (pp. 214–230). Cambridge: Cambridge University Press.

Yuval-Davis, N. (2006a). Belonging and the politics of belonging. *Patterns of Prejudice, 40*(3), 197–214.

Yuval-Davis, N. (2006b). Intersectionality and feminist politics. *European Journal of Women's Studies, 13*(3), 193–209.

Yuval-Davis, N. (2007). Intersectionality, citizenship and contemporary politics of belonging. *Critical Review of International Social and Political Philosophy, 10*(4), 561–574.

Yuval-Davis, N. (2010). Theorizing identity: Beyond the 'Self' and 'Other' dichotomy. *Patterns of Prejudice, 44*, 261–280.

Yuval-Davis, N. (2011). *The politics of belonging: Intersectional contestations.* London: Sage.

Yuval-Davis, N., Kannabiran, K., & Vieten, U. (Eds.). (2006). *The situated politics of belonging.* London: Sage.

Part I

Gender, Sexuality and Belonging

2

Incidental Moments: The Paradox of Belonging in Educational Spaces

Emma Charlton, Leanne Coll, Lyn Harrison, and Debbie Ollis

Introduction

The relationship between bodies, subjectivity and affect in educational spaces is complex, dynamic and messy. Central to this relationship are concepts of belonging: what it means to belong and not belong, who or what can belong or not belong, and the precarious nature of belonging otherwise. To belong in this sense is not inherently positive. Although not always negative, the inclusionary and exclusionary force of belonging can carry certain negative, discriminatory and restrictive expectations for young people that often go unnoticed within the most mundane and incidental moments of school life. These normative forces are so embedded within school rituals, practices and routines that many young people, teachers and members of school communities accept them without questioning their implications.

E. Charlton (✉) • L. Coll • L. Harrison • D. Ollis
Deakin University, Melbourne, Australia
e-mail: e.charlton@deakin.edu.au; e-mail: leanne.coll@deakin.edu.au;
e-mail: lyn.harrison@deakin.edu.au; e-mail: debbie.ollis@deakin.edu.au

© The Author(s) 2018
C. Halse (ed.), *Interrogating Belonging for Young People in Schools*,
https://doi.org/10.1007/978-3-319-75217-4_2

Institutionalised norms surrounding sex-gender-sexuality in educational spaces are particularly problematic. These include the overt and subtle ways in which restrictive sex-gender-sexuality norms and assumptions support inequalities such as homophobia, sexism and transphobia in schools, and designate rules and regulations whereby students, regardless of their gender and/or sexual identity, are told stories about what it is to be 'normal' or 'natural'. Within the field of gender, sexuality and schooling, many scholars have looked at the discursive practices through which young people's subjectivities are constituted, sustained, contested and reinscribed (Blaise 2005; Rasmussen et al. 2004; Renold and Ringrose 2008), yet few have looked at the potential of certain theories of belonging to engage in broader analyses of the many lessons about sex-gender-sexuality that circulate in contemporary schools.

This chapter draws on three theorists—Vanessa May (2011), Sarah Wright (2014) and Nira Yuval-Davis (2006)—to think about belonging as a concept, an experience, a moment, a community, a force, a lens and a politics. As Wright (2014, p. 392) suggests:

> If belonging resonates because it means things to people, if it means different things to different people, if it is used in widely disparate ways, then perhaps what is most important about the term is the texture of how it is felt, used, practiced and lived. These things may be unresolvable. After all, this is a term found in unexpected places and used in unexpected ways. Perhaps what is needed is a reflection on the ways that it is deployed that does not attempt to shut down its multiple meanings and uses.

Wright argues that a focus on belonging as an 'affective act' (p. 400) allows attendance to the ways in which 'belonging is experienced, performed and practised' in the everyday. Drawing on recent work in geography, she points to 'belonging as performance', which allows a focus on 'practices and processes' of belonging rather than seeing belonging as a 'status'.

We continue this discussion of belonging throughout this chapter, in particular in relation to a research narrative from a middle-school and middle-class drama classroom. This is a narrative of a spontaneous moment of slapstick comedy, intended to be insignificant. Drawing on this vignette, we deconstruct the way belonging operates in a microcosm of daily classroom life, considering how it plays out in subtle and messy ways. Through our engagement with the politics of belonging, we argue that normative notions of belonging influence the way teachers view and treat young people, privileging certain types of sex-gender-sexuality belonging over others. Further, we contend that a critical engagement with the politics of belonging provides an important platform to reconsider the conditions of possibility for transformational learning where aspects of sex-gender-sexuality in educational spaces are concerned.

The Landscape of Gender, Sexuality and Schooling

An important platform for this paper is the research and writing of Deborah Youdell (2005, 2006), which focus on school moments when sex-gender-sexualities are constituted, performed, resisted and reinscribed through the day-to-day practices of schooling. Youdell (2005) suggests that although young people are constituted within, and are constrained by, particular discourses and identities, they are also able to reconstitute these discourses. In exploring the regulating effects of heteronormativity, Youdell highlights how constellations of sex, gender and sexuality—which intersect with other identity categories such as class and race—can 'open up possibilities' for young people to be and become otherwise. In this regard, Youdell finds that 'students can be seen to read, remake, and exceed the limits of normative discourse' and, in doing so, 'they are causing sex-gender-sexuality trouble and practising a politics of performative resignification' (Youdell 2004, p. 490). She suggests that:

> the micro exclusions that take place in the most mundane moments everyday inside schools cannot be understood as simply being experienced by students. Rather these must be understood as constitutive of the student, constitutions whose cumulative effects coagulate to limit 'who' a student can be, or even if s/he can be a student at all. (Youdell 2006, p. 12)

Louisa Allen (2011, 2013) also seeks to uncover 'unofficial' sites and ways in which constellations of sex-gender-sexuality inhere in spaces and places in schools. She questions how apparently mundane, spatial and material schooling arrangements constitute particular sexual meanings and identities for students. The young people in Allen's study were invited to create a photo diary of 'how they learned about sexuality at school' over a seven-day period (Allen 2011, p. 489). Young people took photographs of the sports field, toilets, playground and a student fashion show to communicate how sexuality is situated and shaped by these spaces. Allen (2013) described how these sorts of findings are difficult to uncover in word-based methods because of their 'intangible' and 'unmarked' features. She emphasises how the use of these methods reveals the embodied and spatial dimensions of (hetero)sexuality, which inhere in the 'unofficial' details of everyday schooling experiences.

These studies provide a sophisticated theoretical and practice-based understanding of the everyday. They draw particularly on the work of Michel Foucault (1978) and Judith Butler (1990) to explore how students are constituted, or 'subjectivated', within schools, and also how students may 'be otherwise', making compelling cases for showing 'how performative constitutions occur in school contexts' (Youdell 2006, p. 75).

Belonging

Notions of belonging bring something new to this landscape of gender, sexuality and schooling. While 'belonging' is often used to examine issues pertaining to race and citizenship, analyses of gender, sexuality and schooling using belonging as a lens are scarce. We suggest that belonging has been underestimated and underexplored as a concept and lens through which to analyse how micropractices in classrooms and schools make and remake sex-gender-sexuality norms. Further, that it offers insights into how relations of power are played out through these pedagogical practices.

Yuval-Davis (2006) provides a theoretical and analytical framework for the study of belonging and the politics of belonging. Her notion of belonging emphasises attachments and actions. She identifies three types of attachments: those associated with social locations, those associated with identifications and emotional attachment, and those associated with ethical and political values. Historically, specific categories of social location, such as gender, sexuality, race, class, nation, geography, ethnicity and life stage, have implications for particular forms of power relations at particular times. Even in their most stable form, these social locations are rarely constructed along one axis of difference. Analysis therefore requires an intersectional approach that sees these different categories as co-constitutive, with no concrete separate meaning attached to any social division (Yuval-Davis 2006, pp. 199–202). Identifications and emotional attachments relate to the stories people tell about who they are, and who they are not; all of which, Yuval-Davis (2006, pp. 202–203) argues, directly or indirectly relate to what being a member in a grouping or collectivity might mean. These narratives of identity often reflect a duality of being and becoming, belonging and longing to belong. Finally, belonging is about ethical and political values: it is about the ways that social locations and constructions of individual and collective identities are valued and judged.

Hayes and Skattebol (2015) use Yuval-Davis (2006) to consider processes of belonging and education, in particular for young people in an alternative secondary school. Their concern is how processes of belonging underpin disengagement from, and re-engagement with, conventional schooling.

> The politics of belonging involves not only the maintenance and reproduction of the boundaries of the community of belonging by the hegemonic political powers but also their contestation and challenge by other political agents. (Yuval-Davis 2006, p. 205 cited in Hayes and Skattebol 2015, p. 523)

Yuval-Davis offers us a useful framework for considering belonging, as well as a theory of the politics of belonging. It is the maintenance and reproduction of the boundaries of the community of belonging that draws our interest in this chapter; or, specifically, the ways in which notions of belonging co-constitute people and things, processes and places in a middle-school classroom.

Similarly, May (2011) draws on belonging as a lens to consider the connections between the self and society. Distinct from Yuval-Davis, however, May points to the influence of abstract notions such as the construction of the self. May argues that 'our sense of self is constructed in a relational process in our interactions with other people as well as in relation to more abstract notions of collectively held social norms, values and customs' (p. 368). Thus, a sense of belonging is achieved through embodying/internalising unwritten rules and being able to conduct oneself 'acceptably' in front of others.

Wright (2014, p. 393) takes this position further by exploring the importance of the intersection of people and the 'more-than-human'. Wright suggests that 'understanding belonging as emergent co-becoming may allow for hopeful and inclusive geographies that are diversely caring and careful' (p. 391). She argues that belonging is an ontological question, it is not only created by people and 'more-than-humans' but 'co-constitutes people and things and processes and places' (p. 393). For Wright, belonging is not only affective but is a strongly embodied experience and is more than just about the self and identity. Therefore, this chapter is interested in 'entities that come together in relational ways, that define and configure what it means to belong (and not belong) as they define and configure themselves' (p. 393). In this way, belonging

> connects matter to place, through various practices of boundary-making and inhabitation which signal that a particular collection of objects, animals, plants, germs, people, practices, performances or ideas is meant 'to be' in a place. (Mee and Wright 2009, p. 772)

In the research narrative explored in this chapter, we show how processes of belonging shape and are shaped by how young people become subjects of education. We illustrate how certain ways of being are opened up and shut down through processes of belonging; how young people take up or relinquish ways of knowing. We focus on an incidental moment in the classroom that, we propose, reveals much about the production of subjectivity. This incidental moment is an everyday classroom practice that is constitutive of social order yet largely taken for granted: that which is 'seen but unnoticed' (Garfinkel 1967, p. 180, cited in May 2011, p. 370). The layers of schooling are sites where sex-gender-sexuality are constituted, resisted and reinscribed. This occurs even in the most mundane pedagogical moments that work to maintain and reproduce spaces of belonging for students in schools.

Our Data

The data that informs this paper were collected from a mixed-method, ethnographic, year-long study of a grade nine class with 29 students, aged 13–15, and 14 of their teachers. 'Annanhill College' is a pseudonym for the private, P-12 school that the students attended in Queensland, Australia. This school utilised a middle-school structure for students in Years 7–9. One of the consequences of this structure was that each class of students attended all of their subjects together and, therefore, could be considered as a group or community, inhabiting different schooling spaces and with different teachers or sites where processes and practices of belonging are made and contested. Students were filmed in each subject and the film excerpts were converted into narrative vignettes or episodes, drawing on Youdell's work (2006). In addition, students participated in individual and focus group interviews. Individual interviews were conducted with teachers. For this chapter, our emphasis is on the ways the students physically filled their classroom spaces; thus, video data were analysed using an iterative approach identifying themes and instances around learner and gender subjectivities.

The chapter focuses on one vignette created from the larger dataset. The vignette took place at the beginning of a drama class, in a large, carpeted, drama-dedicated room, and was part of a nine-week drama unit. For the most part, the students sat on the carpet in this space and, while the students would usually change into their sports uniform for active classes like drama and physical education, in the vignette discussed here the teacher—Ms Vivien—opted for the students to remain in school uniform to avoid losing class time. Like most Australian secondary schools, the school uniform was different for male and female students. The male students wore shorts or trousers and a button-up shirt with a tie; the female students wore dresses or skirts and blouses. All students wore socks and laced leather shoes. This vignette occurred well into the nine-week programme of drama, when the students were oriented to the teacher, the subject, the space and the associated rituals and procedures, so the students were used to active warm-ups.

Vignette: Slapstick Theatre

Students enter the room to find a mat—like that which would be used for high jump—in their drama space. After some discussion with the group, their teacher, Ms Vivien, explains:

> *We're not going to do what Hugh suggested and jump from the roof onto the mat. And we're not going to be doing what George suggested and pretend it's a boxing thing … I thought because we had the mat we'll do some work on the mat, and do some brief work with slapstick theatre.*

She continues:

> *We are only going to do this briefly, and I'm warning you now this has the potential to be quite dangerous if you're silly. Now if you're silly I'll take you out of the activity straight away.*

Ms Vivien provides instructions to the group: 'The topic of your improvisations is called arguments.… The argument must end with conflict.' Ms Vivien instructs the students on how to make the slapping noise: 'You can slap your thigh. Boys, you can slap your chests if you want to.' While explaining the activity Ms Vivien heard a male student, George, talking about how he would like to tackle someone on the mat. In response, Ms Vivien stated:

> *No, I don't want tackling. I don't want any connection. It needs to be slow and sensible. Gentlemen, I'm concerned. I'm concerned that you're not going to take this seriously and I'm concerned that it could end up with someone actually getting hurt.*

After the students have had time to work on their sketch, Ms Vivien gets George, Larry and Jim to help her lower the mat and then brings the class to the performance space. Ms Vivien asks for volunteers, allows for a moment of silence and then selects the first group to perform: 'Grant's group'. Grant, Chase, Bruce and William were students often marginalised within this class. Six slow claps are heard as they move to the performance space. The boys stand just off the mat and are then counted in, 'three, two, one, action'. There was a quiet wolf whistle as 'one' was stated. The boys aren't ready and are counted in again. There is more groaning. Their chosen conflict is over who bought the last round of drinks at the pub. Grant is the only student who ends up on the mat—he is pushed by Chase and fake-kicked twice by Bruce (but only one kick that Grant notices and thus responds to). Ms Vivien says, 'Stop there, unorganised (sic) but you gave it a go.' Ms Vivien applauds once. There are three slow claps also heard but otherwise little appreciation given to the first group.

The next group called up is Kadie's group. Kadie, Madison, Holly and Suki get up. These girls are generally seen as 'nice girls': studious, not needing to be worried about, well-behaved and quiet. As they move to the performance space, there is some clapping. Ms Vivien says, 'Give them a clap. Girls, start by standing on the mat.' There seems to be lots of students talking. She counts them in again. This group's conflict is about decorating an office and a disagreement about what colours will be used. They stand on the mat in two pairs, and push each other with one hand—there is physical contact. The girls on the mat are laughing. Ms Vivien says, 'Freeze, well done'. She then says something a little hard to discern but relating to more talking than action on the mat.

Ms Vivien then says, 'Who can do this well? I want to see a group that's going to do this well. Larry, your group.' This group are quite popular, as is indicated by Liam, who is heard saying 'Ooh, yeah'. Larry, Jim and George get up and are counted in and start off the mat. Their conflict is a child (George) wanting a snack pack and Larry and Jim denying him this. After some screaming on George's part, Larry and Jim tell him to bend over and then smack him in punishment. George falls onto the mat and then gets up, runs around behind them and pushes both Larry and Jim onto the mat and then tackles Jim when he starts to get up. Except for the smack, in all of these instances there is physical contact. Ms Vivien says, 'Thank you, that was a bit better.' There is some applause from the class.

Ms Vivien then says, 'Alright, next group we go, um, Liam's group.' George jumps on the mat again before returning to his seat. Liam, David, Ethan and Bob, boys who are more popular than marginalised, but not the most popular, get up. Ethan, Bob and Liam start on one side of the mat, and when 'action' is called stand on the mat, David starts on the other side and walks towards the boys. Their scenario is a fight. The group of three harass David. He says he can take them all on. A fight ensues where David punches Bob and Bob falls on the mat. Then Ethan punches David. David flips on to the mat and then, when he gets up, Liam pushes him back down again. The punches don't make contact but the push does. David lifts himself slightly from the ground, says 'I can still take you all on', and then collapses. Ms Vivien says, 'Well done, that was a good one.' The audience clap and have laughed through much of this performance.

Ms Vivien calls on Hugh's group—Hugh, Tim and Darren, also popular boys—but they do not get up. 'We've got nothing Mam', Darren says to Ms Vivien. 'You've got nothing? All right.' Ms Vivien asks for other groups to volunteer. They do not. And the activity ends. (Drama Tape 8 [2/8/04] 7:45–18:00; duration: 10min 15sec)

Boundaries, Hierarchies of Social Location and Emotional Attachments

The slapstick begins with the making of boundaries; Ms Vivien identifies the kinds of behaviour that are not acceptable: 'tackling' and 'connection'. The selection of the scenarios, which included bar brawls and interior design, says a lot about how sex-gender-sexuality is being performed in this classroom. The scenarios are also intertwined with the words and activities that move around and move these students, such as Ms Vivien's suggestion that the female students slap their thighs while the male students can also slap their chests. This produces and reproduces normative gendered binaries, such as active/passive, and encourages male violence regardless of the rules of engagement. Simultaneously, the 'unacceptable' behaviour is positioned as expected of (at least some of) the male students. While this boundary-making may have been established to avoid injury, Ms Vivien's comments and laughter inscribe and construct this behaviour in alignment with normative understandings of male behaviour, and as privileged. From the very first group, the order to perform the 'non-physical' boundary was not maintained. While Ms Vivien claimed to have set boundaries, these were not evident in practice and, it could be argued, not only allowed violence but condoned it.

In this exercise, the students' responses were to position violence as a method of conflict resolution—rather than negotiation or compromise. While pretending violence is an element of slapstick theatre, there is more to this incident and its use by students than the constraints of the activity. It is an illustration of belonging being 'a powerful way of understanding and producing the world' (Wright 2014, p. 399). The group that received the 'well done' was the one that deployed the most physical aggression in their vignette. Hyper-masculine behaviour was reinforced and rewarded. By failing to apply her own rules of engagement, the teacher demonstrated practices of boundary making and these boys' rough and tumble and physical assault of each other was normalised. Ms Vivien allowed them to perform masculinity as violence without question. In contrast, the 'nice' girls depicted group tensions around interior decorating and were positioned as including too much talk and not enough action. It appeared that the gendered nature of their selection of content—conflict over colours and decorating—did not meet Ms Vivien's expectations of what conflict resolution involved. Describing their vignette as having 'too much talk' again marks conflict as inherently violent and girls having too much to say. Although the girls tried to push each other, they found this difficult and uncomfortable, laughing perhaps to mask their discomfort. Ms Vivien's reaction seemed to assume the inevitability of the girls' failure to do the activity as well as the boys, responding to their vignette with a brief 'well done', which was then contradicted by the request for a group that could 'do it well'. In these ways, the practices in the classroom reinforced normative understandings of gender, particularly a privileged hyper-masculinity where violence is reinforced and (re)produced.

It is worth emphasising some of the narratives—the identification and emotional attachments—that dominate this vignette. As Wright (2014, p. 399) has suggested, 'affect and emotion can work to create both inclusive and exclusive belongings and, indeed, belongings that are messily somewhere in between'. There is a relational aspect to the emotions at work. The element of performance in this drama space meant that forms of resistance would have been most visible and, therefore, would open up spaces of vulnerability for those who might resist. For example, as 'marginalised' boys, the first group was already positioned as being inadequate in this space. Being selected to go first and then seen to be unsuccessful by their teacher reinforced their marginal position in the hierarchy of the classroom, positioning them as 'other'; as less popular, less interesting and perhaps less capable. In contrast, the four girls in the second group were constituted as 'nice' girls. They did not volunteer but they were expected to comply, and did what they were asked, without much recognition or applause. Three of the popular boys—Larry, George and Jim—were selected next and the response from the audience, with comments like 'Ooh yeah', indicate their popularity.

In asking for a group who 'can do this well', and then calling on Larry, Jim and George, Ms Vivien further positioned the 'popular' boys as entertaining. George's tackling of Jim was not commented upon, despite tackling being explicitly named as something Ms Vivien did not want to see. The group that did it 'better' (Larry, George & Jim), and the group that was 'good' (David, Ethan, Bob & Liam) both used physical contact; were the girls to do the same, Kadie, Madison, Holly and Suki would have had to reveal what was under their skirts, stepping out of gendered notions about what 'nice girls' do. For these young women, belonging is risky. If they did the activity and displayed the levels of conflict, aggression and physicality rewarded by Ms Vivien, they would not have conformed to gendered expectations of what girls should do. Their social locations as nice, compliant and unsuccessful girls were further constituted in this instance; they simultaneously *belonged* as particular kinds of girls within the hierarchies of this class and *did not belong* as students capable of meeting teacher and peer expectations that they should have the ability to entertain.

These girls, and Grant, Bruce, Chase and William, were positioned as inadequate. The only group to refuse to engage with the task were Hugh, Darren and Tim, 'popular' boys, who argued they had nothing prepared. These students' reluctance to participate may be read in several ways: this refusal may have been the result of not wanting to fail in their teacher's or peers' eyes, particularly following a group that had been identified as being successful and two groups positioned as 'not doing this well'. Or, perhaps, their sense of 'being meant to be in a place', their sense of belonging, provided the confidence, comfort and privilege to refuse. Or, for these boys, it may not have been safe to get up. They may have had too much to lose. The same explanation may be provided for the rest of the girls, who were not asked to perform and, similarly, did not volunteer. The one group who felt able to resist were the more popular boys and the more popular girls were not called upon.

Some of these examples are similar to those offered by Youdell (2006, p. 30), who suggests that students are constituted through constellations, particularly through 'dichotomies of good/bad students and acceptable/ unacceptable and even ideal/impossible learners'. Belonging/not belonging is a fruitful lens to build upon such work as it can provide further insights into the micro-practices of power circulating in the classroom that produce such dichotomies. It operates at two levels. First, Ms Vivien and her construction of particular gendered behaviours and normative notions of boy and girl but, also, the students who take up, reject and supplant the specific gendered constructions Ms Vivien imposes. There are the compliant girls; the groups of boys who assert the normativity of hypermasculinity by ignoring Ms Vivien's directives about behaviour; and the popular boys who refuse to be drawn into the activity and thereby immunise and protect themselves from the teacher's evaluation and the gendered constructions that are integral to this. These constitutions link student identities to school practices, practices/politics, which include some young people and exclude others, thus, as Yuval-Davis suggests, maintaining and reproducing 'the boundaries of the community of belonging' (2000, p. 205). This is a process of becoming where certain ways of being are opened up and other ways of being are closed down.

Between a Mat and a Hard Place— Post-humanism and Belonging

Central to this vignette are the materials, spatial location and institutional traditions and their impact on ways of being in the classroom space. The mat, in particular, is significant as it effects the structure of the task, the 'acting' out of the scenarios and the performance. The use of the mat is also linked to Ms Vivien's perceptions of success from a pedagogical perspective. The purpose of this analysis is not to discuss the impact of the mat as an isolated thing but to emphasise how 'things (or people or places) do not pre-exist, in static ways—their belongings are made through their coming together' (Wright 2014, p. 392). If we are looking at the *how* of belonging then we need to explore the significance of the mat as an object that is agentic, in the sense that it works with the people and place to instantiate a form of boundary making. Paying attention to the material here, we would suggest, also broadens our analysis of the many messages about sex-gender-sexuality that are circulating in the school which often go unremarked; messages that have the power to shape subjectivities in particular normative ways that are often underestimated and unquestioned. By questioning how boundaries between categories, people or things are made, we are forced to grapple with the different positions: student/teacher, good girl/bad girl, good boy/bad boy and successful/unsuccessful learner.

The mat in this vignette became a focal point of discussion for Ms Vivien and her students, as indicated in the opening when Ms Vivien asked the students why they thought the mat was there. They suggested jumping, boxing and tackling, indicating that it did not just arrive but was imbued with a history of how students and Ms Vivien had encountered the mat previously, in drama or other contexts such as physical education. Ms Vivien's disruption of the usual usage of the mat in this context is not insignificant as all struggled to use it in the relatively passive way she proposed. The mat is, therefore, 'a thing that has impact … caught in a circuit of action and reaction' (Wright 2014, p. 393). It had impact on knowing, it affected how learning took place and the experience was a gendered one. The boys used the mat to wrestle, to fight, to fall and to use their bodies with a sense of freedom. For the girls, it was a restrictive and uncomfortable space. This way of seeing the world can help us interfere with and escape from the knowledge that puts the blame and responsibility on the students or Ms Vivien. Objects and things are not inert, fixed or passive matter awaiting 'use' by human intervention; the mat took its place as a material-discursive agent within a classroom space saturated with gendered-sexual meanings. The mat enabled the enactment of physical barriers that constrained who was free to move and, crucially, whose movements were bounded. Attention to the mat draws attention to how objects, bodies and spaces do crucial, but often unnoticed, performative work. This critique is not of the teacher or the use of the mat, but how these aspects of the encounter interplay in order to create a space in which some of the students belong while others do not. The mat was not meant to be there, but it was. The teacher makes use of the mat in an unproblematic way. The mat plays a role in constraining and enabling knowledge processes, local meanings, processes of belonging and relationality and the movement of bodies in space.

The students' uniforms are another material feature of this scenario. A pragmatic decision about time means the students do not change into their sports uniform. A broader decision about gendered fashion, style and institutional imagery sees the female students at this school in skirts and dresses after the early years of primary school. Youdell (2005) writes about the significance of the school uniform. She gives an example of the ways girls and boys sit in assembly and uses this to consider how 'by sitting in particular ways "girls" bodies cite and inscribe particular discourses of heterosexual femininity and simultaneously constitute themselves as embodied subjects within these terms' (p. 256). Enactments of femininity and masculinity entail negotiating normative gender scripts to greater or lesser degrees, showing how young people are not fixed in a particular position. Yet these uniforms, particularly the girls' skirts and dresses, did fix them in certain ways in the activity; they provided an obstacle to their participation and made them feel uncomfortable. In this sense, their uniforms 'do gender' as they shape pedagogies and the performance capacities of students to belong as good students. It was unlikely that the one group of girls who performed were going to flip onto the mat in the way that David did because they were wearing skirts; there was no way that these students could move on the mat in the way that their teacher valued, no way that they could 'do this well'.

It may have been due to these uniforms that instances of gendered differences between students' physical engagement were observed. However, like the symbolic concealment Youdell (2005) noted, rehearsal and cultures of femininity also contributed to this inhibition. The girls' uniforms were shown to be explicitly restrictive in this vignette and this was something that the students were aware of. For example, in an individual interview Meredith commented:

it's kinda hard with skirts.… Yeah, like the guys have got the shorts and stuff so they can get up, they can play the, like the natural disasters game and stuff. When you want to get down and do, when she says, 'Fire', and you have to roll around and stuff. You can't do that in a skirt. (Meredith [19/8/04])

Asked whether their uniforms affected their participation in class, in a focus group interview Kadie and Imogen commented,

Kadie: Well with all the games, like natural disasters, the fire, roll around kind of thing, you can't exactly do that in a skirt.
Emma: So what happens as a result of that then?
Kadie: You just stand there.
Imogen: Oh, not really, but we have to do it carefully. Then we do it slowly and we lose because we're slow.
Kadie: And Chase wins.
Imogen: And Chase wins 'cause he's wearing pants.

(Focus Group #3 [5/11/04] Kadie, Imogen & Suki)

These uniforms are a material constriction; however, they can also be understood as aspects of identification and emotional attachment which forces these girls to make decisions about which subject positions they want to belong to; the good student or the good girl. Being a good girl means you 'just stand there' or 'do it carefully' or 'lose'. These girls did not see their inhibited participation as a consequence of their ability. Rather, it was about their uniforms. However, this inhibited participation is about more than their immediate dress. This rehearsal, and the ways in which it contributes to imagined spaces around bodies, is indicated by Ice who argued that, despite her dress, she would not act 'stupid':

Ice: It [the uniform] doesn't affect me you know.
Emma: It doesn't affect you? Why's that?
Ice: 'Cause every time in drama, I never act silly in any of the things, like the group work, how we have to go together and do something. Like I'd never have to…
Ariel: She's never got the stupid part.
Ice: 'Cause I never want the stupid part.

(Focus Group #7 [23/11/04] Ariel, Ice, Kelsie, Gen & Bob)

Young people are acutely aware of what embodies culturally intelligible femininity and masculinity, whether they choose to enact and/or resist. Kadie, Madison, Holly and Suki could have flipped on the mat, but then they would not have belonged as 'appropriate' girls within the class. Gendered belonging outweighed belonging as students who 'can do this well', which is not to suggest that this was an active, or even a subconscious, choice. Similarly, for Ice, countering a traditional femininity seemed beyond the realm of possibility. This is one of many incidental moments that shape certain ways of belonging and becoming. Which suggests, as Harris (1999, p. 112) writes, that 'the meanings attributed to [female] adolescence, as a bodily process, are deeply embedded in the sociocultural space of patriarchy' (see also Martino and Pallotta-Chiarolli 2005).

Conclusion: Belonging as Becoming, Who Can Resist?

While this vignette is of one instance, it is an instance in a chain of signifiers around the politics of who or what 'belongs' in the spaces of school, and, most significantly, the precarious nature of belonging otherwise and who is authorised to resist. This chapter has considered belonging as a notion, a moment, a politics and a lens for deconstructing the gendered microcosm of daily classroom life. The vignette represents an incidental moment for this group of 14- to 15-year-old students, yet it illuminates the complexity of young people's experiences of sex-gender-sexuality in schools and how the relationship between bodies, subjectivity and affectivity is much more complex than it might first appear. The social norms, materials and hierarchies illustrated within this vignette dictate who and where students are 'allowed' to be in school, who has access to power and belonging in the spaces of school, and the conditions of this belonging. Belonging emerges in the vignette as conditional and as an invisible process of boundary-making that has a direct impact on the everyday school experiences of even the most apparently 'straight' and 'conventional' student. This is a classroom and a set of pedagogic practices that seems to be composed of multiple terrains of belonging and conditions of membership in this community. Using belonging as a lens enables us to reconsider gendered binaries and how particular genders and types of belonging are privileged. The consequence is that other ways of being and becoming are constrained and shut down, such as the ability of the 'nice girls' to position themselves simultaneously as successfully and hegemonically 'feminine' and as successful 'students'. For this class, belonging draws boundaries between and amongst students in terms of gender, bodies, power, success and popularity.

At the beginning of this chapter, we signalled our intention to explore the possibility of transformational learning using belonging as a ubiquitous and problematic concept. In considering this incidental and mundane moment, it may be worthwhile to consider how concepts of belonging can be reconfigured or challenged so that they might open up, instead of close down, certain possibilities to be or become otherwise in educational spaces. Ms Vivien goes ahead despite being aware of the constrictions of the task. There are so many opportunities to challenge normative underpinnings of belonging in this instance and these are opportunities lost. While the normative notions of belonging appear to be hidden, it is difficult to engage in a serious debate about its place: what we want the focus to achieve and at what cost. There is much at stake when we talk about belonging. For example, we might suggest that Ms Vivien could have created space for discussions and for directing student attention towards the cultural norms of the subject and practice in question, including cultural norms that engender and privilege certain behaviours and identities while marginalising others. However, the focus should not be solely on this teacher: belonging constrains what sort of teacher it is possible to be and whether it is even possible to be recognised as a teacher if one was to challenge norms around sex-gender-sexuality. The struggle for belonging in school spaces makes such challenges difficult. The universal institution of schooling functions in ways that maintain and reproduce communities of belonging based on normative ways of being and becoming. Reworking what it means to belong in educational spaces in ways that open up rather than shut down ways of being and becoming, to discover 'geographies of belonging that are diversely care-ing and careful' (Wright 2014, p. 393) is therefore crucial. More importantly, this focus has the possibility of further enriching and responding to the relationship between the self and the social in critical studies of young people, in ways that recognise their potential and places them at the centre of the work that we do.

References

Allen, L. (2011). Picture this: Using photo-methods in research on sexualities and schooling. *Qualitative Research, 11*(5), 487–504.

Allen, L. (2013). Sexual assemblages: Mobile phones/young people/school. *Discourse: Studies in the Cultural Politics of Education, 36*(1), 1–13.

Blaise, M. (2005). *Playing it straight. Uncovering gender discourses in the early childhood classroom.* London: Routledge.

Butler, J. (1990). *Gender trouble, feminist theory, and psychoanalytic discourse.* New York: Routledge.

Foucault, M. (1978). *The history of sexuality, volume 1: An introduction.* New York: Vintage.

Harris, A. (1999). Everything a teenage girl should know: Adolescence and the production of femininity. *Women's Studies Journal, 15*(2), 111–124.

Hayes, D., & Skattebol, J. (2015). Education and the politics of belonging: Attachments and actions. In *Handbook of children and youth studies* (pp. 517–528). Singapore: Springer.

Martino, W., & Pallotta-Chiarolli, M. (2005). *Being normal is the only way to be: Adolescent perspectives on gender and school.* Sydney: University of New South Wales Press.

May, V. (2011). Self, belonging and social change. *Sociology, 45*(3), 363–378.

Mee, K., & Wright, S. (2009). Geographies of belonging. *Environment and Planning A, 41*(4), 772–779.

Rasmussen, M., Rofes, E., & Talburt, S. (2004). *Youth and sexualities: Pleasure, subversion, and insubordination in and out of schools.* New York: Palgrave Macmillan.

Renold, E., & Ringrose, J. (2008). Regulation and rupture: Mapping tween and teenage girls' resistance to the heterosexual matrix. *Feminist Theory, 9*(3), 313–338.

Wright, S. (2014). More-than-human, emergent belongings: A weak theory approach. *Progress in Human Geography, 39*(4), 391–411.

Youdell, D. (2004). Wounds and reinscriptions: Schools, sexualities and performative subjects. *Discourse: Studies in the Cultural Politics of Education, 25*(4), 477–493.

Youdell, D. (2005). Sex-gender-sexuality: How sex, gender and sexuality constellations are constituted in secondary schools. *Gender and Education, 17*(3), 249–270.

Youdell, D. (2006). *Impossible bodies, impossible selves: Exclusions and student subjectivities*. Dordrecht, The Netherlands: Springer.

Yuval-Davis, N. (2006). Belonging and the politics of belonging. *Patterns of Prejudice, 40*(3), 197–214.

3

Becoming and Belonging: Negotiating Non-heteronormative Identities Online and at School

Peter Bansel

Becoming and Belonging

My address to becoming and belonging foregrounds the everyday practices through which young people form and perform sexual subjectivities online and at school. I work with an account of becoming and belonging as ensembles of spatio-temporal practices and socio-cultural relational encounters with others; encounters through which the identities of students are recognised, made intelligible and integrated into the everyday knowledges and practices of the school.

Belonging, as accomplished through everyday practices in multiple locations, is understood as mobile and fluid, rather than stable membership of a group (for example heterosexual, gay, lesbian, transgender). In

Thanks to Dr Emma Keltie for her contribution to my nascent knowledge about digital cultures and digital labour, and to Dan Perell for challenging me to make more explicit theoretical connections between my work on neoliberalism and queer lives.

P. Bansel (✉)
Western Sydney University, Sydney, Australia
e-mail: P.Bansel@westernsydney.edu.au

© The Author(s) 2018
C. Halse (ed.), *Interrogating Belonging for Young People in Schools*,
https://doi.org/10.1007/978-3-319-75217-4_3

resisting the apparent stability of categories of person, I also recognise the centrality of practices of categorisation to identity politics and discourses of equity. For example, the Australian government's Department of Education and Training (DET 2012) identifies six targeted educationally disadvantaged or equity groups in Australia. These categories include people from: (1) low socioeconomic backgrounds; (2) rural and isolated areas; (3) non-English speaking backgrounds; (4) women in non-traditional areas of study; (5) indigenous peoples; and (6) those with a disability. Based on the findings of the *Growing up Queer* study (Robinson et al. 2013), regarding queer young people's experiences of schooling, I argue for the inclusion of LGBTIQ identified young people (henceforth referred to as 'queer') in this list of equity groups. And yet, whilst I am concerned on the one hand with lived experiences of inequality and broadening the categories of disadvantage and equity to include queer young people, I am at the same time resisting the collapse of all forms of diversity into singular stable categories. This is to enact a queer politics; one that queers and undoes categorical conceptualisations of persons at the same time as it mobilises the discourses and politics of categories in order to do so.

This queer politics is predicated on the position that conceptualisations of belonging based on membership of a particular category or community produce static accounts of identity. Such static accounts ignore the multiple ways in which young people might variously conform to, or contest, the practices and boundaries of belonging that operate in any particular spatio-temporal location. Contesting static accounts of belonging also foregrounds the work that is performed when young people actively engage in the production of multiple and fluid identities, over time and in different spaces. Further, since any particular subject's identity and sense of belonging may vary over time, belonging is conceived as a sense of connection to others that is always in the process of being actively achieved (Probyn 1996).

Indeed, for the queer young people I am concerned with, practices of belonging may at certain times and in certain places necessitate disrupting, or at least broadening, the established norms of who one is and how one belongs. For this reason, I am simultaneously *interested in* and *cautious about* cultures of belonging, as I recognise that the normative terms of belonging that operate in any particular context can also reproduce marginalisation and discrimination *both* in that context *and* in any other (for example, bullying and other forms of discrimination happen online as well as at school). This makes static conceptions of belonging problematic and emphasises an account of becoming as indeterminate and irreducible to stable categories.

In taking up an account of belonging as 'experiences of being part of the social fabric' (Anthias 2006), and arguing for a relational understanding of the social and the subject, I foreground the practices through which normative regulatory matrices of intelligibility include some subjects and exclude others (Butler 1993). It is through these matrices of intelligibility that some lives are made recognisable and viable, and others are not; through which some lives come to matter and others do not. Like Rosalyn Diprose (2008, p. 47), I am concerned with 'the preemptive exclusion [...] of others on the basis of the codification of others as outside relation, belonging nowhere, a threat'. In spatialising the becoming subject and belonging in this way, I locate my enquiry in schools, classrooms and online spaces, and consider the ways in which queer young people labour to find themselves in, and occupy, these spaces.

If, as Michel Foucault (1992) suggests, new realms of possibilities for sexual subjectivities are constantly being produced, where might we expect to find them? My discussion draws on qualitative data collected in a national Australian online survey, and interviews and focus groups with young people at Twenty10,[1] a Sydney-based service for people of diverse genders, sexualities and sexes. I consider the material practices through which young people produce and perform the 'truth of themselves' and find spaces of belonging through digital social media and classroom pedagogies and practices. I also articulate points of tension between the truth of the 'self' produced in the heteronormative practices of schooling, and the multiple and possible truths and selves produced in young people's engagement with digital social media. In pointing to these tensions, I capture something of young people's desires to become recognisable and intelligible in communities of belonging as a matter of personal freedom and choice.

Becoming Free, Choosing to Belong

In foregrounding the spatio-temporality of discourses and practices through which subjectivities are constituted and regulated, I contextualise the production of queer lives in the contemporary practices of neoliberalism as a mode of government. For Nikolas Rose (1999), practices of government 'cut experience in certain ways, to distribute attractions and repulsions, passions and fears across it, to bring new facets and forces, new intensities and relations into being' (Rose 1999, p. 31). This is, Rose suggests, partly a matter of the constitution of governable spaces (nations, societies, classes, families, schools, social media, and so on) in which subjectivities are constituted and governed. Reiterating Michel Foucault's (1992) insistence that sexuality is not a natural biological and fixed truth of the self but, rather, constituted and regulated through historically specific and *variable* discourses and practices, I emphasise that possibilities for becoming and belonging are imbricated in constitutive discourses, practices and embodied performances of what is variously fought for, struggled over, won, overcome or accomplished as a project of freedom: including the freedom to be 'oneself' (Rose 1996, 1999). This accomplishment of freedom is made possible, as well as revoked or sustained, through the concordance of the subject with the normative regulatory practices and relations of power through which they are constituted; and constituted as 'free', 'individual' and 'autonomous'. This freedom, individuality, autonomy and self-determination depend on the performance of the subject within normative matrices of intelligibility that variously hold out the promise of recognition, or threaten the possibility of rejection. The powers through which subjects are constituted and regulated are also powers that variously valorise the norm/al and abject those who fall outside it. These practices of valorisation and abjection are variously violent effects of power, or powerful effects of violence: the power to affect who and what counts as human (Butler 2004) along with the terms and conditions of belonging.

Benny LeMaster (2015, p. 4) argues that neoliberalism rhetorically presents all subjects as equally capable of realising their own freedom if they 'make effective life choices to resemble a mythical normative center (e.g., White, cisgender, heterosexual, able-bodied, and so forth)'. Further, those who may be perceived to have made the wrong choices—for example young people who refuse/resist embodying the mythical normative centre—are held responsible and accountable for their own lack of freedom and for any experience of marginalisation or oppression. In this way, oppression is framed as the result of bad life choices, and 'not a systemic means of controlling bodies' (LeMaster 2015, p. 4). Indeed, Penny Griffin (2007, p. 220) argues that sex and gender are not merely 'incidental to the formation and perpetuation of neoliberal discourse, but absolutely central to it', and that neoliberalism 'is entirely predicated on a politics of heteronormativity that (re)produces the dominance of normative heterosexuality' (2007, p. 221).

Trevor Gale and Kathleen Densmore (2002, p. 19) argue for an account of difference that is not based on *assimilation* into the mythic normative centre as the desirable way forward for non-dominant groups, since assimilation perpetuates disadvantage. Rather, they contend that diverse groups should be *integrated* into public life so that all people are able to express their interests and experiences on an equal basis with everyone else. Gale and Densmore point out that such an approach to, or politics of, difference and equity is problematic in the current neoliberal context of the marketisation of schooling, performance pressures and high-stakes testing based on competition and comparison among narrowly framed normative standards. Further, as long as the implicit norms in the current structures and processes of schooling remain invisible and uncontested, inequities for those who are not fully captured within and by the norm will persist. What is required, Gale and Densmore suggest, is creating a space for students to name, critique and develop their own identities within an environment that fosters respect for these: space for students to express and examine their feelings, develop their skills and have these heard and appreciated; and space for students to be involved in the determination of the conditions under which they engage with their education. The simultaneously political and pedagogical task, then, is to encourage differences rather than foreclose or abject their emergence, and engage with broader conceptualisations of becoming and the desire to belong.

Longing to Belong

When the young people who participated in the study *Growing up Queer* were asked what would make a difference to their lives, most suggested that the legalisation of same-sex marriage held the promise of a better future. Recently, in Australia, the issue of legalising same-sex marriage and the Safe Schools initiative (an anti-bullying, anti-homophobia and anti-transphobia programme for schools) have generated highly visible, highly charged, political and public debate. This debate has played out in parliament, departments of education, schools, churches and media, with funding for Safe Schools being withdrawn by the Federal Government and some schools electing to withdraw their name from the Safe Schools website or from the programme itself. The Federal Government has also proposed a divisive plebiscite for a compulsory vote (but a non-binding one with no enforceable parliamentary outcome) 'for' or 'against' the legalisation of same-sex marriage. This provides daily opportunities for public comment that might otherwise pass for hate speech (Butler 1997). A recent by-line accompanying letters to the editor in The Australian newspaper on August 18, 2016, page 13—'Safe Schools is worse than child abuse'—suggests that knowledge about non-heteronormative lives is perceived by some as a clear and present danger to young people. An earlier editorial in the same paper suggested that:

> There have been too many examples of late where social issues once aimed at overcoming prejudice have become progressive causes aimed at promoting alternative lifestyles or even enforcing a new political correctness. We have seen this unfold through the Safe Schools initiative in which admirable efforts to combat bullying of children on any grounds, including sexuality, were hijacked by those with a radical political agenda to "normalise" a wide range of sexual preferences, choices and behaviours… (Editorial, The Australian, August 2, 2016, p. 13)

These recent events have involved significant political and politicised interventions into the freedom to be/come queer. They bring into painfully sharp relief the ways in which competing discourses are mobilised about what is 'normal' and what is 'not'; what is desirable and what is not;

and, ultimately, what differences are acceptable and which are not. These debates inform, intersect with, and intensify conversations about the place of non-heteronormative identities in contemporary Australia and the unequal access queer Australians have to that which they require for a viable or 'good' life. My concern is not so much with elaborating these debates, but with the politics of knowledge through which the viability of queer life is undermined.

Whilst the possibilities for self-expression and self-knowledge about sex, gender, and sexuality that circulate in online spaces suggest multiple, transient, fluid, and mobile identities, these knowledges are in tension with knowledge of the self made available in the heteronormative everyday business-as-usual practices of the classroom. The liminal spaces between the different possibilities for queer identities online and in the classroom instantiate a politics of hope: hope for a place to be 'free to be me', to become and to belong. This search for the 'truth of oneself' is imbricated in the neoliberal fantasy that each of us is alone responsible for realising our potential and becoming what we truly are (Rose 1996, 1999). On the one hand, such fantasies of self-determination and unfettered choice suggest that it is within our power to choose who we are or what we might become. But queer young people tell a different story, especially when it comes to the possibilities opened or foreclosed by their experiences at school. Further, this longing to become, and to belong, is captured by discourses that remind young people that their non-heteronormative lives expose them to a politics that queers their hope for change and the viability of the lives they imagine for themselves and each other.

Remembering that the young people who participated in the *Growing up Queer* study suggested that the legalisation of same-sex marriage held the promise of a better future, one might wonder not only about the possibility of that future arriving, but the troubling road that might take us there, including young people's increased exposure to homophobic and transphobic discourses and practices that cruel their optimism for a better future.

'Cruel optimism', says Lauren Berlant (2011, p. 1), is a relation that exists when 'something you desire is actually an obstacle to your flourishing'. This relation is not, she says, inherently cruel, but becomes such when whatever has become the focus of attachment impedes the realisation of the aim towards that which the attachment is directed. This attachment, she suggests, involves a sustaining fantasy that enables us to expect that '*this* time, nearness to the thing will help you or a world become different in just the right way' (2011, p. 2). But cruel optimism results when the object/aim that ignites a sense of possibility actually makes it impossible to attain the desired transformation. Ironically, such attachment is doubly cruel, insofar as the attachment is sustaining yet exposes one to 'a situation of profound threat that is, at the same time, profoundly confirming' (2011, p. 2).

Berlant draws on this theorising of cruel optimism in order to interrogate citizenship and the public sphere, focusing in particular on how intimate publics work in proximity to normative modes of love and the law. This draws attention to a precarious public sphere where scenarios of possibilities for intimacy are contingent paradigms for a 'good life'. These scenarios also provide opportunities for engaging with the contours of 'what seems possible and blocked in personal/collective life' (2011, p. 4). These are understood as problems of survival made public: of the conditions for a viable life through which queer young people manage 'the incoherence of lives that proceed in the face of threats to the good life they imagine' (2011, p. 10).

> Unless we are prepared to exclude all those sexual constructions that differ from 'our own', or to deny difference by interpreting them as minor variations of an identical phenomenon, we must concede that groups evolve their own sexual culture around which they elaborate coherent lives. (Seidman 2015, p. x)

It is something of this evolution of sexual culture and identity that young people accomplish through online practices of becoming queer that I am foregrounding. Further, I point to the normative practices that determine which 'desires are sexual and which serve as identities, which desires and identities are acceptable, and what forms of sexual intimacy are considered appropriate' (Seidman 2015, p. x)—and thus, which identities and acts are punished, controlled, or considered deviant. I also foreground the tension points between the formation of online identities and communities of belonging and the identities and possibilities for belonging made available and supported in classrooms.

In working with the *Growing up Queer* data, I locate points of tension where practices of identification come into a 'line of sight' that makes differences visible as, simultaneously, points of difference and discrimination. I articulate these tension points as moments of social and emotional disequilibrium and attend to the emotional and symbolic distance they create—distance from a norm and distance between persons. I consider the impact of this disequilibrium on possibilities for becoming and belonging for queer young people, and articulate how this disequilibrium is manifest in the organisation of educational institutions, pedagogical practices and relationships among peers and teachers.

The differences and distances I am preoccupied with are those embodiments and performances of sex, gender and sexuality that fall outside the normative regulation of bodies at school; and with practices of schooling that simultaneously produce discrimination and suggest that certain bodies do not belong in the classroom. To this end, I foreground the ways in which the hetero/normative practices of schooling confirm, for many queer young people, that they neither belong in the classroom nor have any visible place in the curriculum or culture of the school. Where then, if not at school, might non-heteronormative identified students find spaces of becoming and belonging?

Despite the hetero/normative regulation of sexual subjectivity at school, and the silence and invisibility of knowledge of sexual and gender diversity (Robinson and Davies 2008; Ullman 2014, 2015), students are already learning about sexuality in other spaces—including digital social media. Despite teachers' best efforts to normalise students' expressions of sex, gender and sexuality in the classroom, possibilities for non-normative identities are in constant production through the material practices of subject formation that young people undertake online. In addressing the practices through which young people produce gendered, sexed and sexualised subjectivities and find spaces of belonging, both online and in the classroom, I point to tensions between the truth of the 'self' produced in the heteronormative practices of schooling and the multiple and possible truths and selves produced in young people's engagement with digital social media. These are both institutional sites for the production of sexual subjectivity and relations of belonging, each with their own nor-malising and regulatory practices that operate through different relations of freedom and choice. My purpose in pointing to these tensions is not to compare online and classroom practices, but to specifically consider possibilities for non-categorical, non-static possibilities for becoming and belonging at school.

Becoming and Belonging at School

Sara Ahmed (2012a, p. 2) suggests that 'if institutions provide homes in which some bodies gather, then some more than others will be at home in institutions'. Importantly, Ahmed (2012b, p. 13) notes that within any institution the body that causes discomfort is 'the one who must work hard to make others comfortable'. In this way, non-normative bod-ies shoulder the burden of responsibility for 'fitting in' and this pressure to institutionally 'pass' or 'fit in' becomes a matter of 'pressure to become part' (Ahmed 2012b, p. 13). Becoming part of the institution requires participation in the normative practices, embodiments and performances that are privileged in the institution. The normative institutional knowl-edges and practices that I am concerned with here are those that regulate bodies within the matrices of compulsory heterosexuality (Rich 1980)—or heteronormativity.

Broadly, heteronormativity refers to the valuing of heterosexuality as the natural and normative sexual orientation within a framework where gender is viewed as a natural derivative of sex, and males and females are depicted as appropriate and complementary sexual partners for the pur-pose of procreation. When heterosexuality is understood as naturally occurring, the everyday practices through which we learn how to embody and practice it are invisibilised (Ingraham 2005). Indeed, these embodied practices so naturalise heteronormative assumptions about what it means to be human that the extent to which this knowledge is always already heterosexual is elided. This confusion of heterosexuality as naturally occurring rather than institutionalised not only ignores the great variance in its practice across different cultural contexts, but also downplays its role in the distribution of labour and wealth in societies based on the reproductive family unit (Ingraham 2005).

'Becoming family' aligns biological sex, sexuality, gender identity and normative gender roles in ways that do not trouble commonsense understandings of nature, the natural and the normal. This biological alignment of the reproductive couple is foundational to the heteronormative logic of knowledge about gendered bodies, sexuality, biology and desire. Differences from this norm are not taken as evidence of the potential limits or failures of the norm, but rather marked as 'other' or 'deviant'. There is a doubled relation here between those lived experiences of difference that contest the norm, yet can only exist as a category of being different *because* of the norm. There is also a doubled resistance at play in this relation of difference: resistance to the norm and a reciprocal resistance from the norm against that which is different. Interrogation of the imbrication of the everyday practices of schooling in these relations and resistances opens spaces for tracing multiple, contingent and contradictory relationships between the pedagogical, the political and the personal. These everyday practices are sites for exploring the ways in which relations between knowledges, curricula and students are continuously structured and restructured in the institutional arrangements and relations between schools and students.

The *Growing up Queer* report (Robinson et al. 2013) confirms what other studies have a consistently shown: queer students are routinely marginalised at school (Hillier et al. 2010; Ullman 2014, 2015). Bullying, social isolation and homophobic victimisation of queer students have been associated with increased truancy, fear of attending school, diminished educational aspirations and non-completion of schooling (Birkett et al. 2009; Ullman 2014, 2015). Whilst queer young people are often constituted as 'at risk' of drug abuse, depression, suicide ideation and suicide attempts, they are less often articulated as 'at risk' from the hetero/normative practices of schooling themselves.

Kerry Robinson et al. (2013) note that Australian schools can be unwelcoming places for gender and sexuality nonconforming students. Such young people report verbal and physical victimisation and social isolation that frequently goes unnoticed or unpunished by their teachers (Hillier et al. 2010; Ullman and McGraw 2014). These experiences are linked to diminished educational outcomes (Ullman 2014, 2015) that are dependent, in part, on the level of heteronormativity manifest in school culture, curriculum and pedagogy (Wilkinson and Pearson 2009). Whole school curricular silences on sexual and gender diversity, including such topics as diverse families, legal/social equity issues, social construction of gender and sexuality, and other topics which might be linked to the daily lived experiences of queer students, enable the ongoing impact of negative institutional/school culture (Ullman and McGraw 2014). In schools where curricular silences are the norm, and where the general lack of attention to inclusive, bias-free language allows teachers to co-construct a heterosexist world-view, queer students report feeling less positive about their teachers and experience a decreased sense of belonging and identification with the school culture (Aerts et al. 2012; Robinson et al. 2013).

In what follows, I turn to data collected from young people in the study *Growing up Queer* (shown as italicised in the text) to illuminate points of tension between possibilities for becoming and belonging in schools and on social media as homes in which bodies gather. I do so in order to articulate how these points of tension might inform a rethinking of who or what is queer, and of queering possibilities for becoming and belonging at school.

Becoming and Belonging Online

In considering the practices through which young people are engaged in the ongoing negotiation of their own subjectivities—that sexuality is constituted and regulated through historically variable discourses and practices, and that new sexualities are constantly under production and open to revision and invention—I am particularly interested in the ways in which online discourses and practices are produced, consumed, embodied and performed through knowledge of the self, as experiences of self-discovery, becoming and belonging.

Megan Boler (2007) points out that digital representations of self, or digital identities, are more fluid, dynamic and flexible compared with pre-digital representations of self. Similarly, Anthony Giddens (1991,

1992, 2000) characterises the post-modern subject as self-reflexive, unbound by tradition and highly flexible. Giddens suggests that 'the digital revolution' has intensified the practice of self-reflexivity and invited users to change and to continuously reinscribe and reconstitute their identity in a digital world. This leads users to constantly analyse, reflect and strategically change themselves in order to find their place within shifting modes of becoming and belonging.

On February 14, 2014, Facebook (USA) invited users to customise their gender identity on their user profile. Fifty-two gender categories were provided for users to choose from. This invitation engaged users in making active choices in the production and description of both the self and self-knowledge. The purpose of this invitation was explained by Facebook as an opportunity for users to 'feel comfortable being [their] true, authentic self'. As explained by Facebook, a key element of this authenticity is the individual user's 'expression of gender, especially when it extends beyond the definitions of just "male" or "female." So today, we're proud to offer a new custom gender option to help you better express your own identity on Facebook' (Facebook 2013). Fischer (2012, p. 175), in pointing out that Facebook empowers users to contribute 'to their own objectification', signals the extent to which Facebook is a technology for the constitution and regulation of subjects who invent themselves and each other, and express their freedom to become and remain true to 'who they really are'. This is a discourse readily taken up by queer young people who participated in the *Growing up Queer* study: *Facebook has been good for spotting when a friend is in need of reassurance that they are fighting a good fight to stay true to themselves.*[2]

David Buckingham (2008) argues that 'commercial forces both create opportunities and set limits on young people's digital cultures', at the same time as they 'provide young people with symbolic resources for constructing or expressing their own identities' (p. 5). Facebook—as a commercial enterprise and site for the consumption and production of identities, defines and organises identities—enables young people to take up new identities, reaffirms who they already know themselves to be and offers recognition by others (Buckingham 2008, p. 6): *I visit sites that allow me to freely explore my sexuality and find information and read stories, other's stories about growing up and self-discovery.* These discourses and practices of the self are constituted and regulated by neoliberal acts of consumption, production, self-determination and the freedom to be/come one's true self. This 'true self' is made recognisable and intelligible through online communities of belonging.

> When it comes to exploring my own sexual identity, the internet has really helped me realise that there are other people experiencing the same feelings and going through the same repression as I am ... After I overcame the denial of being gay I found www.gayteenforum.org as a way of talking with other gay teens and to feel comfortable with my sexuality.

These practices of becoming and belonging involve labouring over knowledge to locate the truth of an authentic self. The ways in which different knowledge and truths of the self are differently produced online generate diverse truths about sex, gender and sexuality, and open up possibilities routinely excluded from the heteronormative business-as-usual of the classroom. Further, the material effects of classroom discourses and practices instantiate 'problems' that young people negotiate and resolve online. In the *Growing up Queer* data, classroom experiences of alienation, abjection, invisibility, misrecognition and discrimination are materialised in and through discourses of depression, anxiety, suicidal ideation and shame (amongst others). Online experiences of discovery, identification, community and recognition are expressed as discourses of hope, optimism, healing and self-realisation (amongst others). In this way, online practices become a corrective to the problems emergent for the subject who finds that their (queer) life is not viable in the classroom, but which can become viable online:

> I wasn't proud of my sexuality and didn't think I would be accepted or safe. I am now using Facebook to show people that I am proud and that I am very happy with who I am and the choices that I have made.

Jodi Dean (2013, p. 137) highlights the ways in which users of networked media encounter 'the endless possibilities of contemporary reflexivity' through which they are 'propelled to move through a variety of imaginary identities'. We imagine ourselves one way, then another, choosing how we might appear and to whom. Indeed, as Rose notes, neoliberal subjects are '*obliged* to ... construe their existence as the outcome of choices that they make among a plurality of alternatives' (Rose 1996, pp. 78–79). Importantly, the resources through which one might come to know oneself are not inevitably acquired through pure introspection but, as Rose says, 'by rendering one's introspection in a particular vocabulary of feelings, beliefs, passions, desires, values, or whatever and according a particular explanatory code derived from some source of authority' (Rose 1996, p. 32). That is, through a normative, authoritative source that authorises particular possibilities for becoming and belonging, whether online or in the classroom.

I am not so much concerned with comparing and problematising online and offline practices, nor with discontinuities among them, but rather with pointing out the ways in which the erasure of non-heteronormative sexes, genders or sexualities within the pedagogical practices of schooling reduce access to knowledge about the possibilities for alternative subject positions that are readily available to be taken up online:

> When I was younger and still coming out, I found it particularly useful to go onto internet sites and talk to people who had the same feelings as me. I didn't know many gay people growing up and there were certainly none who were open at my school.

Here, I point to the different matrices of intelligibility through which queer young people must learn to know themselves: the heterogeneous possibilities to be found online and the heteronormative matrices of intelligibility of the school/classroom that endorse certain possibilities for becoming and belonging and foreclose others.

Becoming and Belonging in the Classroom

Whilst we might expect to find discourses of individuality that endorse and celebrate difference and diversity in the classroom, we might also find that these celebrations of difference and diversity do not include the multiple and variable iterations of sex, gender and sexuality that young people seek out online. Further, in situations where any celebration of diversity remains both limited and unproblematised in the classroom, so too do the pedagogical practices that re/produce disequilibrium and discrimination. Problematising the heteronormative discourses and practices of schools as institutions, foregrounds the epistemological, ontological and pedagogical practices through which specific relations of power determine what knowledge is presented or not; who is represented and how; who speaks and who is silent; who is visible and who is not; who counts and who does not; and who belongs and who does not.

Student accounts of positive school experiences foreground the importance of both peer acceptance and teacher expectations to their personal sense of attachment or belonging (Aerts et al. 2012; Ullman 2014). It is clear in the *Growing up Queer* data that homophobia, transphobia and other forms of gender violence are experienced by queer young people as more hurtful and alienating when it comes from those who they assume will be their allies: their teachers (Robinson et al. 2013). Judith Butler (2004, p. 5), points out that one's state of managing vulnerability depends on the support one has, and not 'heroic individualism' or resilience figured as an individual capacity. Hence, the culture of the school as an institution is critical to possibilities for queer young people to become and belong. In schools where the curriculum specifically includes positive representations of same-sex-attracted and transgendered people, history and events, queer students experience less victimisation, greater sense of safety and higher reported academic outcomes than those young people whose schools do not include such material (Kosciw et al. 2010, 2013).

Just as young people labour online to negotiate knowledge through which they embody a queer identity, they are not passive consumers of school-mandated knowledge. Further, young people frequently report strong dissatisfaction with what they describe as narrow curriculum and classroom practices, and many report that they do not feel accepted by their peers and teachers (Zyngier 2004). Despite some recognition of the importance of access to a curriculum that encourages choice and diversity, knowledge about multiple sexes, genders and sexualities is conspicuously absent from curricula. Political and public responses to the Safe

Schools initiative suggest that it may be over-optimistic to expect that this will change any time soon.

> I didn't tell anyone I was gay because there were other openly gay students at my school that—people isolated themselves from them. Yeah, there was a guy that went to my school and he was extremely feminine and the boys were really intimidated because they thought he was going to try and put it on them. I saw that so I just thought I'll wait until I finish school and it'll be a lot easier.

The heteronormative practices of the school foreclose discussion of knowledges that disrupt binary constructions of sex, gender and sexuality, and for understanding oneself as becoming other than heteronormal. Further, the invisibility of, and silence about, alternative performances and embodiments of sex, gender and sexuality in classrooms does more than re/produce heteronormativity. Invisibility and silence also produce and endorse homophobia, transphobia and other forms of gender violence, including the symbolic violence of eliding certain possibilities for becoming and belonging. Further, the heteronormativity, homophobia and transphobia of schooling produces effects that consolidate a constitutive relation between non-heteronormative subjects and psychological/emotional trauma:

> I just felt ashamed and awful about myself ... Often it is hard to speak up, as it is very emotionally draining ... When speaking up would require that I out myself, I tended not to say anything, for fear of being stereotyped or thought of as disgusting.

My point here is not to critique the practices and discourses through which shame and disgust are produced, but to emphasise that teachers' pedagogical practices produce 'troubled' young people. This is the materialisation of gender trouble on the bodies, hearts and minds of queer young people. Importantly, any conceptualisations of discrimination and equity through which any subject is simultaneously cast as excluded *and* the problem to be solved, articulate the queer subject as having failed to locate themselves at, or be intelligible as belonging to, the mythic normative centre. This also invisibilises the responsibility of those at the centre—teachers and students alike—who do little more than 'lend a hand' to those in need, without needing to confront and address the ways in which they are complicit in the reinstantiation of the normative centre and practices that specifically aim to bring those who are excluded in towards it (Garbutt 2009).

As I argued at the outset, despite the heteronormative regulation of sexual subjectivity at school and the silence and invisibility of knowledge of sexual and gender diversity, students are already learning about sexuality in other spaces. These practices profoundly disrupt normalised, taken for granted relations between sex, gender and sexuality and reassemble them in a variety of combinations, associations, embodiments, performances and vocabularies of possibility—such as those noted by the young people who participated in the *Growing up Queer* study. In addition to *gay, homosexual, lesbian, queer,* young people described themselves as *heterosexual and queer, asexual, greysexual, greyromantic, gender variant, pansexual, omnisexual, polysexual, heteroflexible, homoflexible, panromantic, pansexual demiromantic, sapiopansexual, heteroromantic and bisexual, open to people*—a lexicon of possibilities unlikely to be acquired or validated in the classroom.

These young people laboured online to find the right vocabularies of intelligibility and categories of personhood through which they might recognise, describe, embody and perform their 'true' or 'real' self. These vocabularies of intelligibility are not, I suggest, signs or reflections of a true sexed, gendered and sexualised self; rather, they are signs that sexuality is not a natural biological and fixed truth of the self but, instead, constituted and regulated through historically specific and variable discourses and practices. These vocabularies of possible bodies, desires, identities, essences, natures, truths and realties are constitutive discourses through which bodies, minds and inner worlds of sensation, desire and feeling are brought together as self-knowledge, and these are more likely found online than in the classroom:

> The vast majority of my knowledge about atypical gender and sexual identities I gained from the internet. I found YouTube to be very helpful when it came to feeling right about myself. Those who were out and proud gave me comfort, hope and support.

Heteronormative discourses of nature and the natural are exclusionary and often irreconcilable with the nature young people ascribe to themselves. The effects of these irreconcilable natures were, in the *Growing up Queer* data, expressed as suicidal ideation, depression, anxiety, shame, humiliation and so on. This was in stark contrast to the more optimistic discourses of recognition and belonging mobilised online. These moments of social and emotional disequilibrium highlight the emotional and symbolic distance they create from the norm, from others and between their online and classroom selves. This is not to romance the production of online identities, but to point out the role that schools might take in both constituting a relation between difference and experiences of trauma and, importantly, in seizing opportunities for constituting difference differently.

Becoming and Belonging Anywhere/ Everywhere

Earlier in this chapter, I flagged my concern with lived experiences of inequality and my intention to broaden the Department of Education and Training's categories of disadvantage and equity to include queer young people. I also articulated a queer politics that resists the collapse of all forms of diversity into singular stable categories: a politics that queers and undoes categorical conceptualisations of persons at the same time as it mobilises the discourses and politics of categories in order to do so. This queer politics is predicated on the assumption that conceptualisations of belonging based on membership of a particular category or community produce static accounts of identity, and it aims to open up multiple and fluid, temporally and spatially shifting possibilities for becoming and belonging. Further, this emphasis on the possibilities for becoming as variable over time and space informs a conception of belonging as a sense of connection to others that is always in the process of being actively achieved (Probyn 1996). Hence, practices and processes of becoming and belonging are indeterminate and irreducible to stable categories. So, what might this recognition of indeterminacy and irreducibility mean for schools as institutions and for the viability of the lives of those students who currently find themselves absent or marginalised in the everyday, heteronormative knowledges and practices of the classroom?

Within the context of contemporary Australian life, contentious and frequently hostile public debates about same-sex marriage and the Safe Schools initiative have simultaneously bolstered and critiqued heteronormative truths about what is natural and normal. These debates have also effaced the broader potential for teachers to engage in democratic deliberation over questions of equity beyond the collapse of equity groups into stable categories of persons. They also unequally expose particular bodies to new opportunities for vilification, abjection and disequilibrium at the very same time as they advocate for their freedom to become and belong. Further, any discourses of equity and diversity that focus on particular categories of person, and hence particular bodies, compromise meaningful discussion about diversity and issues of recognition and intelligibility for those students who have been historically invisibilised or misrecognised in the pedagogical practices and constructions of knowledge embedded in a heteronormative curriculum.

In working with the *Growing up Queer* data, I have drawn attention to tension points in the practices through which queer young people labour to 'pass' or 'fit in' or are subject to elision and discrimination in the school as institution. I have also signalled the extent to which the everyday practices of schooling reinstantiate the peril of both not belonging and becoming responsible for one's own difference. As Edward Said reminds us, to occupy the 'perilous territory of not-belonging' is to develop the 'habit of dissimulation [which] is both wearying and nerve-racking' (Said 2000, p. 177, p. 186).

Given my articulation of the knowledges, discourses and practices through which queer young people negotiate their identities online and at school, and of the significant material violence young people experience in the disequilibrium between them, I contemplate some possibilities for rethinking the truths of sex, gender and sexuality at school. I specifically think beyond anti-homophobia education and equity discourses that, as I see it, reinscribe queer youth within normal/not normal, self/other, same/different, hetero/homo binaries that solidify assumptions of predictable continuities between sex, gender and sexuality. As one participant in our study pointed out: *things would have been better if there was better education in schools about queerness.*

Karen Barad (2012) suggests that all matter, both human and not, is queer: that is, everything is indeterminate and open to multiple possibilities under multiple and variable conditions of possibility. It is something of this spirit of indeterminacy that I hope to mobilise in order to undermine categorical thinking as a hopelessly inadequate account of human becoming and belonging. This is, simultaneously, a pedagogy and politics that aims to 'desubjectivize queerness and to see it in practices that feel out alternative routes for living without requiring personhood to be expressive of an internal orientation or part of a political program advocating how to live' (Berlant 2011, p. 18). I am, then, interested in pedagogies that resist entreaties to find true sexed, gendered and sexualised selves and fix them in place once and for all. Having pointed out the extent to which queer young people labour online to both find alternative possibilities and vocabularies for becoming and belonging as well as manage the material impacts of the heteronormative practices of schooling, I suggest that schools/teachers have an ethical responsibility to *all* young people to ensure that heteronormative curricula and pedagogies do not re/produce binary possibilities for becoming that always, and often painfully, inscribe otherness on particular bodies. Indeed, categorical accounts of becoming and belonging reproduce sexism, racism, classism, and for young people who do not embody the mythic normative centre, experiences of homophobia, transphobia and other forms of discrimination and exclusion. Experiences such as these suggest that queer subjects do not belong at school. In contesting the mythic normative centre and de-centring *all* students from it, at the same time as opening knowledges and practices of human becoming to multiple possibilities under multiple and variable conditions of possibility, I suggest that queer subjects are, and belong, everywhere.

Notes

1. The *Growing up Queer* study included a national online survey of 1230 young people aged 17–26, and interviews and focus groups conducted in 2012 with young people who identify as gender and sexuality diverse. The study was developed in partnership with the Young and Well Cooperative Research Centre.
2. All quotes in this chapter are from the *Growing up Queer: issues facing young Australians who are gender variant and sexuality diverse* (2014) study. They have not been individually identified, consistent with the final report.

References

Aerts, S., Van Houtte, M., Dewaele, A., Cox, N., & Vincke, J. (2012). Sense of belonging in secondary school: A survey of LGB and heterosexual students in Flanders. *Journal of Homosexuality, 59*(1), 90–113.

Ahmed, S. (2012a). *On being included: Racism and diversity in institutional life.* Durham, NC: Duke University Press.

Ahmed, S. (2012b). Whiteness and the general will: Diversity work as willful work. *Philosophia, 2*(1), 1–20.

Anthias, F. (2006). Belongings in a globalizing and unequal world: Rethinking translocations. In N. Yuval-Davis, K. Kannabiran, & U. Vieten (Eds.), *The situated politics of belonging* (pp. 17–32). London: Sage.

Barad, K. (2012). Intra-active entanglements – An interview with Karen Barad, by M. Juelskjaer & N. Schwennesen. *KVINDER FKON & FORSKING NR, 1*(2), 10–24.

Berlant, L. (2011). *Cruel optimism.* Durham, NC: Duke University Press.

Birkett, M., Espelage, D. L., & Koenig, B. (2009). LGB and questioning students in schools: The moderating effects of homophobic bullying and school climate on negative outcomes. *Journal of Youth and Adolescence, 38*(7), 989–1000.

Boler, M. (2007). Hypes, hopes and actualities: New digital Cartesianism and bodies in cyberspace. *New Media & Society, 9*(1), 139–168.

Buckingham, D. (2008). Youth, identity and digital media. In *The J D and Catherine T MacArthur Foundation Series on Digital Media and Learning.* Cambridge, MA: The MIT Press.

Butler, J. (1993). *Bodies that matter: On the discursive limits of 'sex'.* London and New York: Routledge.

Butler, J. (1997). *Excitable speech: A politics of the performative.* New York and London: Routledge.

Butler, J. (2004). *Precarious life: The powers of mourning and violence.* London: Verso.

Dean, J. (2013). Whatever blogging. In T. Scholz (Ed.), *Digital labour: The internet as playground and factory* (pp. 127–146). New York and London: Routledge.

Department of Education and Training. (2012). https://docs.education.gov.au/documents/2012-appendix-2-equity-groups.

Diprose, R. (2008). Where your people from girl?: Belonging to race, gender, and place beneath clouds. *Differences: A Journal of Feminist Cultural Studies, 19*(3), 28–58.

Facebook. (2013, February 13). *Facebook diversity.* Retrieved January 27, 2015, from https://www.facebook.com/facebookdiversity.

Fisher, E. (2012). How less alienation creates more exploitation? Audience labour on social network sites. *Triple C-Open Access Journal for a Global Sustainable Information Society, 10,* 171–183.

Foucault, M. (1992). *The use of pleasure: The history of sexuality: 2.* London: Penguin.

Gale, T., & Densmore, K. (2002). Student success and failure: As a matter of fact or just how they are portrayed? *Asia-Pacific Journal of Teacher Education, 30*(1), 7–23.

Garbutt, R. (2009). Social inclusion and local practices of belonging. *Cosmopolitan Civil Societies Journal, 1*(3), 84–108.

Giddens, A. (1991). *Modernity and self-identity: Self and society in the late modern age.* Stanford, CA: Stanford University Press.

Giddens, A. (1992). *The transformation of intimacy: Sexuality, love, and eroticism in modern societies.* Stanford, CA: Stanford University Press.

Giddens, A. (2000). *Runaway world: How globalization is reshaping our lives.* New York: Routledge.

Griffin, P. (2007). Sexing the economy in a neo-liberal world order: Neo-liberal discourse and the (re)production of heteronormative heterosexuality. *Political Studies Association BJPIR, 9*(2), 220–238.

Hillier, L., Jones, T., Monagle, M., Overton, N., Gahan, L., Blackman, J., & Mitchell, A. (2010). *Writing themselves in 3 (WTi3): The third national study on the sexual health and wellbeing of same sex attracted and gender questioning young people*. Australian Research Centre in Sex, Health and Society, La Trobe University, Melbourne.

Ingraham, C. (2005). Introduction: Thinking straight. In C. Ingraham (Ed.), *Thinking straight: The power, the promise, and the paradox of heterosexuality* (pp. 1–14). New York: Routledge.

Kosciw, J. G., Greytak, E. A., Diaz, E. M., & Barkiewicz, M. J. (2010). *The 2009 national school climate survey: The experiences of lesbian, gay, bisexual and transgender youth in our nation's schools*. New York: GLSEN.

Kosciw, J. G., Palmer, N. A., Kull, R. M., & Greytak, E. A. (2013). The effect of negative school climate on academic outcomes for LGBT youth and the role of in-school supports. *Journal of School Violence, 12*(1), 45–63.

LeMaster, B. (2015). Discontents of being and becoming fabulous on RuPaul's Drag U: Queer criticism in neoliberal times. *Women's Studies in Communication*. https://doi.org/10.1080/07491409.2014.988776.

Probyn, E. (1996). *Outside belongings*. New York: Routledge.

Rich, A. (1980). Compulsory heterosexuality and lesbian existence. *Signs: Journal of Women in Culture and Society, 5*(4), 631–660.

Robinson, K., & Davies, C. (2008). Docile bodies and heteronormative moral subjects: Constructing the child and sexual knowledge in schooling. *Sexuality & Culture, 12*(4), 221–239.

Robinson, K., Bansel, P., Denson, N., Davies, C., & Ovendon, G. (2013). *Growing up queer: Issues facing young Australians who are gender variant and sexuality diverse*. Retrieved June 19, 2017, from http://www.glhv.org.au/files/Growing_Up_Queer2014.pdf.

Rose, N. (1996). *Inventing ourselves: Psychology, power and personhood*. Cambridge: Cambridge University Press.

Rose, N. (1999). *Governing the soul: The shaping of the private self*. London: Free Association Books.

Said, E. W. (2000). *Reflections on exile and other essays*. Cambridge, MA: Harvard University Press.

Seidman, S. (2015). *The social construction of sexuality*. New York: W. W. Norton.

Ullman, J. (2014). Ladylike/butch, sporty/dapper: Exploring 'gender climate' with Australian LGBTQ students using stage-environment fit theory. *Sex Education, 14*(4), 430–443.

Ullman, J. (2015). 'At-risk' or school-based risk? Testing a model of school-based stressors, coping responses, and academic self-concept for same-sex attracted youth. *Journal of Youth Studies, 18*(4), 417–433.

Ullman, J., & McGraw, K. (2014). Troubling silences and taboo texts: Constructing safer and more positive school climates for same-sex attracted high school students in Australia. In D. Carlson & E. Meyer (Eds.), *Gender and sexualities in education: A reader* (pp. 298–312). New York: Peter Lang.

Wilkinson, L., & Pearson, J. (2009). School culture and the well-being of same-sex-attracted youth. *Gender and Society, 23*(4), 542–568.

Zyngier, D. (2004). *Doing education not doing time. Engaging pedagogies and pedagogues – What does student engagement look like in action?* Australian Association for Research in Education Annual Conference, Melbourne, Victoria.

4

Gender, Sexuality and Belonging: Beyond the Mainstream

Tiffany Jones

Introduction

Decades ago, I attended a Catholic all-girls school where lesbians were pelted with Coke cans. Years ago, I was asked by my then university PhD supervisor if I would change my thesis topic from policy on lesbian, gay, bisexual, transgender and intersex (LGBTI) students so that people would not think I was a 'lesbian' (the speaker whispered the word like a snake in a Harry Potter film, as if even its phonemes were toxic)… I changed universities instead. Months ago, I arrived at La Trobe University for grant-work as hundreds of media articles from a few conservative newspapers slammed the university's Safe Schools Coalition (Anderson 2016; Butler 2016; Taylor 2016) and the many LGBTI rights researchers believed to have designed it (almost none of whom had anything even peripherally to do with it but, in an anti-LGBTI press attack, anyone loosely associated with LGBTI students may be cast by extremists as fair game). Weeks ago, I was in UNESCO's headquarters, where we advocated for, and got, education

T. Jones (✉)
La Trobe University, Melbourne, Australia
e-mail: tiffany.jones@mq.edu.au

© The Author(s) 2018
C. Halse (ed.), *Interrogating Belonging for Young People in Schools*,
https://doi.org/10.1007/978-3-319-75217-4_4

ministers of all global regions to release the first ever Call for Action (UNESCO 2016) on homophobic and transphobic violence in education. Days ago, the four Safe Schools Coalition Victoria staff at La Trobe University were told they no longer had a job working to support bullied LGBTI students in schools, as their contracts had been terminated.

So, I come to these chapters in a particularly confused and fraught era where LGBTI identities are currently being used as accusations. And not just from kids in schools but in higher education/media/parliamentary contexts and even by adult journalists and adult parliamentarians. I come to the chapters through my un-belonging, conditional belonging, questioning of belonging and advocacy for broadening belonging. I come to the chapters sharing, at the very least, their suspicion of simplistic notions of 'progress' for LGBTI rights even as I try advance these rights; their suspicion of the impact of 'visibility' even as I live a life as a visible researcher into LGBTI rights themes; and their suspicion of 'identity' even as our research shows LGBTI youth now have a greater proliferation of identifications than ever before, ranging from pansexual through to anti-identity trends (Hillier et al. 2010; Jones 2015; Smith et al. 2014). As theoretical as they seem, these chapters discuss very political and, at times, even painful themes for LGBTI people. They draw particularly on the work of Michel Foucault and Judith Butler to explore how students are constituted, or 'subjectified', within schools, and also how students may 'be otherwise' (Butler 1990; Foucault 1976). They sketch out some of the influences of mainstream thinking on identification and disruptive potentials of queer thinking about the 'truth' of queer identity in education. The chapters inspired me to outline some of the most important ways to support belonging for LGBTIs in education which I have learned from my research. In this paper, I discuss four factors that promote LGBTI belonging in schools or help deal with their nonbelonging: policy protection, activism, direct coverage and alternate spaces.

Policy Protection Promotes Belonging

Emma Charlton, Leanne Coll, Lyn Harrison and Debbie Ollis' chapter highlights how seemingly mundane and incidental pedagogical moments shape sex-gender-sexuality identities in ways that limit the opportunities for learning and for transformational pedagogical experiences. My work has underlined the value of education policies in promoting safety and belonging for LGBTI students in schools and in impacting how teachers and other staff address incidental moments. I analysed online surveys of 3134 LGBTI students (aged 14–21 years, 56% female, 41% male, 3% gender diverse) to understand the value of protections for the group in education policies (Hillier et al. 2010; Jones 2015). Only a quarter of participants reported specific school-level policy protection from discrimination on the basis of LGBTI status (mostly in Victoria and New South Wales where state policy protections also existed). Unsurprisingly perhaps, these students who were protected by school-level policies were more likely to feel safe than students who weren't protected by school-level policies (75% vs. 45%); and safety is a pre-condition for engaging with educational settings and the people one meets there. They were also more likely to be taught anti-homophobia messages in sex education (30% vs. 10%); more likely to feel good about their sexuality (85% vs. 78%); and more likely to report other support features such as posters/library books/support groups for LGBTI students at school (84% vs. 41%).

The practical outcomes were even more concrete, in terms of physical safety for LGBTI students. Most survey participants had experienced some form of homophobic abuse (75%), with most abuse (80%) occurring at school. However, those at schools with no policy protection were more likely to experience physical homophobic abuse at school compared to those at schools with protection (47% vs. 23%). They were more likely to think about suicide on the basis of homophobic abuse (47% vs. 34%), and more likely to attempt suicide (22% vs. 13%). It is, therefore, undeniable that protection for LGBTI people in education policies can contribute to environments where LGBTI students are less likely to be harmed, less likely to harm themselves and more likely to feel they belong. Their teachers were more likely to teach diverse sexuality and gender identity materials. The risks of violence and poor wellbeing for this group are high but the research shows these risks are impacted by the environment rather than being inherent to being an LGBTI person. Education stakeholders (academics, governments, administrators, school staff and parents/guardians) thus have an ethical obligation to argue for LGBTI students' protection in education settings, as a pre-condition to supporting their belonging.

Activism Promotes Belonging

My work has underlined the value of activism as a pathway to belonging in schools. I first became interested in this when I noticed that transgender students were more likely to engage in activism than same-sex attracted students (Jones and Hillier 2013). To investigate this further, we conducted surveys of 189 transgender and gender diverse youth (aged 14–25 years), alongside 16 interviews (Jones et al. 2016b; Smith et al. 2014). Half the participants had identities fitting a male–female binary 'oppositional' to their allocated sex (13% boy/man, 13% girl/woman, 6% trans man, 6% trans woman, 6% female to male (FtM), 5% male to female (MtF) or 1% brotherboy). Half had non-binary identities 16%—genderqueer, 10% gender fluid, 7% agender, 5% trans*, 4% androgynous, 4% questioning, 2% bi-gender and 2% other—such as 15 year old Alex who was agender and reported, '*I don't feel a presence of gender*'. Most of these young people (77%) had begun social transition (affirming their gender identity and preferred pronouns, presentation and role); 7% wanted to in the future. Some (26%) had begun medical transition (accessing hormonal and/or surgical aids); some (33%) wanted to. Few (17%) had legally transitioned (changed birth certificate, licence, proof of age card or passport); most (54%) wanted to. Under 10% changed gender in school records; 41% wanted to.

We found that the overwhelming majority (91%) of transgender and gender diverse students reported participating in at least one activism event. They were more likely to engage in activism that required minimal effort and was anonymous; mainly engaging in online petitions or Facebook/social media activism, for example. In a much smaller number of cases, individuals engaged in activism that required more effort and was exposing; such as giving speeches at school, organising rallies and doing television interviews. Regardless of the type of activism in which the young person engaged, activism made more than half feel better about their gender identity (60%); have fun (57%); and feel part of a larger community (55%). It also had other benefits for a smaller portion of the group, including helping them to feel more resilient (33%); reduce thoughts of suicide (31%); experience less depression (30%); reduce thoughts of self-harm (30%); and stop engaging in a self-harm or suicide attempt (24%). There are a variety of texts school staff can read on how activism can occur for staff and young people, some which rely on claiming LGBTI identities and some which do not (Cohen 2005; Lalor 2015; Ollis et al. 2007; Rasmussen 2006; Rubin 2015). I would argue that it is important educators promote the value of non-exposing, online activism, especially for transgender young people, and activism which does not necessarily require someone to claim a stable LGBTI identity. This might be particularly important in ensuring members of the group can, later on, inhabit identities as adults which do not emphasise an element more important to them now—such as their transgender history—as some adults who have transitioned, for example, might 'go stealth' rather than identifying as transgender directly, or simply see themselves as 'men'/'women' post-transition, for example (Jones et al. 2015). Belonging changes over time and identities can shift and be complex.

Direct Coverage and Support Promotes Belonging

People with intersex variations were born with chromosomal, hormonal or anatomical differences to their sex traits. They are rarely mentioned in Australian schools yet could account for 2–4% of the student body (Jones 2016a; Jones et al. 2016a). I used surveys of 272 people with intersex variations (aged 16–87yrs) to understand their education experiences (Jones 2016a; Jones et al. 2016a). Whilst 52% were allocated a female sex at birth and 41% male (2% X, 2% unsure and 4% another option); fewer *now* used male and more *now* used X or other options. Most participants had two intersex variations (most commonly androgyn insensitivities or Poly-Cystic Ovary Syndrome (PCOS)/PCOS-related hyperandrogynism, although over 30 variations were represented from 5-alpha reductase deficiency/5-ARD to XY-Turner Syndrome). Most preferred to describe their variations using the word intersex (60%) instead of other terms (25% diagnosis, 17% my chromosomes, 7% difference of sex development, 3% disorder of sex development). Less than a third (27%) had disabilities (e.g., anosmia, movement or learning impairments sometimes related to their variations). The majority (64%) learned of their variation aged under 18 years, mainly in relation to medical appointments, in tense, uninformative conversation. Most (56%) now felt positively about their variation; over twice as many as when they had first learned of it—the difference being that, initially, they learned of it in relation to medical appointments and in a stigmatised, medical way suggesting a need for treatment. Over half experienced two medical interventions (commonly hormonal treatment during puberty and genital surgery in infancy or puberty). Most experienced at least one negative impact (scarring, decreased sensation, depression/anxiety/Post Traumatic Stress Disorder (PTSD), septicaemia etc.).

On the basis of having an intersex variation, 42% had considered self-harm and 26% engaged in it; 60% had considered suicide and 19% attempted it—usually around the adolescent period in which they first learned of their variation. A sizeable portion of the group had dropped out of school and, therefore, had a primary school education only (18% vs. 2% in the Australian population). Dropout occurred during grades associated with puberty. It was impacted by medical interventions and lack of support from school staff. Further, 92% reported that their school provided no inclusive sex or puberty education about intersex variations and 95% reported that their school provided no inclusive counselling. Many people with intersex variations did not know if members of their own family shared their variation due to family tension and secrecy. The fact there is, generally, tension and secrecy in families around many LGBTI themes means we cannot rely on family settings for information dissemination. Many people with intersex variations were bullied for how they looked or for the fact that they needed time off from school for medical treatments. The potential for bullying provides additional safety-related reasons why we cannot rely on individual information dissemination methods at school requiring initial disclosure of LGBTI status as an access prompt.

Supportive information about sex traits, gender and sexuality needs to be given to everyone. Indeed, Charlton, Coll, Harrison and Ollis point out, in their chapter, the embodied nature of belonging in pedagogical spaces in schools. Drawing on their vignette, they propose that normative notions of sex-gender-sexuality and belonging are embedded and inherent in the practices and structures of school spaces, which privilege certain types of sex-sexuality-gendered belonging over others. I would argue that scientific data about the diversity in human sex traits (chromosomes, hormones, anatomy), gender and sexuality are fascinating, and relevant to all humans. People with intersex variations (as well as the young LGBT people in my other surveys) wanted schools to mention their broad existence in an inclusive manner to prevent their drop-out. This could easily be achieved in a scientific manner in puberty, sex, health or science education coverage. Training needs to be provided to staff and counsellors to ensure they can assist these students with any particular psychological, medical or other needs (Carman et al. 2011). Belonging is not automatic; it needs to be facilitated.

Alternate Spaces May Help in the Event of Non-belonging

Peter Bansel's paper 'Becoming and belonging' asks where, if not at school, LGBTI students can be recognised, included and belong? Bansel thus spatialises the subject and questions of inclusion and exclusion with prescribed possibilities for being and belonging, and considers how queer young people labour to occupy and find themselves in both schools and online spaces, including social media. Drawing on qualitative survey data, interviews and focus groups, Bansel articulates a constitutive relation between the truth of the 'self' produced in schooling and the multiple and possible selves produced by youth people online. Belonging is cast as an ongoing project of becoming via everyday practices, enacted in multiple and shifting locations, *rather than stable group membership.* LGBTI students are always in the process of actively conceiving connections in ways which broaden various options, disrupt norms or vary in shape or fit over time and as boundaries shift. Both belonging and its policing are effortful yet 'the digital revolution' intensifies opportunities for self-reflexivity, identity change, re-inscription and re-constitution. Young people constantly analyse, reflect and strategically change themselves within shifting modes of being, becoming and belonging. When distant from mythic normative centres, they are held responsible and accountable for their failure, but also for solutions to failure. Alternative spaces for LGBTI students—and their success or failure—should not be solely seen as the responsibility of young LGBTI people.

My own surveys have repeatedly shown the internet as the space where LGBTI people (including adults) now gain information on identities, knowledges and communities (Jones 2015, 2016a; Jones et al. 2015; Jones et al. 2016a). This is especially exaggerated for intersex people, which may seem ironic given their identity is often argued as the most medically and physically grounded. However, the word intersex really only became workably available 'virtually' in the first instance (members of this group have suffered from being labelled with various disorders in medical contexts, or labelled as hermaphrodites or other socially contextual terms, none of which truly fit). The three methods I have discussed for enhancing belonging thus far (policy, activism and direct coverage) were all geared towards changing education systems from the inside or working towards improving them as they currently stand, in what Bansel might term an assimilative way. Education stakeholders (academics, governments, administrators, school staff and parents/guardians) can argue for LGBTI students' protection in policy, can support their activism by providing opportunities to engage in online or in-school events, and can ensure direct coverage of relevant topics in classrooms and staff training for example. This is important because education in Australia and similar countries *is* assimilative, compulsory and delivered *en masse* (regardless of the non-assimilationist politics of Queer theory's ideals). However, sometimes education crises emerge which negatively impact LGBTI people in schools (such as the 2016 attacks on LGBTI people in Australian schools by right-wing media). There needs to be alternate spaces, besides schooling environments, where we deal with the non-belonging of LGBTI people, as Bansel suggests. There have been, and continue to be, examples of LGBTI students who drop out of schools (Jones 2016a; Jones and Hillier 2013). There have been, and continue to be, LGBTI teachers who get fired or legitimately fear being fired due to a lack of policy protection in certain religious schools (Gray et al. 2016; Jones et al. 2014). There have been, and continue to be, LGBTI people in education research, government education department contexts and other education advocacy positions in Australia, for example, who have feared and continue to fear being fired or excluded due to extreme contextual homophobia or pressure from right-wing media attacks (Jones 2016b)—including the four Victorian Safe Schools Coalition staff who were 'let go' at the end of 2016.

We are in a period of what I term a 'volatile shift' in progress in Australia, and globally, on LGBTI rights. Anti-discrimination discourses and laws are emerging but they do not entirely replace the biases against LGBTI people that have long dominated our contexts; they instead exist alongside and in competition with them. We now face a period that will be not unlike that which, as I anecdotally learned from my travels, preceded the dismantling of Apartheid in South Africa; when debates were bitter and violence increased against people of colour (who, like LGBTI people, were seen by their opponents as claiming 'new rights' instead of just 'the same rights as everyone else'). Opponents to LGBTI rights are free to dislike LGBTI people, even if LGBTI people are legally protected in many contexts from their direct expression of their dislike (Australian Parliament 2013; United Nations 2012). Opponents to LGBTI rights are free to imagine LGBTI people as 'hell-bound', even if LGBTI people are members of every faith, religion and spiritualty (Gahan and Jones 2013; Wilson 2013). Some children with intersex variations *still* have their genitals 'medically corrected' without their permission as some clinicians naively attempt to make them fit normative ideals for males or females (Kennedy 2016; Overington 2016), even now when they are protected in international and local law. This can impact on their schooling. There will be times, therefore, when LGBTI people and their allies need to seek each-other out for safety, for recourse, for employment, for education, for spiritual balm, for celebration or simply because there is nobody else to turn to. In seeking belonging in education, alternate spaces for non-belonging must be part of the ongoing contingency plan if people are going to feel safe enough to advocate (and willing enough to lose their employment, or possibly more) for improvement in mainstream education contexts. This is beginning to be seen around the world. In the USA, it comes in the form of a strong network of Gay Straight Alliances in schools run by students, the Gay Straight and Lesbian Education Network funded by a range of donors (so not solely reliant on fickle government funding), and LGBTI-friendly alternative schools like Harvey Milk High. In China, there are online groups and organisations like *aibai* which arrange for mothers to go and speak on behalf of LGBTI people in schools. In the Kingdom of Lesotho in southern Africa, the organisation Fortress provides an alternate environment.

There needs to be an education space where students who are expelled or who drop out, teachers and advocates who are threatened or fired, and other LGBTI people (including those doing academic studies of these issues) can go when there is nowhere else—where non-belonging can be embraced and, therefore, mediated as one of the risks faced in the push for LGBTI rights progress. In Australia at the moment, for example, the main alternate space is online, as identified by Bansel's chapter. In light of the attacks on Safe Schools Coalition online during 2016 (including the creation of the Facebook pages against LGBTI people by unnamed opponents,[1] which sometimes featured death threats or cruel taunts about people's gendered appearance by those who visited and posted throughout the year), internet spaces must be more carefully and protectively conceived than they have been previously to ensure they are secure from homophobia, transphobia and anti-intersex bias. Online spaces need to be more carefully moderated than perhaps they have needed to be in the past, as anti-LGBTI extremists seek to infiltrate and comment negatively on any LGBTI websites like never before (a consequence of visibility is accessibility to attack). We also need to consider the value of seeing alternative online schooling spaces as alternative contexts for employment. I would argue that these should never replace the ultimate goal of increased belonging and safety in mainstream contexts. Instead, they should be a supplement for times when mainstream contexts are too difficult or unsafe for LGBTI people to attend, whilst those spaces are re-negotiated during periods of volatile shift. Online alternative schooling is just one option which could provide temporary employment and education possibilities to those needing aid in any context, could be carefully protected and moderated, and could be facilitated with the aim of getting people back into nearby mainstream contexts as soon as feasible after any reasonable modifications to those spaces have been implemented (in cases of extreme rights breaches).

Conclusion

In sum, the authors of the chapters in this section 'Gender, sexuality and belonging', challenge how belonging, identification, progress, and educative sites—both real and virtual—have been conceived. They question some of the 'truths' often unquestioningly used by media and society in debating LGBTI students, including conceptualisations of progress, visibility and identity processes. Queer subjects are, and belong, everywhere, yet they both identify with queerness through un-belongings in normative centres in schools *and* labour towards other heterogeneous potentials elsewhere. The chapters highlight the value of disruptive, historical, pedagogical and virtual work in re-thinking gender, sexuality and LGBTI people's belonging in relation to education. My own research has shown the value of education policy protection for LGBTI people and of activism (especially anonymous online activism) and direct coverage of LGBTI issues for improving the belonging of LGBTI people in education settings. As Bansel points out, there is potential for the internet to offer further aid in dealing with non-belonging for a variety of LGBTI stakeholders through the development of alternative, LGBTI-friendly, online education supplements, as long as this is done carefully and as a complement only, without seeing alternative spaces as the end-goal for LGBTI people in a way that damages possibilities of mainstreamed belonging.

Note

1. For example, the Facebook page 'Stop the Safe Schools Coalition'.

References

Anderson, S. (2016, February 24). Bill Shorten labels Cory Bernardi a homophobe over opposition to Safe Schools program. *ABC News*. Retrieved from http://www.abc.net.au/news/2016-02-24/shorten-labels-bernardi-a-homophobe-over-safe-schools/7195664.

Butler, J. (1990). *Gender trouble: Feminism and the subversion of identity*. London: Routledge.

Butler, J. (2016, April 12). VIC Premier Daniel Andrews commits to expanding safe schools coalition in his state. *Huffington Post Australia*.

Carman, M., Mitchell, A., Schlichthorst, M., & Smith, A. (2011). Teacher training in sexuality education in Australia: How well are teachers prepared for the job? *Sexual Health, 8*(3), 269–271.

Cohen, S. (2005). Liberationists, clients, activists: Queer youth organizing, 1966–2003. *Journal of Gay & Lesbian Issues in Education, 2*(3), 67–86.

Foucault, M. (1976). *The history of sexuality: Volume one, the will to knowledge*. Harmondsworth: Penguin Books.

Gahan, L., & Jones, T. (2013). *Heaven Bent: Australian lesbian, gay, bisexual, transgender and intersex experiences of faith, religion and spirituality*. Melbourne: Clouds of Magellan.

Gray, E., Harris, A., & Jones, T. (2016). Australian LGBTQ teachers, exclusionary spaces and points of interruption. *Sexualities, 19*(3), 286–303.

Hillier, L., Jones, T., Monagle, M., Overton, N., Gahan, L., Blackman, J., & Mitchell, A. (2010). *Writing themselves In 3: The third national study on the sexual health and wellbeing of same-sex attracted and gender questioning young people*. Retrieved from Melbourne: http://www.latrobe.edu.au/ssay/assets/downloads/wti3_web_sml.pdf.

Jones, T. (2015). *Policy and gay, lesbian, bisexual, transgender and intersex students*. Cham, Heidelberg, New York, Dordrecht and London: Springer.

Jones, T. (2016a). The needs of students with intersex variations. *Sex Education, 16*(6), 602–618. Retrieved from http://www.tandfonline.com/doi/abs/10.1080/14681811.2016.1149808?journalCode=csed20.

Jones, T. (2016b). Researching & working for transgender youth: Contexts, problems and solutions. *Social Sciences, 5*(3), 43.

Jones, T., & Hillier, L. (2013). Comparing trans-spectrum and same-sex attracted youth: Increased risks, increased activisms. *LGBT Youth, 10*(4), 287–307.

Jones, T., Gray, E., & Harris, A. (2014). GLBTIQ teachers in Australian education policy: Protections, suspicions, and restrictions. *Sex Education: Sexuality, Society and Learning, 14*(3), 338–353.

Jones, T., del Pozo de Bolger, A., Dunne, T., Lykins, A., & Hawkes, G. (2015). *Female-to-Male (FtM) transgender people's experiences in Australia*. Cham, Heidelberg, New York, Dordrecht and London: Springer.

Jones, T., Hart, B., Carpenter, M., Ansara, G., Leonard, W., & Lucke, J. (2016a). *Intersex: Stories and statistics from Australia*. London: Open Book Publisher.

Jones, T., Smith, E., Ward, R., Dixon, J., Hillier, L., & Mitchell, A. (2016b). School experiences of transgender and gender diverse students in Australia. *Sex Education, 16*(2), 156–171.

Kennedy, A. (2016). Fixed at birth: Medical and legal erasures of intersex variations. *UNSW Law Journal, 39*(2), 813–842.

Lalor, K. (2015). Making different differences: Representation and rights in sexuality activism. *Feminist Legal Studies, 23*(1), 7–25.

Ollis, D., Mitchell, A., Walsh, J., Hillier, L., & Watson, J. (2007). *Safety in our schools: Strategies for responding to homophobia*. Retrieved from http://www.latrobe.edu.au/ssay/assets/downloads/safety_in_our_schools.pdf.

Overington, C. (2016). Carla's case ignites firestorm among intersex community on need for surgery. *The Australian*. Retrieved from http://www.theaustralian.com.au/national-affairs/health/carlas-case-ignites-firestorm-among-intersex-community-on-need-for-surgery/news-story/7b1d478b8c606eaa611471f70c458df0?csp=4f59d201ee2c7ae8983925404ca8ea97.

Rasmussen, M. L. (2006). *Becoming subjects: Sexualities and secondary school settings*. New York: Taylor & Francis Group.

Rubin, D. A. (2015). Provincializing intersex: US intersex activism, human rights, and transnational body politics. *Frontiers, 36*(3), 51–83.

Sex Discrimination Amendment (Sexual Orientation, Gender Identity and Intersex Status) Act 2013 (Cth) (SDA Amendment Act). (2013).

Smith, E., Jones, T., Ward, R., Dixon, J., Mitchell, A., & Hillier, L. (2014). *From blues to rainbows: The mental health and well-being of gender diverse and transgender young people in Australia*. Melbourne: Australian Research Centre in Sex Health and Society.

Taylor, L. (2016, March 17). Caving in to the right on Safe Schools could undermine Turnbull's greatest asset. *The Guardian*.

UNESCO. (2016). *Call for action by ministers: Inclusive and equitable education for all learners in an environment free from discrimination and violence*. Paris: UNESCO.

United Nations. (2012). *Born free and equal: Sexual orientation and gender identity in international human rights law*. New York and Geneva: United Nations Human Rights Office of the High Commissioner.

Wilson, G. (2013). Intersex and religion. In L. Gahan & T. Jones (Eds.), *Heaven Bent: Australian lesbian, gay, bisexual, transgender and intersex experiences of faith, religion and spirituality* (pp. 42–46). Melbourne: Clouds of Magellan.

Part II

Race, Class, Citizenship and Nation

5

'I am Korean': Contested Belonging in a 'Multicultural' Korea

Jessica Walton

Introduction

In an age of globalisation characterised by increased transnational mobilities, the presence of people from diverse racial, ethnic and cultural backgrounds are complicating and countering hegemonic national representations of identity and the boundedness of state citizenship (Eriksen 2010). These demographic changes also present challenges for belonging (Yuval-Davis 2011). As more people cross national boundaries as temporary visitors, migrant workers or to immigrate with the intention to live and work long-term in the host country, what it means to belong for both 'newcomers' and existing residents and citizens, the terms by which belonging is defined and how that belonging is represented are highly contested.

For the purposes of this paper and for stylistic reasons, hereafter, 'Korea' and 'Koreans' will refer to the Republic of Korea/South Korea and South Koreans.

J. Walton (✉)
Deakin University, Melbourne, VIC, Australia
e-mail: jessica.walton@deakin.edu.au

© The Author(s) 2018
C. Halse (ed.), *Interrogating Belonging for Young People in Schools*,
https://doi.org/10.1007/978-3-319-75217-4_5

93

In the case of Korea, domestic factors, including a declining fertility rate, an aging workforce and a highly educated population, have warranted government policies to encourage international migration as a way to address short-term labour shortages (primarily in manufacturing and construction) (Kim et al. 2012). One of the major forms of international migration to Korea has been marriage migrants. Since the early 1990s, there has been an increase of female marriage migration, especially from China, Japan, Vietnam and the Philippines (Kim 2011; Korean Educational Statistical Service [KESS] 2014). This shift toward international marriages coincided with intraregional migration from rural to urban areas. Such migration occurred due to rapid industrialisation in the 1970s, when many Korean women worked in factories, and democratic transformation from the 1980s, as women began to seek and demand better career and educational opportunities (Cho 2002).[1] These social changes also resulted in a gender imbalance with an excess of men, particularly in rural areas. With the support of the government and through a burgeoning international matchmaking market (Kim 2011), many Korean men pursued international marriage as an alternative way to find a partner, have children and continue the patrilineage (Lee 2008). These children and their parents are referred to in government policies as 'multicultural families' (*damunhwa kajeong*).

In South Korea, there are 48,225 children from 'multicultural families' enrolled in primary schools (KESS 2014). Despite this, previous research on multiculturalism issues in Korea has predominantly focused on migrant labourers, foreign wives and policy and media analysis. There are a few studies that examine children's experiences, such as a quantitative study about children's reports of bullying, social adaptation and welfare (Kim et al. 2012) and a recent study that analysed 'multicultural' Korean children's personal narratives submitted for a regional essay contest (Lee 2016). This chapter makes a contribution by providing an in-depth ethnographic examination of 'difference' in the context of children's social relations in schools as shared spaces of forced togetherness. In doing so, the chapter engages with a politics of belonging by demonstrating how children's identification and understanding of Korean identity, within the context of peer social relations, highlight the ways in which Korean society is grappling with what it means to belong in an increasingly ethnically diverse country.

National Identity and 'Multicultural' Belonging

As Paul Connolly (1998) emphasises, to understand children's experiences and social relations, it is important to understand how children's lives inside the 'school gates' are influenced and always situated in relation to broader historical and contemporary social issues and debates. To understand the current challenges that increased racial, ethnic and cultural diversity pose to a politics of belonging in contemporary Korean society, it is helpful to briefly consider the political and affective underpinnings of a Korean national identity.

Prior to the division of the Korean Peninsula, a nationalised Korean identity arose primarily in response to external threats, especially Japanese colonialism and imperialism (Shin et al. 1999). Since then, significant historical events have presented an ongoing dilemma for Korea's national identity including the Korean Peninsula's Liberation from Japan in 1945 and the subsequent division into two nation states after the Korean War as a result of Cold War imperialism. As well, there is a long history of emigration. This history has contributed to Korea's staunch ethnic nationalism that equates national identity with ethnic and cultural identity aligned along Korean patrilineal bloodlines (Han 2016; Shin 2006).

As a form of 'strategic essentialism' (Spivak 1990), an essentialised Korean ethnic national identity was not only politically operationalised in the face of imperialism and colonialism, it also involved affective strategies by drawing on collective feelings of togetherness. This collective feeling relates to Raymond Williams's concept of 'structures of feeling', which refers to structured 'meanings and values as they are actively lived and felt, and the relations between these and formal or systematic beliefs' (Williams 1977, p. 132). Drawing on this concept, Townsend Middleton (2013, p. 611) argues that for Nepali-Indians (Gurkhas), feelings of national identity and belonging persist in varied ways over time because they have deep historical roots and are steeped in a 'collectively embodied "structure of feeling"'. Middleton (2013) describes how this deep embodied history causes even seemingly mundane remarks or events suddenly to reactivate the question of Gurkha identity and land rights. This was similarly the case in a unified Korea pre-1953. Gi-Wook Shin et al. (1999, p. 469) explain that Korean identity is based on a 'belief in a common origin in pre-history, producing an intensely felt collective sense of "oneness"'. Due to the precarious circumstances under which Korean national identity was initially formed, subsequent challenges to this sense of 'oneness' raise ontological anxieties or insecurities, during which national identity is strategically activated and reinforced. This is most apparent during pressure points, particularly current tensions with North Korea and Japan.

Ontological anxieties are also apparent in the government's response to immigration and growing ethnic diversity within Korean society. The government's policies, which focus primarily on 'multicultural families' and multicultural education, relate less to reconceptualising a Korean national identity and more toward reinforcing an existing Korean national identity as a form of 'national-engineering' (Norman 2004). Wayne Norman (2004, pp. 88–89) broadly defines national-engineering as involving 'deliberate nation-shaping activities' focused on shaping 'national identities through subtle and not-so-subtle attempts to instil, eliminate, modify, strengthen, or weaken the beliefs, sentiments, and values that make up individuals' sense of national identity'. Of course, as Norman also points out, the nation cannot simply impose a feeling of national identity on individuals and assume a specific interpretation of national identity will be something individuals automatically and wholeheartedly feel as integral to their sense of self. Instead, a feeling of national identity also has to be something through which individuals develop in ways that may or may not align with the nation state's view.

By drawing attention to characteristics of the Korean government's 'national-engineering' approach toward incorporating racial, ethnic and cultural diversity within Korean society, it becomes clearer who and why particular groups are targeted (Norman 2004). The next section examines the Korean government's response to diversity through educational policies targeted at children of international marriages from 'multicultural family' backgrounds.

Educational Context

Children of international marriages are positioned at the centre of a politics of belonging that conjures a neoliberal hope for the future of Korea, evidence of a difficult historical past and the impact of globalisation. The government's primary approach toward these children has been through educational policies in schools, beginning with the 2006 Educational Support Plan for Children from Multicultural Backgrounds (Ministry of Education and Human Resources Development [MEHRD] 2006). Given the intention of these plans was to reduce linguistic and cultural gaps between multiethnic children and their Korean monoethnic peers, funding schemes and support services have included afterschool programmes to learn Korean as a Second Language and to become more familiar with Korean culture (see Grant and Ham [2013] for a summary of the plans). In the Ministry of Education, Science and Technology (MEST) 2012 plan, a recommendation for textbook revisions was introduced to address a lack of understanding in schools (and among the general population) about people from different ethnic and cultural backgrounds and, secondly, as an attempt, at least superficially, to begin to address a dominant national imaginary as ethnically and culturally homogenous. However, such plans are ultimately less concerned with reflecting on what it means to be Korean and more focused on ensuring the future and prosperity of the Korean economy, given declining fertility rates and an aging workforce. Understood within the broader historical context of Korea's still unsettled national identity, it becomes apparent why the Korean government has invested so much time and money on incorporating 'multicultural families' and, particularly, on children (Draudt 2016).[2] There is an expectation that, through educational approaches, children from 'multicultural' backgrounds will assimilate and be able to contribute, as trained, culturally competent individuals, to Korea's domestic and global future (Kim 2011; Park 2014).

Because of this predominantly one-sided focus on incorporating multiethnic children, the ways in which these plans are framed, as something separate that multiethnic children must do to assimilate or as an 'add-on' for all students to learn, also activate a politics of belonging that draws on 'dichotomous notions of identity and difference' (Yuval-Davis 2010, p. 263). By trying to 'do good' primarily in ways that represent people from multiethnic backgrounds as needing help rather than also taking into consideration their own needs and expectations, the cultural paternalism and fetishism of 'difference' that underlies the dominant group's attitudes (Kim 2011) maintain a racialised hierarchy of 'us' versus 'them'. As is the case with dichotomous approaches to identity, children from multiethnic backgrounds tend to be lumped together under the label, 'multicultural person', including the majority who were born in Korea, with the assumption that they also identify as 'multicultural'. This does not take into account children's sociality and situated processes of identification and, instead, treats them in much the same way their non-Korean parents are treated, as children that simply need to be educated about Korean culture and to speak the language. Although linguistic capabilities are clearly important for daily life, this one-size-fits-all approach does not account for children's multiple or alternative claims to belonging that are not necessarily centred on ethnic or cultural identity. It also overlooks children's normative claims to belonging as a Korean person that reject the pre-defined and often stigmatised 'multicultural' category imposed on them.

Drawing on Nira Yuval-Davis' (2006) politics of belonging, assumptions embedded in the category 'children from multicultural families' neglect to account for the differentiation between social location or positioning, identification and ethical and political values. By placing 'multicultural' people in opposition to, or apart from, 'Korean people', the impetus is on the former to assimilate. First, by placing 'multicultural families' and their children outside a bounded Korean identity from the outset, the agential and diverse ways people may identify as Korean are marginalised. Secondly, mainly focusing on language and cultural acquisition does not address the social inequalities, racism and prejudice experienced by multiethnic children and their parents that interrupt feelings of belonging regardless of language and cultural capabilities (Kim et al. 2012; Kim and Won 2015).

In a review of Korean multicultural education policies, Grant and Ham (2013, p. 84) found that teaching about cultural diversity tends to be about 'the exceptional and the culturally different and [takes] a human relations approach to multicultural education'. This approach focuses on building harmonious relations, which tends to avoid conflict, anxieties and other forms of interpersonal tension in favour of directing students to simply 'get along', without necessarily taking into account how such directives may fail to 'stick' because children's social dynamics are not taken into consideration. This approach also does not adequately challenge a cultural hierarchy of 'difference' because 'difference' is understood in opposition to that which is 'not different' and so 'getting along' becomes a matter of those whose bodies are read as 'different' to be in a state of always striving toward *becoming* 'not different'. This inadvertently reinforces structures of power that impose a conditional belonging determined by the dominant group in terms of who is 'too different' to claim unconditional belonging.

For multiethnic children, hierarchies of difference are determined by skin colour and the origin of the non-Korean parent (Lee 2016). For example, broader social stigma associated with 'multicultural families' as financially poor and from a perceived lower social status (e.g., lower education and undesirable jobs) is more strongly associated with people from countries in Central and Southeast Asia. As Aihwa Ong (1996, p. 737) argues, 'hierarchical schemes of racial and cultural difference intersect in a complex, contingent way to locate minorities of color from different class backgrounds'. For multiethnic children and their non-Korean parents, these hierarchies exist along a 'dual racial order—their parents' place of origin [place-based hierarchy] and their skin colour [colour-coding hierarchy]' (Lee 2016, p. 14).

Because of these hierarchies of difference, there is vested interest in keeping the stigma of 'difference' hidden if possible. However, there is also a vested interest on the part of people who are from diverse ethnic backgrounds who are not recognised or who choose not to be recognised by the government's 'multiculturalism' policies. These people include migrant labourers and ethnic Chinese living in Korea who have tended to 'distance themselves from the multicultural explosion to avoid the stigmatisation associated with being beneficiaries of multiculturalism' (Kim 2012, p. 106). By refusing to be targeted as 'multicultural', they also choose to maintain a stance outside of the government's assimilating efforts to focus on other issues such as migrant labour working rights

(Prey 2011). Conversely, children from multiethnic family backgrounds are less able to work outside of a Korean 'multicultural' framework at school due to their less mobile and less powerful positioning. However, in my study, they were acutely aware of the social stigma attached to being identified as 'multicultural' and asserted themselves in ways that refused to fully embrace this external positioning as only 'multicultural'. This chapter analyses how multiethnic children experienced 'difference' at school and considers the ways they navigated their perceived or felt sense of 'difference' in relation to their monoethnic and other multiethnic peers, situated within a broader politics of belonging about Korean national identity.

Methodology

The overall aim of the research on which this chapter is based, was to analyse inter-ethnic relations among Grade 5/6 Korean children from both monoethnic and multiethnic backgrounds at primary schools in urban contexts. This chapter draws on ethnographic school-based observations, interviews and PhotoVoice data conducted in 2015 with 11- to 12-year-old children (12- to 13-years-old in Korean age[3]) at three government primary schools in Gyeonggi province, about 1 to 2.5 hours outside of Seoul (refer to Table 5.1).[4]

Children who participated in my study were all born in Korea except for one student who was born in Germany and they all had at least one Korean parent. There were seven children with one non-Korean parent (hereafter referred to as multiethnic students/children) and 13 children with two Korean parents (hereafter referred to as monoethnic students/children). All of the multiethnic children could speak Korean as fluently

Table 5.1 Multicultural student demographics at research schools

School	Total multiethnic students	Total students
Baram	10	807
Hosu	34	833
Namu	8	727

as a native speaker and all of them had Korean names. Ethics approval was acquired and pseudonyms have been used for all participants and the schools.

From May to July 2015, I conducted observations every day during classroom lessons, 10-minute breaks between lessons and before and after school. During classroom-based lessons, children's behaviour was structured and surveilled by the teacher's presence at the front of the classroom. As such, I was also limited as to how much interaction I could have with the students. I usually sat in the back of the classroom at one of the student desks or in a chair at the side of the room by the window. For classes that did not take place in the homeroom, such as English and Physical Education, there were more opportunities to interact with the students. For example, during gym class, when there was an odd number of students, the teacher would ask me to pair up with a student to do one of the activities, such as rope jumping, playing catch and throwing frisbees. As an adult but not a teacher, these moments during structured class activities helped to lessen the hierarchy between the students and me.

However, it was mainly during lunch breaks and breaks between lessons when the teacher left the classroom to go to the staffroom that I could get to know the students and they could ask me questions in a casual way. When the bell rang, signalling the end of class, the classroom was instantly transformed and without the teacher there to discipline them, the room became the students' territory—playing games, laughing and shouting. I joined in their activities and also sat with the students during lunch rather than with the teachers and hung out with them in the schoolyard during the lunch break. Girls and boys mainly kept to themselves and so, over time, I was adopted into some of the girls' groups. However, I often crossed over into the boys' territory to kick a soccer ball with them or to challenge them to a lightning fast game of Rubik's Cube, which they always won. In addition to my Korean physical appearance, at times I was even momentarily mistaken for one of the students by both staff and students despite our significant age difference. At the same time, I was also always an adult and a researcher and so I needed to be reflexively aware of my behaviour and my assumptions in relation to how the students were responding to me and how I interpreted their behaviour.

After I had been at the schools for almost two months and the students and I had become more comfortable around each other, I conducted interviews with twenty students across the six classes using the photos they took. For the photos, I gave students disposable cameras and over a seven to ten-day period, I asked them to take photos of people, places and things around their home, neighbourhood and school that were important to them or evoked feelings of happiness, anger, sadness and so on. This approach allowed the students to guide part of the interview to talk about experiences that were not always captured by the interview questions. For the other part of the interview, I used a semi-structured interview schedule and asked them questions about their interests, hobbies, things they like or do not like, worries and dreams, friends and family and experiences of ethnic and cultural diversity. To understand their friendship groups and to confirm whether or not my observations of their friendships were accurate, I asked them to draw a friendship circle[5] (Smith 2005). This involved drawing concentric circles with their name in the centre and then continuing with their closest friends, next closest friends and acquaintances on the outer circle. I used the friendship circle to discuss in more detail how and why they became friends with different students and who they wish they could spend more or less time with. The following sections provide an analysis of the children's sense of identity and belonging in the context of particular modes of sociality, which centred on friendships and forms of exclusion. First, I will begin with analysing both monoethnic and multiethnic students' understanding of and feelings toward cultural difference.

Unspoken 'Difference'

In designing the interview schedule with the students, I did not want to assume that ethnic and cultural diversity was something that was significant to their everyday experiences at school and home. Instead, I took a more open-ended approach by asking questions about what was important to them and what they usually do with their friends and family. I also asked them about whether they have been on holidays with their family around Korea or to other countries. Most students had only travelled around Korea. Exceptions were some monoethnic students whose families could afford to go on overseas holidays and multiethnic students who tended to go overseas to visit their mother's country.

When asked if they knew anyone or if they were friends with people from different ethnic backgrounds, multiethnic students mentioned family members or said that they knew of people in their neighbourhood but did not know them personally, whereas monoethnic Korean students said they either did not know anyone or mentioned one of the multiethnic students at school. For the monoethnic students, culture was closely tied to place and so they assumed that people from a different cultural background would also be from a different country, would speak a different language and could not speak Korean. For example, Min-a, a monoethnic student, explained that it is difficult to get to know people from different cultures 'because they use different languages and lifestyles' (Girl, Hosu, Grade 6). In response to whether or not it is easy or hard to become friends with people from different cultures, another monoethnic student, Shi-woo said, 'It is hard. We have different cultures and languages, so it is hard'. When I asked if anything was easy, he said, 'Nothing' (Boy, Namu, Grade 5).

During the interviews, students identified multiethnic students as examples of people who may also be from a different cultural background. However, there was also some uncertainty around whether multiethnic students at school are from a different cultural background in the same way as people who speak a different language. Since all the multiethnic students could speak Korean fluently and all but one were born in Korea, the main difference that distinguished them from other students was whether or not they *looked* like they were from a different 'cultural background'. One monoethnic student at Hosu School, Min-a, said she had not met anyone from a different culture but also said that Ha-eun, the Japanese Korean student in her class, has a mother or grandmother from Japan. When I asked if she talks with her about Japanese culture, she said, 'No, a male [Korean] classmate likes Japan so I talk about it with him' (Girl, Namu, Grade 6). In this case, Ha-eun was recognised as someone who has a connection with a different cultural background because of her extended family members but when it came to talking about Japanese culture, she did not talk about it with Ha-eun. Min-a and Ha-eun were friends and often hung out together during breaks. They also both included each other's names in their friend maps as one of their closest friends. When I asked Ha-eun if other students knew about her mother being Japanese, she said, 'Only three or four of them know.' I asked if she was okay if others know. She explained, 'I'm okay. I even want to show off that but I worry others don't like me showing off. I'm proud of her. I want to tell my classmates.' Her hesitancy is reflected in the way she compared herself to Joo-won's experiences (Nepalese Korean student). She said, 'If it doesn't show that you are from a different culture like me it is okay, but if it shows like Joo-won, those kids get bullied a lot and have a difficult time becoming friends with others.' Ha-eun's hesitancy seemed to stem from an underlying feeling that other students might bully her like she sees them doing to other multiethnic students like Joo-won. Because she could not know how each student might feel, she did not talk about her Japanese mother.

When I initially spoke to the Korean teachers about observing their classrooms and interviewing multiethnic students, some thought that I was researching how well adjusted they were and so they told me that there would not be a 'problem' because the students could speak Korean fluently and that the teachers saw them as 'Korean'. At Namu School, when I inquired as to which Grade 5/6 classes included multiethnic students, some of the teachers realised only after some investigation that one of the students, Yun-seo, has a Thai mother. At Hosu School, Joo-won was said to have a mother from the Philippines but during the interview, the student said that his mother was from Nepal and they had visited family there. From a teacher's perspective, because the multiethnic students had been through the Korean schooling system since kindergarten and were completely fluent, there was no difficulty teaching them in the sense that they were not necessarily any more or less difficult than another student from only a Korean background.

Nevertheless, whether or not a student's 'difference' was known, there was a palpable feeling of 'difference' (Tilbury and Lloyd 2001) that was apparent among the students. Some of the multiethnic students were intent on not drawing attention to that 'difference', particularly those like Yun-seo, the Thai Korean student, who could effectively pass as only Korean compared to others who had more distinct racialised features (e.g., darker skin, rounder eyes, lighter hair). When I was around these students, I had to be careful not to mention their non-Korean background around other students because they did not want others to know. In this sense, at least for students whose physical difference was not apparent, the notion of 'encounter', or according to the Oxford English Dictionary Online (2016), 'to meet (someone) unexpectedly', was not occurring. Rather, it was the *possibility* of encounter that was either being avoided by not allowing other students to know about their 'difference', or, more blatantly avoided particularly in the case of multi-ethnic students whose 'difference' was already 'known' by their racialised bodies.

For all multiethnic students, this palpable feeling of difference affected the extent to which they allowed others to know about their sense of difference and also affected the extent to which others interacted with them. This exclusion by their peers (and fear of potential exclusion) contrasted with everyday modes of sociality among the children's friendship groups. At school, children's relationships were characterised by *uri* (우리) or a sense of togetherness or we-ness. Rather than conceiving of a group as composed of individuals, *uri* describes a quality that exists between and through people. The word for human being in Korean, *ingan* (인간), is based on Chinese characters that 'literally means "between men"' (Chung and Cho 2006, p. 48). Based on this conceptual understanding of what it means to be 'human', human beings are not simply individuals who exist in relationships with each other but are fundamentally relational beings (Strathern 2005). The importance of *uri* was also reflected in the monoethnic students' relationships. During the breaks, the monoethnic students always played together unless they made it clear that they wanted to keep studying or if they were reading a book or drawing. Even then, their friends either checked to make sure they were fine being left alone or lingered quietly by their desk drawing pictures together or playing with their toys. This contrasted with the everyday racism (Essed 1991) enacted by the way students avoided interacting with some of the multiethnic students particularly those whose skin was darker.

Min-jae, the student at Hosu School with a Russian mother was also often on the periphery. Although he had a lighter skin colour, his mother was from Russia and so his background was not considered to be ideal compared to, for example, having a lighter skin colour and being from the United States (Lee 2016). In addition to his racialised difference, his interest in computers and how they work separated him from the other boys who were more interested in sport and K-pop (Korean pop music). His dissimilar interests added an extra sense of 'difference' that prevented him from being included in the *uri* feeling of togetherness that was shared by the other students.

Min-jae moved schools when he was in third grade because he was being bullied. He said other students frequently called him a 'loser'. At Hosu School, it has been slow for him to make friends. He told me he once had a friend in fourth grade but that friend moved away and left the school. During the first month of classroom observations, he was mostly on his own despite his efforts to include himself in other students' games. During breaks, he sometimes lingered around other boys and laughed when they laughed at things to try to interact, but they were more involved with their own friends. In June, he began hanging out with another boy a bit more. They tended to choose each other as partners during gym class and, during class breaks, they started hanging out more at each other's desks as well. During the interview, Min-jae included this student as one of his friends. He said the friendship developed recently when they began working on a school project together. However, they were not close and he said that his best friend, if he is honest, is his cat. Compared to the other students with two Korean parents, he did not take pictures of any friends. Most were of himself or objects he enjoyed playing with like his PlayStation 3 game console.

These multiethnic students' experiences demonstrate that there is an affective politics of belonging, based on racialised differences, that persist despite linguistic and cultural similarities. Rather than only looking at addressing nationalised forms of 'not belonging' (that is, a policy focus on linguistic and cultural skills), greater focus on how students create an affective sense of belonging (that is, *uri*/togetherness, such as through the exchange of school supplies and physical proximity) is required. By drawing attention to this affective dimension of belonging, aspects of peer relations that counter this feeling of belonging are highlighted, namely a physical sense of distance due to racialised differences which rub up against the physical proximity of *uri*/togetherness.

In terms of developing a theoretical understanding of belonging in a Korean context, an affective politics of belonging needs to be taken into account. The following section analyses this affective dimension in relation to 'anxious belonging' (Middleton 2013) and demonstrates the need to address these racialised feelings of 'difference' that shape monoethnic and multiethnic students' interactions and relationships. The section concludes with multiethnic students' efforts to belong as Korean and to not be regarded as 'different' despite their experiences of rejection and marginalisation.

Affective Politics of Belonging

Among the students' interactions with multiethnic students, there was a sense of difference that was at once unfamiliar and familiar, foreign and not foreign. The multiethnic students were 'just like' the other monoethnic students in the sense that they were all born in Korea or had moved to Korea at a very young age, could speak Korean fluently and were socialised to observe Korean cultural behaviours. Yet, there was an embodied lack of intimacy that contrasted with everyday expressions of *uri* or 'we-ness' among the majority of monoethnic students. At school, multiethnic students were treated as 'Other', but they were also not so easily categorised as definitively 'Other' because of their cultural and linguistic similarities to the monoethnic students. This relates to Yuval-Davis' (2010, p. 279) argument that 'the boundaries of self, or even of "us", do not necessarily depend on dichotomous divisions of "self" and "other", "us" and "them" … the realm of the "not-me" is much more multiplex and multilayered'. In other words, the realm of 'not-me' is both self and other. I argue that it is precisely this blurriness between self and other that required boundary-making to enforce a clearer demarcation between self and other among the students. This needs to be understood within the broader context of ontological challenges to Korean national identity, which informs children's social relations and how they determine who is 'us' in the sense of *uri* (together-ness) and who is not-*uri*.

To hone in on this unsettling feeling that existed between belonging and not belonging, I asked all the students (both monoethnic and multiethnic) if they felt Korean and to explain why. Some went further to say who could be Korean and on what basis, which captured both the 'sentiment … [and] the content of … national identity' (Norman 2004, p. 95). Most monoethnic students found the question surprising because their Korean identity had never been questioned. When asked to explain why they felt Korean, monoethnic students drew on racial, ethnic and cultural characteristics as illustrated by Hye-jin:

> Yes. I feel like I'm Korean. Because my mom and dad, my mom and dad are Koreans, and I'm Korean, too, I'm Korean. Uh … my … uh … my ancestors are Koreans, too, and as a Korean, I speak well, too, I speak well because I've spoken Korean since I was born, and I look like Korean, right. My skin is Korean color, and like my body, too, and things like the color of my eyes, everything is Korean. (Girl, Hosu, Grade 5)

This description of 'Koreanness' draws on racialised ethno-nationalistic characteristics that do not distinguish between ethnicity and culture and race, thus evoking a primordial collective identity (Shin 2006).

Another monoethnic student, Hyun-jun also cited Korean language and culture and living in Korea as evidence of his Koreanness. In the interview excerpt below, he also explained how someone could become Korean if they came from a different country:

> *Jessica: Do you think that if somebody else comes from a different country and lives here, do you think they can be Korean?*
> *Hyun-jun: Yeah, if they were kind and work hard, they could also be Korean. They will do same thing as Koreans too.*
> *Jessica: If they work hard?*
> *Hyun-jun: Yeah.*
> *Jessica: What do you mean 'work hard'?*
> *Hyun-jun: Like understanding our culture or history … learn our language, and they could also be Koreans. (Boy, Baram, Grade 6)*

The effort required toward becoming Korean is described as something that can be acquired through skill and determination. Based on these criteria, multiethnic students are also Korean and, in fact, they used similar criteria to describe why they are Korean. Both Joo-won (Boy, Hosu,

Grade 6) and Ye-jun (Boy, Baram, Grade 6), who are multiethnic students, also said they felt Korean:

Jessica: *Do you feel Korean?*
Ye-jun: *Yes, because I've lived in Korea for a long time.*
Jessica: *Do you feel you are Japanese?*
Ye-jun: *No, I am living in Korea so I feel I am Korean.* (Boy, Baram, Grade 6)
Jessica: *Do you feel Korean?*
Joo-won: *Yes, because I was born in Korea.* (Boy, Hosu, Grade 6)

Both Joo-won and Ye-jun had been to visit their mother's family in Nepal and Japan, respectively. Min-jae also talked about going to Russia to visit his mother's family. He was there for one month so I asked him if he liked living in Russia and he said, 'I even cannot live there half a month. I want to go back to Korea … to see my father, go eat Korean food'. He explained:

I feel I'm really Korean … because I was born here, in this place, in this ground and like one of my parents is Korean, like my father. And that's the reason why feeling myself like a real Korean. (Boy, Hosu, Grade 5)

He said he only feels Russian when he wants to feel 'strong' after he has said 'something weird' and feels 'embarrassed'. Only one student made an explicit reference to her multiethnic background when explaining why she does not feel completely Korean. During the interview, Yun-seo (Thai Korean student) gestured to her face and put her hand in front so it divided her face in half and said she feels only 'medium … half' Korean because of 'my mother' (Girl, Namu, Grade 5).

According to the children's conceptualisation of what it means to be Korean, the multiethnic students I interviewed were Korean because they were born/raised in Korea, spoke Korean as a first language, and understood the cultural nuances of someone who has been culturally socialised in Korea. In this sense, they have effectively 'achieved' the aims of the government's assimilationist 'multicultural family' plans and therefore, according to these criteria, should be regarded no differently from their monoethnic Korean peers. However, based on Hye-jin's earlier remark about looking Korean, the multiethnic students' racialised difference interrupted a unified, primordial, national identity and prevented an affective sense of belonging among their peers.

Zembylas (2014, p. 10) suggests 'affective citizenship' as a way to complement a critical approach to citizenship and belonging by identifying 'more effectively and critically the multiple emotional affiliations of students and their implications in everyday life'. By directing attention to this affective dimension, 'underlying ambivalences of 'embracing the other'—that is, both the desires and anxieties' can be examined and these factors which influence children's social relations in terms of proximity and distance can be considered (Zembylas 2014, p. 12). To date, Korean educational policies have focused on mainstream linguistic and cultural capabilities and have not accounted for what it means to affectively belong in Korea that go beyond a monocultural national identity. Findings from this present study have demonstrated that monoethnic and multiethnic children's (limited) interactions are hampered by feelings of distance in the face of an overwhelming feeling of *uri* or togetherness characterised primarily by interactions among monoethnic students. This affective sense of belonging based on *uri* or togetherness goes beyond the individual and draws on a sense of Koreanness grounded in 'an intensely felt collective sense of "oneness"' long before the Korean War (Shin et al. 1999, p. 469), but which has since been reinforced in more nationalistic ways.

When multiethnic children say, 'I am Korean', their claims to Korean identity draw attention to a politics of belonging that go beyond individual feelings of belonging. Their assertion becomes a radical statement of belonging that requires a reconceptualisation of both the ethno-nationalistic and affective parameters by which Koreanness is used to include and exclude. Rather than accepting that those in positions of power (that is, monoethnic Koreans) have the power to determine inclusion and position them as people who need to be included, or have inclusion done to them, the multiethnic students I interviewed are saying they are Korean and always have been and therefore, do not need to be included. In one sense, the children are refusing exclusionary forms of 'multicultural' representation. They also assert that they feel Korean and highlight the fact that there is no 'difference' between themselves and their monoethnic Korean peers because they were also born in Korea, have Korean family, speak Korean and live in Korea. Of course, at the same time, the extent to which they can refuse to be identified in ways that stigmatise them is limited given other students' perceptions of and behaviours toward them are structured by an unequal playing field. Additionally, in ascribing to normative criteria for Korean identity, they also contribute to the exclusion of people who feel they are Korean but do not necessarily fit those criteria.

Nevertheless, when understood within a broader historical context of national engineering and ontological insecurity, their racialised presence and adamant assertion that they are Korean and do not need to prove this, radically shakes up a dichotomy of belonging and not belonging, inclusion and exclusion. It requires a different Korean national identity that includes people who do not all look 'the same', meaning people that do not necessarily share the same racialised features that makes someone 'look Korean'.

Conclusion

Overall, for most of the monoethnic students, ethnic and cultural diversity did not feature strongly in their everyday lives. For students from multiethnic backgrounds, while their non-Korean ethnic background was not something they frequently talked about or highlighted, their perceived difference still affected the extent to which they were able to develop friendships with a similar sense of intimacy as students who were not multiethnic. Their embodied sense of self as Korean and therefore 'not different' and their perceived racialised bodies as 'different' served to counter dichotomous conceptualisations of belonging and not belonging evoked by the government's 'multiculturalism' approach of assimilation.

Although monoethnic students did not have explicit 'encounters' with ethnic and cultural diversity beyond playing and working alongside their multiethnic peers, broader social debates about ethnicity and identity weighted heavily in the background and informed how children related to each other. It affected the extent to which multiethnic children were included in feelings of *uri* or togetherness. It affected how both monoethnic and multiethnic children spoke about Korean identity. In relation to past and current nation-engineering endeavours within an intensifying global context, children were also caught up in contested meanings of belonging. Through their everyday interactions at school, they also reinforced and challenged the boundaries by which belonging is determined.

Despite multiple forms of citizenship that are not understood only in terms of liberal state citizenship, the 'resilience of the nation-state as the major tool of governance' remains, and hence draws attention to 'the continuous critical importance of state citizenship as a political project of belonging' (Yuval-Davis 2011, pp. 48–49). In Korea, the uncertain and anxious belonging of the nation-state, exemplified by militarised tensions with North Korea and territorial disputes with Japan, is challenging the way in which Korean identity is defined and informing the extent to which it adapts to changes such as the question of a 'multicultural' Korea. As illustrated by multiethnic students' claims to an unconditional Korean identity, the way 'difference' is defined by an ethno-nationalistic conceptualisation of Korean identity is unacceptable as it does nothing to disrupt the unequal social relations that exclude those based on the same criteria by which they are meant to be included. Instead, what is perhaps required is an 'acceptance of difference, a recognition that what we have *in common* are "partial connections"' (Tilbury and Lloyd 2001, p. 84). In this sense, 'difference' is understood as the space through which relations are formed rather than existing outside of oneself or 'the other'. Rather than requiring 'difference' to be subsumed into 'one identity' as is the case with assimilative approaches, it can be reconceptualised as 'the grounds for, and the product of, all human connections and transformations' (Tilbury and Lloyd 2001, p. 82). In Korea, a primordial ethnic national identity cannot withstand processes of social change without severely marginalising people who are positioned as 'different'. So long as this is the case, those people who exist on the margins will continue to reject a category that stigmatises 'difference' and assert a politics of belonging, in which the statement, 'I am Korean' does not need to be accepted or included but can simply exist in its alterity.

Notes

1. The possibility for these opportunities was supported by increased democratic reform especially after the inauguration of the first democratically elected civilian president Kim Young-sam in 1993.
2. In 2012, 95% of the budget for social integration programmes (about $1 billion) was allocated to multicultural families (Draudt 2016, p. 15).
3. In Korea, a person is one-year-old when they are born. Also, on the first day of the Lunar New Year, everyone becomes a year older.
4. Based on 2014 statistics, the average number of students from multiethnic backgrounds at elementary schools in Gyeonggi province is about 9.7 per school (KESS 2014). Gyeonggi province has the highest number of multiethnic elementary school students compared to the other provinces. However, in terms of the proportion of total multicultural students to the total number of elementary students, other provinces have a higher ratio (e.g., Jeollanam province is 3.46 and Gyeonggi province is 1.59) (KESS 2014).
5. This method is based on an exercise used by Smith (2005) with 9–11 year old children to understand friendship networks and issues of belonging from their perspectives.

References

Cho, H. (2002). Living with conflicting subjectivities: Mother, motherly wife, and sexy woman in the transition from colonial-modern to postmodern Korea. In L. Kendall (Ed.), *Under construction: The gendering of modernity, class and consumption in the Republic of Korea* (pp. 165–195). Honolulu: University of Hawai'i Press.

Chung, C. K., & Cho, S. J. (2006). Conceptualization of jeong and dynamics of hwabyung. *Psychiatry Investigation, 3*(1), 46–54.

Connolly, P. (1998). *Racism, gender identities and young children.* New York: Routledge.

Draudt, D. (2016). South Korea's national identity crisis in the face of emerging multiculturalism. *Georgetown Journal of International Affairs, 17*(1), 12–19.

Eriksen, T. H. (2010). *Ethnicity and nationalism: Anthropological perspectives* (3rd ed.). London: Pluto Press.

Essed, P. (1991). *Understanding everyday racism: An interdisciplinary theory.* Newbury Park: Sage.

Grant, C. A., & Ham, S. (2013). Multicultural education policy in South Korea: Current struggles and hopeful vision. *Multicultural Education Review, 5*(1), 67–95.

Han, G. S. (2016). *Nouveau-riche nationalism and multiculturalism in Korea: A media narrative analysis.* New York: Routledge.

Kim, J. K. (2011). The politics of culture in multicultural Korea. *Journal of Ethnic and Migration Studies, 37*(10), 1583–1604.

Kim, N. H. (2012). Multiculturalism and the politics of belonging: The puzzle of multiculturalism in South Korea. *Citizenship Studies, 16*(1), 103–117.

Kim, H., & Won, S. (2015). Experiences of discrimination and its effect on life satisfaction: understanding differences within subgroups of foreign spouses from multicultural families in Korea. *Asian Social Science, 11*(26), 64–74.

Kim, E. M., Ok, K. Y., Lee, H. Y., & Cho, H. L. (2012). *South Korea advances toward a multicultural society.* Paju Book City, South Korea: Nanam.

Korean Educational Statistical Service (KESS). (2014). *Basic statistics on schools: Multicultural students.* Retrieved September 10, 2015, from http://kess.kedi.re.kr/eng/publ/publFile/pdfjs?survSeq=2014&menuSeq=3894&publSeq=2&menuCd=62384&itemCode=02&menuId=1_3_14&language=en.

Lee, H. K. (2008). International marriage and the state in South Korea: Focusing on governmental policy. *Citizenship Studies, 12*(1), 107–123.

Lee, C. S. (2016). Narratives of 'mixed race' youth in South Korea: Racial order and in-betweeness. *Asian Ethnicity.* Retrieved August 31, 2016, from https://doi.org/10.1080/14631369.2016.1219940.

Middleton, T. (2013). Anxious belongings: Anxiety and the politics of belonging in subnationalist Darjeeling. *American Anthropologist, 115*(4), 608–621.

Ministry of Education and Human Resources Development (MEHRD). (2006). *damunhwa gajeong janyeo gyoyuk jiwon daechaek* [Educational support plan for children from multicultural backgrounds]. Retrieved August 25, 2015, from http://125.60.48.13/home4/dl_files/edu/001/IM006954.pdf.

Ministry of Education, Science and Technology (MEST). (2012). *damunhwa haksaeng gyoyuk seonjinhwa bangan* [Advanced plan for Multicultural Family Student]. Retrieved September 5, 2016, from *moe.go.kr/web/100026/ko/board/download.do?boardSeq=66030.*

Norman, W. (2004). From nation-building to national engineering: On the ethics of shaping identities. In A. Dieckhoff (Ed.), *The politics of belonging: Nationalism, liberalism and pluralism* (pp. 87–106). Oxford: Lexington Books.

Ong, A. (1996). Cultural citizenship as subject-making: Immigrants negotiate racial and cultural boundaries in the United States. *Current Anthropology, 37*(5), 737–762.

Park, K. (2014). Foreigners or multicultural citizens?: Press media's construction of immigrants in South Korea. *Ethnic and Racial Studies, 37*(9), 1565–1586.

Prey, R. (2011). Different takes: Migrant world television and multiculturalism in South Korea. *Global Media Journal – Canadian Edition, 4*(1), 109–125.

Shin, G. W. (2006). *Ethnic nationalism in Korea: Genealogy, politics and legacy.* Palo Alto, CA: Stanford University Press.

Shin, G. W., Freda, J., & Yi, G. (1999). The politics of ethnic nationalism in divided Korea. *Nations and Nationalism, 5*(4), 465–484.

Smith, G. (2005). *Children's perspectives on believing and belonging.* London: National Children's Bureau for Joseph Rowntree Foundation.

Spivak, G. C. (1990). *The postcolonial critic: Interviews, strategies, dialogues.* New York: Routledge.

Strathern, M. (2005). *Kinship, law and the unexpected: Relatives are always a surprise.* Cambridge: Cambridge University Press.

Tilbury, F., & Lloyd, M. (2001). Friendship and relationships in everyday life. In C. Bell (Ed.), *Sociology of everyday life in New Zealand* (pp. 70–88). Palmerston North, New Zealand: Dunmore Press.

Williams, R. (1977). *Marxism and literature.* Oxford: Oxford University Press.

Yuval-Davis, N. (2006). Belonging and the politics of belonging. *Patterns of Prejudice, 40*(3), 197–214.

Yuval-Davis, N. (2010). Theorizing identity: Beyond the 'us' and 'them' dichotomy. *Patterns of Prejudice, 44*(3), 261–280.

Yuval-Davis, N. (2011). *Politics of belonging: Intersection contestations.* London: Sage.

Zembylas, M. (2014). Affective citizenship in multicultural societies: Implications for critical citizenship education. *Citizenship Teaching & Learning, 9*(1), 5–18.

6

Young People on Asylum Seekers: The 'Dirty Work' of Boundary Making in the Politics of Belonging

Christine Halse, Rosalyn Black, and Claire Charles

Introduction

Around the world, polarised views pervade political, social and media debates about the swelling, transnational flows of asylum seekers. As a group, asylum seekers are invariably viewed as strangers. Georg Simmel (1908, p. 185) describes the stranger as not the 'wanderer who comes

---

The terms 'asylum seekers' and 'refugees' are invariably elided in public discourse and the academic literature. For clarity, we adopt the distinction articulated by the United Nations Refugee Agency (see http://www.unhcr.org/asylum-seekers.html) and used in Australia and the UK, whereby an asylum seeker is an individual seeking protection from persecution in her/his own country but whose claims have yet to be assessed. The granting of refugee status is governed by the 1951 United Nations Convention on the Status of Refugees. If a claim is assessed favourably, the asylum seeker is granted refugee status and this is usually accompanied by the right to remain in the country granting asylum.

C. Halse (✉)
The Education University of Hong Kong, Tai Po, Hong Kong
e-mail: chalse@eduhk.hk

R. Black • C. Charles
Deakin University, Melbourne, VIC, Australia
e-mail: rosalyn.black@deakin.edu.au; c.charles@deakin.edu.au

© The Author(s) 2018   **117**
C. Halse (ed.), *Interrogating Belonging for Young People in Schools*,
https://doi.org/10.1007/978-3-319-75217-4_6

today and goes tomorrow'; s/he is the stranger 'who comes today and stays tomorrow' but who can never be indigenous. In the twenty-first century, the stranger is more than the traveller who comes but does not go. S/he is the individual whose identity locates them permanently beyond the possibility of acceptance and belonging. For Zygmunt Bauman (2004, p. 80), asylum seekers and refugees are 'the outsiders incarnate' because they have 'no realistic prospect of being assimilated and incorporated' into the social body of their new land or returning to their homeland (pp. 77–78). They are constituted and confirmed as strangers—the alien Other—by their racial, ethnic, religious, or other differences from the social majority because their presence divides societies into native/other, same/different, insiders/outsiders, friend/enemy, belonging/not belonging.

In contrast to the permeability of national boundaries evidenced by the global flow of consumer goods, communications, technologies and ideas, conferring an identity of strangerhood on asylum seekers has bolstered the status of the nation-state as a potent physical, symbolic, emotional, and political unit. The consequence has been an intensification of the *politics of belonging* (Yuval-Davis 2006, p. 197). These are the strategies that social groups use to define and differentiate themselves from others, to establish who belongs/does not belong to their social group, and to manage strangers, particularly within 'the imaginary boundary line of the nation' (Yuval-Davis 2006, p. 204; see also Bauman 1996).

The politics of belonging around asylum seekers generally pivots on two axes of anxiety. First, the implications for the nation's economy, employment, welfare expenditure, and its social and cultural identity and cohesion. Second, the ethical, moral and political responsibilities of nations for asylum seekers. In Europe, these anxieties are evident in the different and changing positions of nations to the flow of asylum seekers from Syria, Afghanistan, Iraq, Sudan and elsewhere: from an initial welcoming tolerance, to deprivation, border closures and deportation.

In Australia, the politics of belonging around asylum seekers has focused largely on those arriving without authorisation by boat from Indonesia. During the national election of 2013, all political parties vied to demonstrate their superior capacity to manage/halt the arrival of asylum seekers and refugees. Over the ensuing years, Australia's approach to asylum seekers has drawn increasing political, media and public attention following riots and the death of an asylum seeker on the Manus Island processing centre in Papua New Guinea; exposure by a Human Rights Commission Inquiry of unconscionable levels of mental ill-health, sexual abuse, inadequate medical care, and inadequate living conditions on Christmas Island; public condemnation of Australia's treatment of asylum seekers by a United Nations Human Rights Council Periodic Review; and the decision by the Papua New Guinean Supreme Court that Australia's detainment of asylum seekers on Manus was 'unconstitutional' and 'illegal'.

Set against this context, a growing body of research has sought to understand the experiences of asylum seekers in general in Australia (e.g., Brough et al. 2013; Christie and Sidhu 2006; Croston and Pedersen 2013; Forrest et al. 2013; Fozdar and Hartley 2014; Lenette 2014; Pickering 2001; Schweitzer et al. 2005; Wilson 2011). Others have focused on community attitudes in Australia towards asylum seekers (e.g., Fozdar and Low 2015), often identifying patterns of prejudice (e.g., Leask et al. 2006; Lenette 2014; McKay et al. 2011; Pedersen et al. 2005a, b) fuelled by racist representations by politicians and the media (Clyne 2005; Pedersen et al. 2005a, b).

Yet, nationally and internationally, the issue of asylum seekers has been 'largely neglected by educationalists, even those concerned with social justice, critical analysis or ethnic issues', in schools (Pinson et al. 2010, p. 4). Research with teachers has focused on their attitudes and actions for social justice (Arnot et al. 2009), and pedagogies to support asylum seekers and refugees (Block et al. 2014; Ferfolja and Vickers 2010; Hughes and Beirens 2007; Keddie 2011; Matthews 2008; Pinson et al. 2010). In contrast, research with school students has focused largely on the efficacy of interventions to improve students' attitudes (e.g., Cameron et al. 2006; Turner and Brown 2008), empathy and respect for their human rights (e.g., Candappa et al. 2014; Spiteri 2013), and their sympathy and understanding of the plight of refugees (e.g., Watts 2004).

Largely lacking is any empirical or theoretical analysis of how young people *construct* asylum seekers, even though this group's attitudes, values and behaviours help shape the politics of belonging in the present and future. There are some exceptions. For instance, a study in the United

Kingdom of 11- to 24-year-olds' perspectives on the rights of young asylum seekers found that young people were more likely to endorse religious than nonreligious rights (Tenenbaum and Ruck 2012); an ethnography in an Australian rural high school found consensus that two Sudanese students would 'fit in' better in an urban school (Edgeworth 2014); and a study in Greece revealed that students held largely negative views of migrants except as a source of cheap labour (Dimakos and Tasiopoulou 2003).

This chapter seeks to add to this literature. It examines how primary and secondary students constitute asylum seekers and their entitlement to belong/not belong in Australia. Our discussion draws on focus groups conducted as part of a larger, multi-method study of intercultural understanding in 2013 and 2014. This was a time of intense public and media debate about Australia's responsibilities to asylum seekers and their rights to national belonging. The focus groups comprised ethnically diverse students from a socio-economic cross-section of six primary (Years 3–6) and six secondary (Years 7–10) schools in Melbourne, Australia. Students were invited to discuss two questions that directly relate to the conceptual issue of belonging:

> There's a lot of discussion in the media and politics about asylum seekers arriving in Australia by boat, and what Australia should do. *If you were the Prime Minister, what would you do about the asylum seekers?* (2013)

> Asylum seekers arriving in Australia by boat are now refused entry and housed in a detention centre on Manus Island in Papua New Guinea. During a recent protest by asylum seekers on Manus Island about their situation, the police and dog squad were brought in and gunshots fired. Several asylum seekers were injured and one died. *If you were Prime Minister, would you allow refugees to settle in Australia?* (2014)

Although our questions focused on Australia and the Australian context, the discourses deployed by our students align with those evident around the world, and we capture these under three headings: 'Excluding the Stranger'; 'Caring for the Stranger'; and 'Containing the Stranger'. In each section, we describe the identities students assign to asylum seekers, the logic they use to rationalise/justify the entitlement of asylum seekers to belong/not belong, and the theoretical issues these raise. Finally, in our conclusion, we highlight the provocations that the discourses deployed by students pose for teachers, schools and education systems.

Excluding the Stranger

The idea of belonging has little meaning without the idea of *not* belonging. In terms of nations, belonging has always presumed the existence of 'the insider' and 'the outsider, the other, against which the nation is itself defined and constructed' (Spencer and Wollman 2002, p. 96). Similarly, the concept of citizenship has always been as much about who is *not* entitled to belong as who is (Shaheed 2007), the 'entitled insiders and de-privileged outsiders' (Eckert 2011, p. 311). The tensions and dynamics of inclusion/exclusion feed the creation of boundaries that nurture and exacerbate the politics of belonging. This politics determines not only who is recognised as belonging but who is deemed a *desirable* citizen, who can access the resources of national membership, and who remains a stranger and outsider to the nation's normative social, legal, racial and cultural order.

Arguably, the asylum seeker is the most recent—and perhaps most emblematic—representation of the *dangerous* stranger. Within potential host nations, asylum seekers are often trapped in a stateless, 'nether world' of refugee camps or detention centres where belonging is either impossible or 'on hold' or prohibited by their status as 'absolutely foreign [and] absolutely alien' (Rundell 2004, p. 93) strangers.

This construction was echoed in the ways that some young Australians in our focus groups configured asylum seekers as shadowy, unknowable strangers who carry within themselves the threat of unspecified, unknown dangers:

> They say they are fleeing war but they have no background, no passport. How does Australia have any idea whether they are going to come in and shoot? (Kirkswood, Years 7 and 8)

There's a lot of incidences where people aren't actually who they are. (Kirkswood, Years 7 and 8)

If I was Prime Minister I could allow people that I would trust, not people that I don't know what they'd do. (Blackmede Primary, Year 5)

For some young people, this threat was an unintended consequence of the asylum seekers' condition, for example they might be 'carrying a disease' (Haskell Peak, Year 9). Previous studies show that communities distrust asylum seekers if they are considered 'bogus' (Pinson et al. 2010, p. 2) or a potential 'enemy' (Balibar 2006, p.1). Similarly, and reflecting the rhetoric of contemporary political and media debates, some of our students constitute the unfamiliar, unknowability of asylum seekers as central to their identity and a threat to Australia's social and legal order. After all, these students maintained, asylum seekers had disregarded the nation's laws by 'just trying to sneak in without anyone knowing' (Jardleigh College, Years 9 and 10), and 'you never know what they may do here, you never know what could happen, they might do something bad' (Blackmede Primary, Year 5). More than this, they 'might be trouble makers' (Claire Creek Primary, Years 3 & 4) or 'horrible people [who] have grudges against Australia' (Claire Creek Primary, Years 5 & 6) or 'have guns' (Claire Creek Primary, Years 3 & 4) or be 'dealing drugs' or 'smuggling drugs' (Haskell Peak, Year 9).

These students take up a discourse that constitutes asylum seekers as risky strangers whose unknowability threatens 'the dissembly of order' (Bauman 1995, p. 11), and this potentiality renders asylum seekers unacceptable candidates for citizenship and national belonging. In contrast, the *desirable* citizen was one who adheres to the normative social, ethnic, cultural, legal and political values of the nation, and is therefore recognised/recognisable as a citizen who belongs to the nation-state. Of course, students' anxieties are framed against an illusionary view of the 'real' Australia as a place and space occupied by law-abiding citizens who share a homogenous cultural identity, a commitment to 'a common destiny' (Fozdar and Low 2015, p. 524), and who conform to the cultural and legal expectations of this social majority.

In nations like Australia, this common destiny has historically been used to racialise and construct boundaries that exclude those constituted as 'Other' because their race, ethnicity, culture or religion do not align with those of the social majority. The contemporary shift has been to *augment* these exclusions with a discourse of civic nationalism which stresses that asylum seekers and migrants must 'follow the law' (Fozdar and Low 2015, p. 524). This discourse constitutes itself as colour-blind, non-discriminatory and non-racist, yet it makes adherence to the Law 'central to national belonging' and a 'proxy' for the normative behaviours of the desirable citizen (Fozdar and Low 2015, p. 532). It simultaneously excludes new arrivals by associating them with a propensity for either 'breaking the law and/or changing it' (Fozdar and Low 2015, p. 524). In these ways, asylum seekers are constructed as strangers who stand outside the social and legal frameworks that constitute belonging in Australia and as strangers who are 'culturally incompatible with a modern liberal democracy' (Fozdar and Low 2015, p. 524) and the ideals and norms of the 'homogenous nation' that civic nationalism evokes (Fozdar and Low 2015, p. 533).

Students reflect this conflation of cultural and legal acceptability by eliding the notion of belonging based on compliance with the law with the presumed, normative 'insider culture' (Amin 2004, p. 37) of the nation. This elision reinforces the expectation that those accepted as belonging in Australia will adopt the legal and cultural values and behaviours of the social majority, and that those who are different and fail to do so are seen as culturally deviant, warranting distrust or alienation:

> If you're Australian, there are laws. It's like the burka issue. I just don't think that if you come to Australia you should try and make your own laws again to improve the system. Because—it's going to sound so petty—but we're Australians, like, we were here first. So if you're going to come to Australia and you get this opportunity—this amazing opportunity to start your life again—you're going to have to follow, kind of, our way. (Kirkswood, Years 7 & 8)

Such comments ignore the history of British invasion, occupation and colonisation of Indigenous lands, yet assert a common expectation among the students that asylum seekers must leave all alien cultural baggage at the nation's door. This is the cost of transition from stranger to entitlement to belong and be a citizen: to become a blank slate on which the (presumed) cultural norms of the nation can be inscribed and to start one's life again. The imagery of a new start and new life as integral to belonging was a persistent theme in this focus group:

> Yeah, Australia is a very multicultural country, so I agree that people should have a right to speak their own language that their ancestors or previous family members have spoken and to carry on that kind of tradition, in a way. But I also don't agree when you see—I'm not picking on this because this is the least thing I want to be racist about, but, oh god—men with multiple wives! That's one big issue that I have a really big problem with in Australia, especially. In their own country I think that they should be allowed to uphold their tradition and custom, but once you come into another country, isn't that meant to be a symbol of a new beginning and new life? … Like you wouldn't want, like, 60,000 wives following you around every day because that's not our way of doing it here. (Kirkswood, Years 7 & 8)

A parallel narrative among students concerned the other ways by which these unknowable strangers might be rendered knowable and eligible to be desirable citizens. A number of the students describe the need for Australia to 'know [the] stories' of those who are applying for asylum (Haskell Peak, Year 9). While this narrative is still laden with the trope of the dangerous stranger, the implication is that the detention process could be used to discover—or uncover—the hidden and potentially lawless histories of those seeking asylum in Australia:

> Why should they be immediately let in without us figuring out who they are or what their past experiences have been like. (Haskell Peak, Year 9)

> The detention centres should stay, because it's just to help identify who they are. (Haskell Peak, Year 9)

Students elaborated on this theme by summoning up the strategies of exclusion and assimilation that have marked White Australia's race relations with its Indigenous peoples: from forced removals of all Aboriginal people to reserves under the guise of 'protection' since the nineteenth century, to the advocacy of biological absorption to 'breed out the colour' as a route to assimilation in the first half of the twentieth century (McGregor 2002). Bauman (1993a, 1996, 2004) argues that contemporary societies use two key strategies to deal with those it constitutes as strangers because they do not align with racial, ethnic, cultural or religious norms of the social majority. These are an *anthropophagic* strategy of annihilation whereby the stranger is absorbed and assimilated into a society; and an *anthropoemic strategy* of exclusion through border protection, ghettoisation and placement in detention centres that are 'guarded enclaves where they can be safely incarcerated without hope of escaping' (1993a, p. 163).

In our focus groups, several students reveal the 'immanence of the past in the present' and how closely racialised discourses and remnants of racialised thinking from the past bleed into and resurface in the present to shape the course of lives and the future (Halse 2017). They suggest that asylum seekers should not be accepted for admission or residency in Australia until they show compliance with the social and cultural norms by, for example, 'respect[ing] our language rather than just coming and demanding things' (Dalmorning Primary, Years 5 & 6). Others proposed that detention can serve as an enculturation process for asylum seekers whereby the stranger can be transformed into a 'proper Australian' (Claire Creek Primary, Years 3 & 4) who is fit and acceptable to 'come here and live a proper life like anyone else' (Haskell Peak, Year 8).

Caring for the Stranger

The configuration of the desirable citizen draws on an ethics derived from Kantian rationalism and moral theory combined with the social contract theories of liberal philosophers like Thomas Hobbes, John Locke, and John Rawls. This model of social relations underplays issues of racial, ethnic, cultural or religious difference and diversity by presuming that the expectations and rules of society can be universally and impartially applied to all people regardless of their circumstances. This is a problematic worldview, particularly for race relations and feminist scholars, because it can breed blindness and insensibility to the issues that affect one's life and one's relations to others (Gilligan 2008; Leonardo 2009). Thus, Margaret Walker (1997) criticises such 'law-like moral principles or procedures' as transhistorical, transcultural, and couched in the language of scientific objectivity to appear dispassionate and authoritative (1997, p. 36) even though they privilege some groups and disadvantage others.

In contrast to this dominant model of social relations, some education researchers have focused on compassion as the desirable trait for engaging with refugees and asylum seekers (e.g., Arnot et al. 2009; Pinson et al. 2010), informed by the thinking of Paul Gilbert (2005) who describes compassion as:

> being open to the suffering of self and others, in a non-defensive and non-judgemental way. Compassion also involves a desire to relieve suffering, cognitions related to understanding the causes of suffering, and behaviours—acting with compassion. Hence, it is from a *combination* of motives, emotions, thoughts and behaviours that compassion emerges. (p. 1)

Compassion configured in this way focuses on the sentiments and behaviours of *individuals* but, as Martha Nussbaum (2001) argues, this form of compassion can be unreliable, partial, and 'motivate self-indulgent and self-congratulatory behaviour, rather than real helpfulness' (p. 399). Nor does compassion as an individual attitude and mode of behaviour address the question of the institutional and societal enactment of compassion.

Drawing on Carol Gilligan (1977), an ethics of care is one approach for addressing these limitations. An ethics of care involves both empathy with *and* responding to the specific 'concrete, physical, spiritual, intellectual, psychic, and emotional needs of others' (Jagger 1995; Tronto 1989, 1993). It is a 'morality based on responsibility and relationships' that 'is grounded in concrete circumstance', expressed as an 'activity of care' (Halse and Honey 2005, p. 128), and that focuses on 'how to respond' to the concrete particularity of others in all individual, institutional and social interactions.

Wittingly or otherwise, small pockets of young people across all schools invoked an ethics of care that argued that asylum seekers were entitled to belong in Australia. They observed that asylum seekers had experienced the 'hard times' and the horrors of war in countries where they 'weren't safe' (Jardleigh College, Years 7 & 8), and that they had 'no choice' but to flee, even though they had no money and did not want to leave (Kirkswood, Years 9 & 10). For these reasons, students argued, asylum seekers should not be 'treated differently just because they're different' (Blackmede Primary, Year 5) but deserved to be 'rewarded with safety and food and, like, taken as people' (Mallore Hills College, Years 9 & 10) and were also entitled to have a house, a living, and equal rights with other Australians 'because they're human beings' (Blackmede Primary, Year 5).

In contrast to those students who focused on asylum seekers' ineligibility to belong and undesirability as citizens because they posed a potential threat to the nation's existing social order, other students took up a discourse of inclusion. They argued that asylum seekers were exactly the sort of people who make 'good' citizens and are entitled to belong in Australia: they are 'innocent' (Claire Creek Primary), 'hard working people' who just want a job, money, and to help others overseas (Jardleigh College, Years 9 & 10). For these students, care was an ethical and moral orientation and mode of practice towards the Other for both individuals and for the nation (see Sevenhuijsen 1998; Tronto 1993). They extrapolated from their own experiences to apply the same moral stance to the institutions and behaviours of wider society: 'most people are taught, like ever since they were young, you know, to share and to be nice to each other' (Kirkswood, Years 7 & 8). For these students, Australia's privileged social and economic status meant there was no justification for *failing* to care. They argued that, geographically, Australia has plenty of land to accommodate asylum seekers (Kirkswood, Years 7 & 8; Years 9 & 10) and that, economically, it is a 'safe and wealthy place' (Kirkswood, Years 9 & 10) 'because of the all the taxes we're paying' the government (Claire Creek Primary).

These students echoed the principles captured by Joan Tronto (1989, 1993) that care defines 'the shape of social and political institutions', is an essential virtue of participation in public life, and is a moral obligation of a nation's governments and political leaders. Our students were highly critical of the Australian government and then Prime Minister, Tony

Abbott, for their lack of empathy for the experiences of asylum seekers (losing their families and homes, being forced to flee their homelands, suffering a treacherous sea voyage to Australia) and their current plight (confined 'in cages' in detention centres and 'treated like dogs'). For these students, the *absence* of care by the nation's political leadership was incompatible with the moral foundation of a liberal democracy. They argued that the government ought to spend the taxes it raised on 'people who are in need, not just for themselves all the time' (Claire Creek Primary) and that the Prime Minister ought to visit Afghanistan to better understood the former lives and conditions of asylum seekers and enable him to make more caring decisions about their wellbeing and future (Leighburns College, Years 9 & 10).

In targeting the Prime Minister as an individual *and* as representing the generalised public institution of government, students unknowingly echo Nussbaum's (2001) call for compassion and care in public life at 'both the level of individual psychology and the level of institutional design' (p. 403). In doing so, these students intuitively recognise the centrality of care as part of the social structures and institutions of the nation (Jagger 1995). Reflecting the content of the school curriculum secondary, older students reinforced this point by insisting that the nation's obligation to care was also part of Australia's legal and political obligations as a signatory of the Declaration of Human Rights and a member of the United Nations.

Containing the Stranger

A third group of students struggled to reconcile the competing notions of exclusion and inclusion underlying the discourses deployed by their classmates. Key to their efforts were the notions of boundaries and an alternate configuration of space. For these young people, permitting asylum seekers entry into Australia was possible—even desirable—but they constructed clear geographical boundaries around where asylum seekers ought to be housed within the national space, and named particular and geographically distant places in Australia as acceptable, permissible sites for asylum seekers. One student, for example, reported: 'I heard on A Current Affair [a commercial TV news program] about the idea of taking

them to Tasmania and it will save them. I think that is a very good idea'
(Blackmede Primary, Year 5). This was a good idea, the student explained,
because we should let them 'at least go somewhere because their country
may be in war and they may be suffering a lot'.

In a similar vein, one student said: 'I would allow the asylum seekers
to come, and I would build an area for them where they can stay, maybe
near the top of Australia' (Claire Creek Primary, Years 5 & 6). Another
student in the same group commented: 'I would probably get rid of all
the detention places and build new ones that were nicer, because detention centres are, from what I've heard, absolutely horrible'.

One secondary school student put forward the most elaborate of these
configurations of space, when he suggested that he would build an estate
in Western Australia for the asylum seekers to live:

Student 1:	Personally I would make a massive estate and put all the refugees in it, build like a McDonalds, build houses, … and then just dump, like just put them all there, so they're separated from us, but they still live in Australia.
Student 2:	So it's not like a detention centre-
Student 1:	Yeah it's not really a detention seeker, they still have freedom-
Student 2:	It's more comfortable.
Student 1:	More comfortable, more of a society, a community.
Student 3:	But would you really want them separated from other people?
Student 1:	Well they wouldn't be separated, because it would just be their town where they lived.
Student 2:	Their area.
Student 3:	They can still leave it.
Student 1:	Yeah they can still leave it… you could have obviously schools there and education
Student 2:	Like tutors…
Student 4:	But then again that's going to cost so much.
Student 3:	Yeah that's going to take a lot of the government's money up though. Like aren't they paying for other stuff as well, they're paying for the whole detention centre thing to go ahead.
Student 1:	Yeah the detention centre they still don't have freedom they're locked up in cages and stuff… well not cages…
Interviewer:	Alright. So where do you think you might build this estate that you–
Student 1:	Western Australia
Interviewer:	W.A. Any particular part of W.A?

Student 1:	Right in the middle … because isn't it just like all country in the middle of WA, like no one there, so … and then like, there could be teachers there, there could just be everything there, they could make their own Coles, their own little shopping centre, little school.
Student 4:	It would still be pretty hard to build on there.
Student 2:	Yeah
Student 1:	Well this could be a plan, it doesn't matter if you take 10 years, 20 years, it's still in the future, [it] will be a success.
Interviewer:	So you'd build a whole—sounds like you'd build a whole new community from the ground up, from nothing–
Student 1:	Yeah
(Haskell Peak, Year 9).	

The spatial solutions proposed by these particular young people sought to reconcile the competing ideas of exclusion (distancing the stranger) and inclusion (caring). Implicit in their proposals is the view that life *within* Australia would be more hospitable than the off-shore detention centres on Manus, Nauru or Christmas Islands, that Australia has a moral obligation to care for asylum seekers, and that this is best be achieved by allowing them into our national space.

For these students, the compromise solution was to propose that asylum seekers be cared for in communities located in physically distant and isolated spaces and landscapes, and that are geographically and socially 'far away' from the social majority who live in the densely populated suburbs of eastern and southern mainland Australia. As a Year 9 student explained: 'they're separated from us but they still live in Australia'. Yet, despite their intentions, these students deployed clear configurations of space and boundaries that constructed asylum seekers as belonging in a *very particular way* that precluded them from the rights of political and social participation conferred on citizens, and simultaneously Othered them by reinforcing their identity as marginalised and excluded strangers.

Space and boundaries have an influential place in the politics of belonging (Curtis and Mee 2012; Hage 1998; Perera 2009; Trudeau 2006; Wright 2015; Yuval-Davis 2011). Yuval-Davis describes the politics of belonging as 'constructing belonging to particular collectivities' by establishing 'boundaries [that] are often spatial and relate to a specific locality/territoriality and not just to constructions of social collectivities' (2011, p. 10).

It is the social majority, however, who 'codify landscapes and define the terms of belonging' (Trudeau 2006, p. 437) so that the boundary between 'us and them' is not simply imagined but 'articulated on the ground, in the construction, reconstruction and contestation of spaces' (p. 434) and thus operates in very concrete and material terms. Ghassan Hage, in *White Nation* (1998), illustrates this phenomenon by revealing how white Australians assume the right to direct and determine who belongs within the national space as well as particular local spaces, and the clear sense of entitlement about their own belonging within these spaces.

In a similar way, our students' 'solution' asserted their hegemony as the dominant social group. At the same time, it reworked the ghettoisation (Bauman 1996, 2004) that has marked the history of peoples constituted as Other and excluded from mainstream society, such as Jews, and the Indigenous Australians who were forcibly removed from their own land and contained on reserves or as state wards under the guise of care and protection. Students reinforced this identity by invoking the geographical sites for the asylum seekers' new towns as unwanted, empty, uninhabited spaces with 'no-one there', ignoring the custodial rights of its traditional, indigenous owners and the interests of any present-day inhabitants. In doing so, they unwittingly resurrect and reassert the colonial discourse and practices used to justify the invasion and occupation of Australia: that it was *terra nullius* or 'nobody's land'. These students' *intention* is to care and, in seeking to cater for asylum seekers, they imagine towns equipped with all the resources that young people consider essential for daily life—a school, a supermarket, a McDonald's restaurant. Nevertheless, the effect of their strategy is to reinforce the power dynamics that are central to the politics of belonging by affirming the social majority's power to prescribe the Other's identity and belonging, and to inscribe this in geographical/spatial terms of national and political membership.

Discussion

Yuval-Davis (2011) argues that the politics of belonging—and conversely the politics of non-belonging (see Everatt 2015)—involves contestation along three, intersecting axes: the positions and locations of individuals/groups according to their different social categorisations and social power; the social, cultural and symbolic practices that individuals/groups identify with and have emotional attachment to; and the ethical and political values that are used to judge who belongs/does not belong.

Our students, however, show just how deeply the politics of belonging are entangled with the physical and metaphorical notions of space and geography that determine how national belonging is 'experienced, enacted, ordered and resisted' (Anderson and Taylor 2005, p. 13). Yet, the authority to decide who belongs/does not belong lies with the social majority who *already* belong, even though the exercise of their power is disguised under a cloak of seemingly rational, reasonable common sense. The persuasiveness of this approach, however, hinges on constructing asylum seekers as a particular *species* of persons—the alien, racialised stranger who can never be understood, trusted or able to 'fit in'—and applying this identity to *all* asylum seekers regardless of their individual and collective differences and diversity.

The discourses taken up by our students suggest that the asylum seeker is always/already the stranger, the outsider who already does not belong. This pre-existing identity is reinforced through the discourse of 'Excluding the Stranger' by imbuing the asylum seeker with the possibility of menace to the nation's cultural norms and legal and social order. This threat, however, is always ambiguous and provisional: a menace that cannot be confirmed and therefore needs to be guarded against. This elaboration of the asylum seeker's identity works to define and divide individuals/groups into native/Other, desirable/non-desirable citizens and, therefore, those who belong and do not belong. Implicit in these binaries is a recasting of the logic for the racism and prejudices of the social majority as the protection and preservation of societies' legal, social and cultural norms. Such deployment of logic and language is common among young people (see Halse 2017). It is used to convey, legitimate, deflect and deny personal and structural responsibility for exclusionary, racist attitudes and behaviours, while also perpetuating the social divisions that privilege the majority group but disadvantage and discriminate against those marginalised as Other (Halse 2017).

In contrast, students who take up the discourse of 'Caring for the Stranger' advocate that questions of belonging must attend to the common humanity and connectedness of all peoples, and that an ethics of care is integral to how individuals and nations ought to engage with asylum seekers. This discourse also universalises asylum seekers but not as risky, threatening strangers. Rather, it constitutes asylum seekers as individuals who share the same desires and aspirations as themselves and all peoples, and who are entitled to be welcomed and belong because 'they're human beings'. Of course, there is always a risk that focusing on the common humanity of all peoples might erase actual alterity and cultural difference. Nevertheless, these students propose that care, as a more developed modality of practice than compassion, should be a guiding principle of public life and of the actions and behaviours of a nation's government and political leaders.

The discourse of 'Containing the Stranger' tries—and fails—to resolve the tension between excluding and including the stranger. Rather than configuring belonging as an affective and intellectual site created by accepting the diversity and differences of Others, this discourse remains shackled to the physical notion of space, geography and the nation-state, and to particular geographical sites that are deemed further away from the hegemonic majority and therefore more acceptable for locating strangers. This is a paradoxical stance given that these young people live in an increasingly diverse, transcultural and transnational world of globally mobile populations. In part, we propose, this paradox testifies to the stickiness of divisive, racialised ideas and practices from the past, and their embeddedness in the national consciousness and psyche in contemporary social conditions (see Halse 2017).

Conclusion

The discourses summoned by the primary and secondary students in our focus groups have different moral, political and practical effects. They constitute asylum seekers as strangers who are Other to the social majority, and belonging in terms of space and the geographical boundaries of the nation-state. Extending John Crowley's (1999) idea of 'boundary maintenance', each discourse actively contributes to the 'dirty work of boundary *making*' by inscribing and reinscribing the politics of belonging in different ways to define who is included/excluded and entitled/not entitled to belong with the nation in ways that simultaneously assert and affirm the asylum seekers' identity of Other and as stranger. Thus, as Sara Ahmed describes, the other as stranger is not simply someone we do not yet know or understand, but 'an effect of processes of inclusion and exclusion' which simultaneously reinforce, challenge, and (de)construct the boundaries of our 'homes' (2000, p. 6).

Our analysis also suggests that young people in Australia are not passive actors in the politics of belonging. Rather, their attitudes, values and behaviours are political, and they play into how asylum seekers and the future of asylum seekers are configured and experienced. Yet, students do not present a unitary voice on how Australia should respond to asylum seekers. Rather, their values and attitudes resonate with the same views that have marked history and that percolate through contemporary public policy, media coverage and popular understandings about asylum seekers. This analysis, we propose, has implications for teachers, schools and Australia's education systems, for the account of the national imaginary they communicate, and for the role of schooling in facilitating the capacities of future generations to recognise and resist the repetition of stigmatising identities that perpetuate unjust exclusions. These implications underline the imperative for educators and education to think anew about how we can address the central problematic of belonging. This is what Bauman (1993b) describes as the 'burning question' of contemporary life, namely 'not how to give the stranger a temporary residence, but how to live with strangers daily and permanently' (p. 399).

References

Ahmed, S. (2000). *Strange encounters: Embodied others in post-coloniality*. London: Routledge.

Amin, A. (2004). Regions unbound: Towards a new politics of place. *Geografiska Annaler: Series B, Human Geography, 86*(1), 33–44.

Anderson, K., & Taylor, A. (2005). Exclusionary politics and the question of national belonging: Australian ethnicities in 'multiscalar' focus. *Ethnicities, 5*(4), 460–485.

Arnot, M., Pinson, H., & Candappa, M. (2009). Compassion, caring and justice: Teachers' strategies to maintain moral integrity in the face of national hostility to the 'non-citizen'. *Educational Review, 61*(3), 249–264.

Balibar, É. (2006). Strangers as enemies: Further reflections on the aporias of transnational citizenship. Retrieved from http://www.artcentersf.org/fall2016/parallaxdrift/wp-content/uploads/2017/04/Strangers.pdf.

Bauman, Z. (1993a). Racism, anti-racism, and moral progress. *Arena Journal, 1*, 9–21.

Bauman, Z. (1993b). *Postmodern ethics.* Cambridge: Blackwell.

Bauman, Z. (1995). Making and unmaking of strangers. *Thesis Eleven, 43*, 1–16.

Bauman, Z. (1996). *Alone again: Ethics after certainty.* London: Demos.

Bauman, Z. (2004). *Wasted lives: Modernity and its outcasts.* Cambridge: Polity Press.

Block, K., Cross, S., Riggs, E., & Gibbs, L. (2014). Supporting schools to create an inclusive environment for refugee students. *International Journal of Inclusive Education, 18*(12), 1337–1355.

Brough, M., Schweitzer, R., Shakespeare-Finch, J., Vromans, L., & King, J. (2013). Unpacking the micro-macro nexus: Narratives of suffering and hope among refugees from Burma recently settled in Australia. *Journal of Refugee Studies, 26*(2), 207–225.

Cameron, L., Rutland, A., Brown, R., & Douch, R. (2006). Changing children's intergroup attitudes toward refugees: Testing different models of extended contact. *Child Development, 77*(5), 1208–1219.

Candappa, M., Arnot, M., & Pinson, H. (2014). 'I don't know how you can say 'no' to them really': 'Citizen' students' negotiation of the social morality of asylum. In L. Chisholm & V. Delgiann-Kouimtz (Eds.), *Changing landscapes for childhood and youth in Europe* (pp. 208–230). Newcastle upon Tyne: Cambridge Scholars Press.

Christie, P., & Sidhu, R. (2006). Governmentality and 'free speech': Framing the education of asylum seeker and refugee children in Australia. *Oxford Review of Education, 32*(4), 449–465.

Clyne, M. (2005). The use of exclusionary language to manipulate opinion: John Howard, asylum seekers and the reemergence of political incorrectness in Australia. *Journal of Language and Politics, 4*(2), 173–196.

Croston, J., & Pedersen, A. (2013). 'Tell me what I want to hear': Motivated recall and attributions in media regarding asylum seekers. *Australian Journal of Psychology, 65*(2), 124–133.

Crowley, J. (1999). The politics of belonging: Some theoretical considerations. In A. Geddes & A. Favell (Eds.), *The politics of belonging: Migrants and minorities in contemporary Europe* (pp. 15–41). Aldershot: Ashgate.

Curtis, F., & Mee, K. J. (2012). Welcome to woodside: Inverbrackie alternative place of detention and performances of belonging in Woodside, South Australia, and Australia. *Australian Geographer, 43*(4), 357–375.

Dimakos, I. C., & Tasiopoulou, K. (2003). Attitudes towards migrants: What do Greek students think about their immigrant classmates? *Intercultural Education, 14*(3), 307–316.

Eckert, J. (2011). Introduction: Subjects of citizenship. *Citizenship Studies, 1*(3-4), 309–317.

Edgeworth, K. (2014). Black bodies, white rural spaces: Disturbing practices of unbelonging for 'refugee' students. *Critical Studies in Education, 56*(3), 351–364. https://doi.org/10.1080/17508487.2014.956133.

Everatt, D. (2015). The politics of non-belonging in the developing world. In J. Wyn & H. Cahill (Eds.), *Handbook of children and youth studies* (pp. 63–78). Netherlands: Springer.

Ferfolja, T., & Vickers, M. (2010). Supporting refugee students in school education in Greater Western Sydney. *Critical Studies in Education, 51*(2), 149–162.

Forrest, J., Hermes, K., Johnston, R., & Poulsen, M. (2013). The housing resettlement experience of refugee immigrants to Australia. *Journal of Refugee Studies, 26*(2), 187–206. https://doi.org/10.1093/jrs/fes020.

Fozdar, F., & Hartley, L. K. (2014). Civic and ethno belonging among recent refugees to Australia. *Journal of Refugee Studies, 27*(1), 126–144.

Fozdar, F., & Low, M. (2015). 'They have to abide by our laws … and stuff': Ethnonationalism masquerading as civic nationalism. *Nations and Nationalism, 21*(3), 524–543.

Gilbert, P. (Ed.). (2005). *Compassion: Conceptualisations, research and use in psychotherapy*. East Sussex: Routledge.

Gilligan, C. (1977). In a different voice: Women's conceptions of self and morality. *Harvard Educational Review, 47*(4), 481–517.

Gilligan, C. (2008). Moral orientation and moral development. In A. Bailey & C. Cuomo (Eds.), *The feminist philosophy reader* (pp. 467–476). Boston: McGraw-Hill.

Hage, G. (1998). *White nation: Fantasies of White supremacy in a multicultural society*. Annandale: Pluto Press.

Halse, C. (2017). Responsibility for racism in the everyday talk of secondary students. *Discourse: Studies in the Cultural Politics of Education, 38*(1), 2–15.

Halse, C., & Honey, A. (2005). Unravelling ethics: Illuminating the moral dilemmas of research ethics. *Signs: Journal of Women in Culture and Society: Special Issue on Dilemmas in Feminist Social Research, 3*(4), 2142–2161.

Hughes, N., & Beirens, H. (2007). Enhancing educational support: Towards holistic, responsive and strength-based services for young refugees and asylum-seekers. *Children and Society, 21*(4), 261–272.

Jagger, A. (1995). Caring as a feminist practice or moral reason. In V. Held (Ed.), *Justice and care: Essential readings in feminist ethics* (pp. 179–202). Boulder, CO: Westview Press.

Keddie, A. (2011). Supporting minority students through a reflexive approach to empowerment. *British Journal of Sociology of Education, 32*(2), 221–238.

Leask, J., Sheikh-Mohammed, M., MacIntyre, C. R., Leask, A., & Wood, N. J. (2006). Community perceptions about infectious disease risk posed by new arrivals: A qualitative study. *Medical Journal of Australia, 185*(11/12), 591–593.

Lenette, C. (2014). 'I am a widow, mother and refugee': Narratives of two refugee widows resettled to Australia. *Journal of Refugee Studies, 27*(3), 403–421.

Leonardo, Z. (2009). *Race, whiteness, and education.* New York: Routledge.

Matthews, J. (2008). Schooling and settlement: Refugee education in Australia. *International Studies in Sociology of Education, 18*(1), 31–45.

McGregor, R. (2002). *'Breed out the colour' or the importance of being white. Australian Historical Studies, 33*(120), 286–302.

McKay, F. H., Thomas, S. L., & Blood, R. W. (2011). 'Any one of these boat people could be a terrorist for all we know!' Media representations and public perceptions of 'boat people' arrivals in Australia. *Journalism, 12*(5), 607–626.

Nussbaum, M. (2001). *Upheavals of thought: The intelligence of emotion.* Cambridge: Cambridge University Press.

Pedersen, A., Attwell, J., & Heveli, D. (2005a). Prediction of negative attitutdes toward Australian asylum seekers: False beliefs, nationalism, and self-esteem. *Australian Journal of Psychology, 57*(3), 148–160.

Pedersen, A., Clarke, S., Dudgeon, P., & Griffiths, B. (2005b). Attitudes towards indigenous Australians and asylum seekers: The role of false beliefs and other social-psychological variables. *Australian Psychologist, 40*(3), 170–178.

Perera, S. (2009). *Australia and the insular imagination: Beaches, borders, boats, and bodies.* New York: Palgrave Macmillan.

Pickering, S. (2001). Common sense and original deviancy: News discourses and asylum seekers in Australia. *Journal of Refugee Studies, 14*(2), 169–186.

Pinson, H., Arnot, M., & Candappa, M. (2010). *Education, aslyum and the 'non-citizen' child: The politics of compassion and belonging.* Hampshire: Palgrave Macmillan.

Rundell, J. (2004). Strangers, citizens and outsiders: Otherness, multiculturalism and the cosmopolitan imaginary in mobile societies. *Thesis Eleven, 78*(1), 85–101.

Schweitzer, R., Perkoulidis, S. A., Krome, S. L., Ludlow, C. N., & Ryan, M. (2005). Attitudes towards refugees: The dark side of prejudice in Australia. *Australian Journal of Psychology, 57*(3), 170–179.

Sevenhuijsen, S. (1998). *Citizenship and the ethics of care: Feminist considerations on justice, morality and politics.* London: Routledge.

Shaheed, F. (2007). Citizenship and the nuanced belonging of women. In J. Bennet (Ed.), *Scratching the surface: Democracy, traditions, gender* (pp. 23–38). Lahore: Heinrich Böll Foundation.

Simmel, G. (1908 [1971]). The stranger. In D. N. Levine (Ed.), *On individuality and social forms: Selected writings.* Chicago: University of Chicago Press.

Spencer, P., & Wollman, H. (2002). *Nationalism: A critical introduction.* London: Sage.

Spiteri, D. (2013). Can my perceptions of the 'other' change? Challenging prejudices against migrants amongst adolescent boys in a school for low achievers in Malta. *Research in Education, 89*(May), 41–60.

Tenenbaum, H. R., & Ruck, M. D. (2012). British adolescents' and young adults' understanding and reasoning about the religious and nonreligious rights of asylum-seeker youth. *Child Development, 83*(3), 1102–1115.

Tronto, J. (1989). Women and caring: What can feminists learn about morality from caring? In A. Jaggar & S. Bordo (Eds.), *Gender/body/knowledge: Feminist reconstructions of being and knowing* (pp. 172–187). New Brunswick: Rutgers University Press.

Tronto, J. (1993). *Moral boundaries: A political argument for an ethic of care.* New York: Routledge.

Trudeau, D. (2006). Politics of belonging in the construction of landscapes: Place-making, boundary drawing and exclusion. *Cultural Geographies, 13,* 421–443.

Turner, R. N., & Brown, R. (2008). Improving children's attitudes toward refugees: an evaluation of a school-based multicultural curriculum and an anti-racist intervention. *Journal of Applied Social Psychology, 38*(5), 1295–1328.

Walker, M. (1997). *Moral understanding: A feminist study in ethics*. New York: Routledge.

Watts, M. (2004). Telling tales of torture: Repositioning young adults' views of asylum seekers. *Cambridge Journal of Education, 34*(3), 315–329.

Wilson, E. (2011). Much to be proud of, much to be done: Faith-based organizations and the politics of asylum in Australia. *Journal of Refugee Studies, 24*(3), 548–564.

Wright, S. (2015). More-than-human, emergent belongings: A weak theory approach. *Progress in Human Geography, 39*(4), 391–411.

Yuval-Davis, N. (2006). Belonging and the politics of belonging. *Patterns of Prejudice, 40*(3), 197–214.

Yuval-Davis, N. (2011). *The politics of belonging: Intersectional contestations*. London: Sage.

7

Privileged Bonds: Lessons of Belonging at an Elite School

Adam Howard and Hoa Nguyen

It took me longer than expected to find the dining hall, despite it being prominently located on campus. I had an hour to roam around the campus that sprawls over nearly 150 walled acres (about 61 hectares) on a hilltop overlooking the surrounding arid land. Landscaped in such a way, the towering perimeter wall is invisible from the inside. More a symbol than a meaningful barrier, discreet members of the school's security staff are the real protection, patrolling the school grounds constantly to make sure students from prominent families and their classmates remain safe in a region of the world that has seen violence and instability over the years. While on campus, the outside world recedes. With swathes of greenspace, lush gardens surrounded by olive, palm and jacaranda trees, and Levantine-style buildings with red tile roofs and wooden balconies, I feel separated from life outside the campus.

Upon exiting one of the gardens located near the sporting fields, I spot a group of students heading in the same direction. I follow their lead until I run into Tariq, one of our student guides. 'Just come with me. I'll show you

A. Howard (✉) • H. Nguyen
Colby College, Waterville, ME, USA
e-mail: mahoward@colby.edu

C. Halse (ed.), *Interrogating Belonging for Young People in Schools*,
https://doi.org/10.1007/978-3-319-75217-4_7

to your table', he offers when we make eye contact. Entering the crowded dining hall, the atmosphere dramatically shifts with hundreds of chair legs moaning over the tiled floor, teachers and students scurrying to their assigned tables, some students fulfilling their lunchtime duties, and seemingly everyone engaged in lively conversations. Despite a lot going on, everyone seems intimately familiar with the rituals that give meaning to this all-school gathering.

An older man, perhaps in his eighties, who is introduced to me as 'the elder' of the community, steps onto a small elevated platform at the front of the room. After taking his position, he stands silently for a few seconds before he rings a bell that immediately brings silence to the room. He speaks softly, yet with authority, into a microphone to give a blessing. Students and faculty listen attentively and keep their eyes on him until he steps down from the platform. Conversations instantly erupt among the 'family members' sitting together. As one of the students serves us food, the headmaster kicks off the conversation at our table ('OK, how's everybody?') and lets it flow for a few minutes. Concise and thoughtful, students go around the table to share what's most pressing on their minds. Three students are about to graduate and were just notified of admissions decisions. Two of these students share that they got into their first choice but don't seem as thrilled as one would expect.

I quickly learn that they are concealing their excitement out of respect for Ahmed, another student sitting at the table, who was not as successful in the admissions process. He lets us know, 'I got into two places but waitlisted at my top choice. I have no idea what to do now'. The headmaster brings me into the conversation by asking, 'Any advice for this confused young man?' I ask a few questions to gather the necessary details to offer an informed response. Then I give a typical professorial suggestion, 'All the schools are really good ones, go where you think you'll be the happiest for the next four years'. My response did little to comfort Ahmed. Others at the table chime in to reassure him that everything is going to work out. For the rest of the meal, we all join together in supporting a member of our table family.

'If you want to get a real sense of who we are as a community, you only need to go to the dining hall when we're all there, especially during lunch', Mr. Meyer, language teacher and assistant headmaster, insists. The dining hall at Olive Grove Academy, an elite coeducational boarding school in Jordan, is often described as 'the heart of the school'. Much more than just a place where students and faculty eat three meals a day, it is a space for the community to come together 'to strengthen friendships, exchange ideas and build the community spirit that distinguishes the school', as Dr. Thomas, the headmaster, explains. Mr. Meyer adds that lunchtime, in particular, provides a time and space for 'sharing conversation, engaging in meaningful interactions with students and faculty, paying attention to manners, taking an interest in one another, and reinforcing the sense that we are all contributing to make the experience meaningful'.

All students take turns waiting on tables; teachers and administrators emphasise that members of royal families who attend the school are no exceptions. When it is a student's turn on the schedule, they retrieve food from dining staff, serve that food to the seven other students and teacher or administrator sitting at their table, and clear the dishes when everyone is finished. Students fulfil these tasks for the purpose of developing 'a sense of camaraderie' and encouraging 'service to the school'. Table assignments rotate every three weeks to provide students opportunities to meet and engage in conversation with different peers and teachers. These family-style meals are just one of the ways in which students at Olive Grove are encouraged to feel 'at home' and form an emotional attachment to the school and others within the school community (Yuval-Davis 2011). This sense of belonging to a 'family' within Olive Grove is essential for fomenting a collective identity (Gaztambide-Fernández et al. 2013). Within this context, sense of belonging not only refers to the emotional attachment of individuals that allows them to feel accepted, valued and a meaningful part of their community, but it is also a crucial means by which individuals form particular self-understandings and 'individuals and social formations are reciprocally constituted' (Harding and Pribram 2009, p. 10).

Sense of Belonging in Educational Contexts

Roy Baumeister and Mark Leary (1995) suggest that a need for regular contact and an understanding that relationships have stability, affective concern and continuity, characterise a sense of belonging. They argue that belongingness is a fundamental human motivation: 'human beings have a pervasive drive to form and maintain at least a minimum quantity of lasting, positive, and significant interpersonal relationships' (p. 497). Others similarly contend that belonging to groups positively affects a number of key factors that contribute to individuals' overall well-being and healthy development (e.g., Haslam et al. 2009; Holt-Lunstad et al. 2010). Although individuals can form this sense of belonging in multiple contexts (such as family and community), Kelly Allen and Terry Bowles (2012) point out that schools, in particular, play 'an important role in building social networks for individuals and offer unique opportunities for influencing belonging for school-aged children' (p. 108).

Unsurprisingly, given the positive impact of belonging on individuals, research points to a strong and positive link between students' sense of belonging in school and both their participation and achievement (e.g., Cemalcilar 2010; Gibson et al. 2004; Osterman 2000). In fact, scholars argue that the need for belonging is one of the most important needs of students to perform and function well in the schooling context (Goodenow 1993). Moreover, studies suggest that students who feel that they belong to learning environments report higher levels of enjoyment, enthusiasm, happiness, interest and confidence (e.g., Furrer and Skinner 2003). Although scholars emphasise different positive outcomes of students developing a sense of belonging to their school community, there is general agreement that students should feel 'accepted, valued, included, and encouraged by others (teachers and peers) in [school] and of feeling oneself to be an important part of the life and activity of the [school]' (Goodenow 1993, p. 25). Carol Goodenow further contends that this sense of belonging is 'more than simple perceived liking or warmth, it also involves support and respect for personal autonomy and for the student as an individual' (p. 25).

As a research focus and school priority, the concept of belonging has received relatively little scholarly interest, especially given its significance in students' wellbeing and healthy development, which is consistent, as several scholars note, with other areas that promote students' overall health and their emotional worlds in the schooling context (e.g., Allen and Bowles 2012). Moreover, the body of work existing to date has focused primarily on the role that belonging (and sense of belonging) plays in the educational experiences and academic performance of disadvantaged students. The role of belonging in elite schools remains virtually unmapped terrain. However, studies on the emotional geographies of elite schools highlight the importance of students' emotional investments in their school (Kenway et al. 2013) and identification with their school (Gaztambide-Fernández et al. 2013). Research suggests that the processes involved in instilling a sense of belonging in students play an incredibly important role in the production of privilege at elite schools.

Examining how students at an elite boarding school construct identification with the eliteness of their school, Rubén Gaztambide-Fernández (2009), for example, offers a framework for understanding elite identification. This framework, what he calls the 'five E's' of elite identification, includes the interrelated processes of exclusion, engagement, excellence, entitlement and envisioning that contribute to how students come to see themselves as members of an elite school and how they internalise elite status. Similarly, Adam Howard (2008) explores the ways that belonging to an elite institution influence how students come to see themselves, others and the world around them and how these understandings reflect particular ideological moves in justifying advantages. These and other studies on elite schools propose that the processes involved in students' forming a sense of belonging position them to surrender their individualism; thus, offering a different perspective to the respect and support for autonomy and individualism facilitated through processes involved in instilling belongingness in non-elite educational contexts (e.g., Goodenow 1993).

More specifically, boarding schools like Olive Grove put much effort into stripping students of their individuality to form a collective identity within the school community. As 'total institutions' (Goffman 1961), boarding schools regulate students' lives in ways to develop a particular character. In their seminal study of elite boarding schools in the United States, Peter Cookson and Caroline Persell (1985) observe,

> Since their inception the elite schools have had the responsibility of melting down the refractory material of individualism into the solid metal of elite collectivism. By isolating students from their home world and intervening in their development, it is hoped that they will become soldiers for their class … The total institution is a moral milieu where pressure is placed on individuals to give up significant parts of their selves to forward the interests of the group … Thus the requirement that students eat, sleep, and study together creates and continuously reinforces a sense of collective identity. (p. 124)

As students 'give up significant parts' of themselves to form a collective identity, they learn important lessons about themselves, others and the world around them. In this chapter, we explore the ways in which these kinds of lessons instil a sense of belonging in students at Olive Grove to reinforce privilege as a collective identity within their school community. We examine how these lessons embrace particular norms, perspectives, dispositions, ways of knowing and doing and ideologies that give shape and meaning to students' self-understandings. All of these reveal how privilege is affectively and ideologically produced within this elite educational context.

Research Project

To explore these lessons of belonging, we draw from a multi-sited global ethnography (e.g., Kenway 2015; Kenway et al. 2016) of the lessons students are taught about their place in the world, their relationships with others and who they are at elite secondary schools in six countries: Australia, Chile, Denmark, Ghana, Jordan, and Taiwan. There are no common criteria to determine what constitutes an elite school (Maxwell and Aggleton 2016). The schools involved in this study are identified as elite based on their high standing and prestigious reputation within their society and, for some of the schools, across the world due to their high academic standards, well-resourced education and notable track record of sending their students to highly-selective universities (Kenway and Fahey 2014).

Our method includes conducting a series of interviews over Skype before our two-week visit at each school: three in-depth, phenomenological interviews (Seidman 2006) with four students and one in-depth interview with two alumni. While in each school, two to four members of our research team generated data through conventional ethnographic techniques including observations of classes, events (such as all-school gatherings, sporting competitions, and graduation) and faculty meetings, semi-structured follow-up interviews with the four students and structured interviews with four to six teachers, the head of school and two to four other members of the school's governing body. We also employed creative methods by photographing the schools to capture the social aesthetics of those sites (Fahey et al. 2015), filming our travelling experiences to document the important role travel plays in global ethnography (Epstein et al. 2013) and blogging about our embodied encounters and experiences to facilitate ongoing reflexivity.

In exploring these lessons, the data reported in this chapter were generated primarily from the group interviews with four students: Tariq, Layla, Fatima and Karim. They are from families with characteristics of those whom Jean Anyon (1980) classified as members of the affluent professional and executive elite classes. The students' parents are either executives or high-status professionals and are university-educated. Their families also have an annual income that places them in the top ten percent in Jordan.

Although Olive Grove draws students from diverse ethnic, geographic and religious backgrounds, the six hundred plus students come from similar economic backgrounds. However, the school sets aside around thirty percent of its tuition revenue to provide forty percent of its students with some form of financial aid for the nearly $40,000 (USD) annual tuition. Since its founding, Olive Grove strives to be one of the most distinctive boarding schools in the region: the campus was modelled on the culture of a prestigious American boarding school; the student body comes from nearly forty countries; the faculty represent an equally international mix, most of whom have worked all over the world; the primary language of instruction is English; students are required to participate in local community service and international service trips, as well as in the sports programme; and the academic programme offers a college-preparatory course of study based on the American Advanced Placement Curriculum. These distinctive features are what makes the school commonly referred to as 'an oasis of learning in the desert'.

Privilege as Identity

Privilege is a contested concept and, as Aaron Koh and Jane Kenway (2016) point out, 'a slippery term often mobilised to speak to all sorts of individual and group advantage' (p. 1). Yet, scholars, mostly from the fields of cultural anthropology, social psychology, cultural sociology and multicultural education, primarily construct commodified notions of privilege. Privilege, in other words, has been understood extrinsically, as something individuals have or possess, rather than as something more intrinsic, as something that reveals who they are or who they have become in a fundamental sense. Although intrinsic aspects of privilege are acknowledged (e.g., Khan 2011; Loh 2016), such as the influence of advantages on people's identities, the prominent views of privilege, informed mainly by groundbreaking work that emerged nearly three decades ago (e.g., McIntosh 1988), continue to be focused mainly on what people have rather than on who they are.

Moving beyond the conception of privilege as a commodity, we approach this exploration of the lessons students are taught at Olive Grove with an understanding of privilege as identity (Howard 2008, 2010; Howard et al. 2014). As an identity or an aspect of identity, privilege is a lens through which individuals with economic, social and cultural advantages understand themselves, others and the world around them. Their values, perspectives, assumptions and actions are shaped, created, re-created and maintained through this lens of privilege. This view of privilege is more concerned with people's self-understandings than with what advantages they have. To think about privilege in this way is not to deny or diminish the importance of advantages that certain individuals and groups have over others but it is, in fact, to underline the relationship between advantages and identity formation and, thus, to understand the ways individuals actively construct and cultivate privilege.

Identity is rarely addressed explicitly in the study of elites and elite education, instead scholars use related concepts such as identification, membership and social category (e.g., Gaztambide-Fernández 2009). However, an implied view of identity emerges from this body of work that challenges traditional ways of thinking about identity as a distinctive and stable set of characteristics belonging to an individual or group. Instead, the common thinking is that identities develop within social and cultural groups and out of the socially and culturally marked differences and commonalities that permeate interactions within and between groups. According to this perspective, identities are marked by many categories: gender, race, ethnicity, sexuality, nationality, class, religion and ability—to name the dimensions most commonly discussed. These different categories have meaning in the material and symbolic structures that organise social and cultural groups in societies. Groups are positioned in particular ways to put some groups at an advantage (and, therefore, others at a disadvantage) in the accumulation of power and resources. However, larger structures in societies are constantly in flux and, consequently, identities are not fixed.

What may be meaningful at a particular moment or in a certain context may not be so meaningful at another moment or in another context. Because of this continuous placement and displacement of who people are, identities are viewed as multiple, contextual and contingent. As Nira Yuval-Davis (2011) argues, identities 'can be more or less stable in different social contexts, more or less coherent, more or less authorized and/or contested by the self and others, depending on specific situational factors, and can reflect routinised constructions of everyday life' (p. 15). Identities, therefore, are constantly in transition through the combined processes of being and becoming, belonging and longing to belong (Fortier 2000; Probyn 1996).

In previous work, Howard (2008, 2010) extends this view of identities as not fixed and as being constantly influenced by various contexts, structures and interactions to establish a more useful framing for exploring the intrinsic aspects of privilege. From this perspective, identities are understood as forms of *self-understanding*: 'People tell others who they are, but even more important, they tell themselves and then try to act as though they are who they say they are' (Holland et al. 1998, p. 3). These self-understandings are not, however, simply individual, internal, psychological qualities or subjective understandings that emerge solely from self-reflection. Identities, instead, link the personal and the social—they are constituted relationally (Wexler 1992); they entail action and interaction in a sociocultural context (Penuel and Wertsch 1995); they are social products that live in and through activity and practice (Holland et al. 1998); and they are always performed and enacted (Butler 1990).

With a primary focus on the intrinsic aspects of privilege, this conception of privilege redirects attention towards the agency of privileged individuals. Even though human agency exists within the contradiction between people as social producers and as social products (Holland et al. 1998), self-understandings are neither imposed nor stable. Individuals mediate cultural meanings and have the capacity to transform these understandings in order to interrupt the cultural processes that validate and support privilege and, therefore, oppression. With the agency to form their own self-understandings, privilege is not something one is passively given or possesses but something one actively constructs and cultivates.

Privileged Lessons

Both within and outside the classroom context, Olive Grove students learn important lessons about themselves, others and the world around them that reinforce privilege as a collective identity within the school community. In the following sections, we explore five of these *privileged lessons* that are attached to a sense of belonging. These lessons highlight various emotions and ideologies involved in students developing and maintaining a sense of belonging to their school community.

Despite Individual Differences, We Are More Alike than Different

Olive Grove takes great pride in the diversity of its community. The approximately six hundred and sixty students come from thirty-six countries, and the faculty represent an equally international mix, most of whom have worked all over the world. The school puts a tremendous amount of effort and resources into making sure the community is as diverse as possible to prepare students for the interconnectedness of the world that seems to be shrinking, with fading boundaries characterised by difference. As Dr. Thomas, the headmaster, explains,

> We know that students are going to operate in an environment where they need to be able to work with and understand people who speak different languages, people who come from different backgrounds, people who come from different cultures and operate on different belief systems so that ability to cross boundaries and to do so with grace, to work with people and share their beliefs is built into the DNA of the school.

In concurrence with this, all four of the students we interviewed as a group point to the valuable lessons they are learning about forming relationships across differences within their community.

Tariq, for example, argues that this diversity is one of the most important factors in forming an 'unified community'. He explains, 'All these cultures, all these religions, all these languages come together to form the Olive Grove community. I think that's what makes us a different school from any other school in the community. This diversity bonds us'. These bonds develop, in part, by practices and events celebrating the diversity of the community. Annual events, such as 'Arab Night' and 'Chinese New Year', allow students of different cultural backgrounds to be celebrated 'in the spirit of one large community', Fatima says. All the students claim that the school places an importance on discovering 'common ground' across the differences existing within their community. Fatima adds that engaging in the same activities, like these cultural events as well as sports and co-curricular activities, breeds a sense of familiarity and similarity.

Although Olive Grove is undoubtedly a diverse community in many respects, students share particular commonalities that make finding 'common ground' easier. Despite the relatively high percentage of students receiving some level of financial aid, which the school advertises as forty percent, the students claim that the student body is more alike than different when it comes to social class. Layla observes, 'Most of my friends and students here in general are really similar to me and we carry the same values that we've been taught. I really find myself feeling like I fit in perfectly as most other students do. We are from different places but most students here are from my social class'. Sharing similar social class backgrounds allows students to easily 'focus on our similarities and not think about our differences in other regards', Karim explains. The students also believe that their common class privilege shapes common plans for the future. Tariq jokes, 'You have two options for a career later on: being a doctor or an engineer'. Although students have more than these two options in reality, all of them have a clear path laid out before them: accumulate the credentials necessary to gain admissions to a selective university; maintain high academic performance and gain valuable life experiences during university; either continue on to graduate school or enter a prestigious career; and achieve success in their respective professions.

In following this path, Fatima believes that students at Olive Grove place tremendous pressure on themselves. She feels, 'All students here really want to be something, like they want to be extraordinary. Everyone goes to college; I haven't heard of anyone who hasn't or doesn't want to. But students want to go to the best colleges and are working toward that goal'. Even though students 'are pursuing their individual dreams for the future', Fatima adds, 'We usually all have things in common with overall goals and we all have similar interests'. Students believe that their pursuits to be 'extraordinary' and the 'best' feed competition within the school community. Layla claims, 'There is huge competition for everyone at the school to be the best'. This competition, however, is part of what brings the students together and what fosters their bonds and sense of belonging. As Karim concisely puts it, 'We're all working to be the best. Competition brings us together'.

Everyone's Voice Matters

As a school modelled on the distinctive culture of a prestigious American boarding school, Olive Grove uses similar educational approaches adopted in many U.S. elite schools. For example, 'Harkness' tables are found in most classrooms to encourage inquiry-based learning, critical thinking and open-ended discussions. Classrooms are spaces where both students and teachers actively contribute to the teaching and learning process. According to Layla,

I think the students talk more than teachers. I think as students, we are the people who decide how the class looks, or what we're going to talk about. I think the teachers have a say, and they give their opinions, but they give their opinions and we don't have to agree with what they say. We have the freedom to voice our opinions.

Students believe that this 'freedom' is another feature of their educational experiences that sets Olive Grove apart from other schools. 'You're expected to follow teachers' instruction closely at other schools, but it's different here', Tariq claims. Karim adds, 'Teachers constantly encourage students to voice their opinions. In every class, they try to always focus on multiple perspectives'. He contends that the school purposefully creates an environment where students are 'able to have a real dialogue with the teachers'.

According to students, the most important way the school encourages students to engage in such meaningful conversations with their teachers is 'to make it comfortable for students to voice opinions', Fatima explains. Teachers using specific pedagogical approaches and developing close relationships with students make this comfort possible. For example, she claims that she is graded mainly on sharing her opinions and contributing to class discussions instead of 'memorising teachers' opinions'. She continues, 'A lot of teachers focus on thinking from different perspectives and getting all the students to say their opinion. That is what's emphasised, not just saying other people's opinions'. Karim adds, 'Teachers want you to develop your own opinions and share them during class. Our classes are organised around students sharing their ideas'. Students' close relationships with their teachers allow them to feel comfortable enough to actually express their ideas openly. 'You know teachers here and they know you. You believe them, trust them, when they say they want to hear what you think', Tariq claims.

Outside the classroom context, students believe their opinions are equally respected and valued. They point to the number of student-run events and projects as evidence that 'everyone's contribution and voice matters', Karim explains. He points out, 'Usually events on campus are initiated by students. The school as a whole is very much focused on students organising their own initiatives'. Similar to students' experiences in the classroom, he and other students believe that their individual contribution to the school community is 'making an impact on what happens here and how things move forward'. As Tariq further explains, Olive Grove is place where 'I'm respected, which is the most important thing, and also where I'm taken seriously; my points and thoughts are taken seriously'. Being 'taken seriously' motivates him to do even more for the community. For all students, the feeling of being of value to the school community invokes a strong desire to make further connections and be a part of that community.

Success Is Achieved by Working Together

'Skills like teamwork and collaboration and abilities to work and talk with other people respectfully and effectively are really important to us', Dr. Thomas claims. Although students attribute individual success to personal choices and hard work, they similarly value the importance of working together not only for individual success but also for the greater success of the school community. As Tariq explains, 'Success is all about teamwork and coming together for a common purpose and to work toward similar goals. It's about your own success and the overall success of Olive Grove'. Using 'a pride of lions' as a metaphor for the school community, he adds, 'We form as lions as if we are one body. "We may not have it all together, but together we may have it all". This is the motto that I think captures why we work together and form as one'. On the sporting fields, Tariq believes that this motto is especially reinforced. 'We are lions that prey on other schools', he contends, 'we come together as lions to eat our prey. Through teamwork, we become the predators. We form this monster together to win and beat others. This is what makes us the best'.

This spirit of teamwork also drives what students do within the classroom context. As Fatima points out, 'We all work together to complete projects and other assignments. We talk together about what we need to complete and plan how we're going to complete that work together. Cooperating together is very common'. Karim adds, 'We cooperate with others to attain common goals and get what we need to get done finished'. In surviving the demands that Olive Grove places on students, he believes, 'This cooperation is key to being successful here. You can't do all things on your own'. Fatima further explains, 'We talk about everything with our classmates. We go through nervous breakdowns together. We rely on each other to get through all this'.

According to the students, working together is necessary not only for individual and collective success but also for fostering feelings of accomplishment. 'I feel like I can accomplish more when I'm working with others. Even if I could finish it on my own I wouldn't feel the same about what I accomplished', Tariq believes. Fatima similarly feels, 'Working together with other people makes me proud of what I'm doing and what others are doing'. She further explains that collaboration allows students to have shared experiences, which 'make my bonds with my friends and everybody here stronger'. Similar to other students, Fatima claims that these common experiences enable students to form a closer community. As Tariq simply puts it, 'Working together brings us together'.

Others Are Too Different for Us to Relate to

In their daily lives, the students are mostly isolated from the world outside the 'bubble' of Olive Grove, surrounded by others who seem more similar than different. However, they encounter others who are different from themselves by stepping outside their immediate world on a regular basis, travelling extensively, engaging in community service and other extracurricular activities and attending social events. Through global citizenship practices (Dill 2013), the school emphasises the importance of students leaving campus and travelling to develop awareness and knowledge of differences, build relationships across differences and form a sense of obligation toward others different from themselves. Service activities, in particular, are designed to provide students the kinds of opportunities to build these competencies and 'to encourage students to feel what others feel', Tariq explains.

Even though service is not mandatory, Tariq claims, 'Community service is encouraged a lot at Olive Grove'. Karim further points out,' Community service has become part of the social life at the school. You don't have to do it, but you do it because everyone just wants to. You would feel sort of left out if you don't go on these service trips and do other community service'. All four students are actively involved in service and emphasise the important role these activities play in what they are learning about themselves and others. During one of the community service trips offered at Olive Grove, Layla, for example, believes that she learned important lessons about a 'different world' than the one with which she is most familiar. Fatima similarly believes that her service work teaching children at refugee camps how to read exposed her to an unfamiliar environment and provided her opportunities to become aware of her own privilege and the disadvantages of others.

Tariq claims that his community service, especially raising money for 'less fortunate people' in an impoverished community in a nearby urban area, allowed him to develop deeper understandings about himself and others. He explains,

> I learned some valuable things [through my service], especially how fortunate I am. If I have one fear and an obstacle in life, then those who aren't as fortunate as me have millions. As a person, I want to help them because they need somebody like me and other students here to help them. We should feel how other people who are less fortunate feel. We should help them out.

Even though students identify important lessons they are learning about themselves and others through their community service efforts, they acknowledge difficulties in identifying enough in common with others outside their community to build relationships.

In fact, as they become more aware that 'we are the privileged ones and most people are not as privileged', as Fatima puts it, they cast others outside their community as being too different. As Tariq explains,

> It's sometimes hard to find similarities with other people not at Olive Grove. It's hard to know what their lives are like because our school is a bubble from the outside. Sometimes big events happen around us and we're just living our everyday life. We're not impacted by what's happening to others. It's hard to keep aware of things. It's just not a part of our world.

Fatima echoes this, saying, 'As students, we love Olive Grove. But we also understand that it's a bubble from the outside. Sometimes big events happen and we're just living our everyday life'.

Karim also feels the school is 'sort of a bubble in Jordan' and claims, 'If you live at the school, you are not really living in Jordan. You're living in a different world'. Layla similarly believes that the realities of the world outside Olive Grove seem very distant from the realities and circumstances that give meaning to her life. She elaborates,

> It's as if our little world here is not related to the world outside. So, sometimes big events happen and it's hard to get the whole campus into the mood of what happened or to face the reality of what happened because we're just living our everyday life. The school is in a way isolating us from other people in Jordan and what's going on in Jordan.

She continues, 'I think when I go outside or meet other people, I'm going to need mentalities that are similar to mine. I think we're isolated, and because of that we also create our own society within'. Seeing others outside Olive Grove as too different to relate to, Layla emphasises the similarities within her own community.

We Are Superior to Others

Olive Grove promotes a competitive culture within and outside the classroom context to prepare students for the demands of the world beyond its school walls and to give students the necessary skills to have a competitive edge in life. Outside the classroom, students are required to participate in the athletics programme in order to hone their competitive attitudes and skills. The sporting fields are sites for students to strengthen their competitive character. All students believe that their participation in sports is not only teaching them valuable skills and lessons to be successful now and later on in life but also placing them ahead others outside their community, especially students at non-elite schools. As Fatima claims, 'Public schools here aren't as great as private schools'. She further explains that when it comes to sports equipment, facilities, training and coaching, 'we are simply better'. Tariq concurs, 'Our athletic teams tend to outperform other ones at different schools. We are just better. They don't have a chance against us'.

This sense of superiority, especially in comparison to public schools, reverberated through students' discussions of peers outside their community. Layla is the only one who had attended a public school during her educational career; 'I went to a public school for a short time when we moved, waiting until I got into Olive Grove', she clarifies. In reflecting on her experiences as a student at a public school, she claims, 'I had a limited point of view of life. The school sucked. It's not even a school really. It's like half a building. The classes are small. It's horrible in public schools'. She adds, 'Students at public schools are not getting a good education like we are. They don't know how to debate ideas or think for themselves'. When asked about the friends she made during her time at a public school, Layla responds, 'I rarely talk to them or hang out with them because I don't feel they're on my level any more. I was in their shoes at one point. I hate to say it but seriously before I went to Olive Grove, I was ignorant'. Although she refrains from using derogatory language in describing others, she makes an implicit criticism of them as 'ignorant'. Thus, she positions herself as superior to other students who do not have the same advantaging circumstances in education as Olive Grove students enjoy.

The rest of the students similarly see their education at Olive Grove as better than that offered at other schools. For example, Fatima understands her English-based education as a form of advantage that provides her greater access to knowledge and experiences than what is available to her peers at other schools in Jordan, including other elite schools. Tariq describes Olive Grove as 'drastically different from other schools [in what] we learn and the skills we develop through our education and the type of environment that's created here'. Karim emphasises the distinctive opportunities that are available at Olive Grove. He says, 'Olive Grove provides us with experiences that broaden our views and exposes us to different perspectives. When we go somewhere else, for example, Turkey, U.S. and other places, we get the opportunities to experience something new and different'. According to all the students, travelling experiences, English-based curriculum, well-resourced athletic programme, highly-qualified teachers and motivated peers are just some of what makes Olive

Grove 'better' than other schools. These qualities are also what, as Tariq explains, 'makes us proud and feel fortunate to be here'.

Privileged Belonging

Shamus R. Khan's (2011) ethnography about the making of a 'new elite' at St. Paul's School, a boarding school in the U.S., finds that privilege remains a constant, powerful influence on students' learning at elite schools. Specifically, he draws out lessons of privilege that students learn through their elite education. Among these lessons, students are taught that 'privilege is not something you are born with; it is something you learn to develop and cultivate', and, therefore, 'experiences matter' (p. 15). Students also learn to interact with others within their communities in such a way that hierarchies are enabling rather than constraining and where they feel comfortable in almost any social situation. Similarly, Gaztambide-Fernández (2009) demonstrates that the practices and meanings at an elite school influence the ways in which students become a part of that school's culture. His work reveals the processes involved in students not only learning to identify with their school but also with eliteness. Likewise, Sarah Chase's (2008) analysis of gender performances at an elite boarding school highlights how affluent adolescents learn to preserve their privilege. Her work reveals the ways in which elite schools shape shared values, needs and desires through their meanings and practices.

Although a sense of belonging is not the focus of inquiry (but is addressed) in these and other studies on elite schools, this body of work demonstrates that the privileged lessons students learn influence their dispositions, values, interactions, and ways of knowing and doing and are crucial for cultivating a sense of belonging to such institutions. Consistent with other studies, the five lessons above play an incredibly important role not only in forming Olive Grove students' self-understandings but also in developing their emotional attachments to the school.

Students' feelings of belonging to the Olive Grove 'family' are related to the core values promoted by the school, which are revealed through these lessons and expressed in a variety of ways and contexts (e.g., in their ideals, curriculum, school culture, residential life, co-curricular activities and classrooms). On one hand, these values reveal the kind of excellence that is often associated with elite schools. They promote working together toward a common goal, respecting differences within the community and building relationships across those differences. However, on the other hand, the values that reflect their excellence also encourage students to differentiate themselves from others outside their own communities and to see themselves as uniquely worthy of their advantages. This is central to the processes involved in justifying and legitimising advantage/s (and, therefore, others' disadvantages) (Brantlinger 2003; Howard 2010; Thompson 1990) and for forging a sense of *privileged belonging*. All five lessons, to varying degrees, surface the interpellation of ideologies and emotions that give meaning to and shape and reinforce students' self-understandings and privilege.

Ideology plays a critical role in maintaining and advancing the dynamics of power and oppression (Brantlinger 2003) through the 'production of principles, ideas, and categories that support unequal class relations' (Apple 1992, p. 127). Dominant ideologies within a particular context often work like a 'network of templates or blueprints' (Geertz 1973, p. 11) through which actions, experiences and understandings of individuals are expressed and constituted. As familiar and respected systems of representations and complexes of narratives, ideologies mediate people's self-understandings in profoundly influential and, often, unconscious ways. However, the meanings imbedded in these ideologies take on different values and forms as individuals mediate these cultural meanings in constructing their self-understandings. Ideology and self-understandings meet at the boundary between individuals' inner and outer worlds. Their self-understandings are produced in relation to, and in coordination with, the ideologies which they adopt and give meaning to.

Although ideology is a crucial component of the processes involved in creating the lens of privilege that shapes students' self-understanding, affect is equally important. Affective responses or emotions are structured by people's forms of understanding and, specifically, by their self-understandings (Howard et al. 2014). Lutz (1988) argues that although most emotions are predominantly viewed as universal experiences and natural human phenomena, emotions are anything but natural or universal. Even though people may experience similar emotions, meanings for those emotions are implicated by one's self-understandings. However, just as self-understandings link the personal and the social, emotions are more than individual responses: they are constituted relationally in sociocultural contexts. Emotions, Catherine Lutz contends, 'can be viewed as cultural and interpersonal products of naming, justifying, and persuading by people in relationship to each other. Emotional meaning is then a social rather than an individual achievement—an emergent product of social life' (1988, p. 5).

Olive Grove's affective production of belonging plays a crucial role in constructing and reinforcing privilege as a collective identity. This production of privilege aligns emotions with particular narratives that the school reinforces through the lessons they teach students. These lessons, and the narratives and emotions behind them, are a crucial means by which students and the school community are reciprocally constituted. Sense of belonging interfaces between particular ideologies and self-understandings to facilitate a means through which students actively construct their own privilege—not, fundamentally, as what they *have*, but, rather, as *who they are* (e.g., Howard 2008; Howard et al. 2014).

However, as noted earlier, identities are neither constant nor stable. They are continuously shaped and reshaped by the complex interactions of everyday realities and lived experiences. As students mediate their sense of self-understanding, they can be taught alternative lessons about themselves, their place in the world and their relations with others in engendering their sense of belonging to their school community. They can be taught lessons that are not only typically more aligned with intended goals for student learning (such as building meaningful relationships with others different from oneself) but that also offer alternatives to privilege.

References

Allen, K., & Bowles, T. (2012). Belonging as a guiding principle in the education of adolescents. *Australian Journal of Educational & Developmental Psychology, 12*, 108–119.

Anyon, J. (1980). Social class and the hidden curriculum of work. *Journal of Education, 162*, 67–92.

Apple, M. (1992). Education, culture, and class power: Basil Bernstein and the neo-Marxist sociology of education. *Educational Theory, 42*(2), 127–145.

Baumeister, R. F., & Leary, M. R. (1995). The need to belong: Desire for inter-personal attachments as a fundamental human motivation. *Psychological Bulletin, 117*(3), 497–529.

Brantlinger, E. (2003). *Dividing classes: How the middle class negotiates and rationalizes school advantage.* New York: Routledge–Falmer.

Butler, J. (1990). *Gender trouble: Feminism and the subversion of identity.* New York: Routledge.

Cemalcilar, Z. (2010). Schools as socialisation contexts: Understanding the impact of school climate factors on students' sense of school belonging. *Applied Psychology, 59*(2), 243–272.

Chase, S. (2008). *Perfectly prep: Gender extremes at a New England prep school.* New York: Oxford University Press.

Cookson, P. W., & Persell, C. H. (1985). *Preparing for power: America's elite boarding schools.* New York: Basic Books.

Dill, J. (2013). *The longings and limits of global citizenship education: The moral pedagogy of schooling in a cosmopolitan age.* New York: Routledge.

Epstein, D., Fahey, J., & Kenway, J. (2013). Multi-sited global ethnography and travel: Gendered journeys in three registers. *International Journal of Qualitative Studies in Education, 26*(4), 470–488.

Fahey, J., Prosser, H., & Shaw, M. (Eds.). (2015). *In the realm of the senses: Social aesthetics and the sensory dynamics of privilege.* Singapore: Springer.

Fortier, A.-M. (2000). *Migrant belongings: Memory, space, identity.* London: Bloomsbury.

Furrer, C., & Skinner, E. (2003). Sense of relatedness as a factor in children's academic engagement and performance. *Journal of Educational Psychology, 95*(1), 148–162.

Gaztambide-Fernández, R. A. (2009). *The best of the best: Becoming elite at an American boarding school.* Cambridge, MA: Harvard University Press.

Gaztambide-Fernández, R., Cairns, K., & Desai, C. (2013). The sense of entitlement. In C. Maxwell & P. Aggleton (Eds.), *Privilege, agency and affect: Understanding the production and effects of action* (pp. 32–49). Hampshire: Palgrave Macmillan.

Geertz, C. (1973). Ideology as a cultural system. In C. Geertz (Ed.), *The interpretation of culture* (pp. 197–207). New York: Basic Books.

Gibson, M., Bejínez, L., Hidalgo, N., & Rolón, C. (2004). Belonging and school participation: Lessons from a migrant student club. In M. Gibson, P. Gándara, & J. Koyama (Eds.), *School connections: U.S. Mexican youth, peers, and school achievement* (pp. 129–149). New York: Teachers College Press.

Goffman, E. (1961). *Asylums: Essays on the social situation of mental patients and other inmates.* New York: Anchor.

Goodenow, C. (1993). The psychological sense of school membership among adolescents: Scale development and educational correlates. *Psychology in the Schools, 30,* 70–90.

Harding, J., & Pribram, E. (2009). Introduction: The case for a cultural emotion studies. In J. Harding & E. Pribram (Eds.), *Emotions: A cultural studies reader* (pp. 1–23). London: Routledge.

Haslam, S., Jetten, J., Postmes, T., & Haslam, C. (2009). Social identity, health and wellbeing: An emerging agenda for applied psychology. *Applied Psychology: An International Review, 58,* 1–23.

Holland, D., Lachicotte, W., Jr., Skinner, D., & Cain, C. (1998). *Identity and agency in cultural worlds.* Cambridge, MA: Harvard University Press.

Holt-Lunstad, J., Smith, T., & Layton, B. (2010). Social relationships and mortality risk: A meta-analytic review. *PLoS Med, 7*(7), e1000316.

Howard, A. (2008). *Learning privilege: Lessons of power and identity in affluent schooling.* New York: Routledge.

Howard, A. (2010). Elite visions: Privileged perceptions of self and others. *Teachers College Record, 112*(8), 1971–1992.

Howard, A., Polimeno, A., & Wheeler, B. (2014). *Negotiating privilege and identity in educational contexts.* New York: Routledge.

Kenway, J. (2015). Ethnography 'is not what it used to be': Rethinking space, time, mobility, and multiplicity. In S. Bollig, M.-S. Honig, S. Neumann, & C. Seele (Eds.), *MultiPluriTrans in educational ethnography: Approaching the multimodality, plurality and translocality of educational realities.* Transcript-Verlag: Bielefeld.

Kenway, J., & Fahey, J. (2014). Staying ahead of the game: The globalising practices of elite schools. *Globalisation, Societies and Education, 12*(2), 177–195.

Kenway, J., Fahey, J., & Koh, A. (2013). The libidinal economy of the globalising elite school market. In C. Maxwell & P. Aggleton (Eds.), *Privilege, agency and affect: Understanding the production and effects of action* (pp. 15–31). Hampshire: Palgrave Macmillan.

Kenway, J., Fahey, J., Epstein, D., Koh, A., McCarthy, C., & Rizvi, F. (2016). *Class choreographies: Elite schools and globalization.* London: Palgrave Macmillan.

Khan, S. R. (2011). *Privilege: The making of an adolescent elite at St. Paul's School.* Princeton, NJ: Princeton University Press.

Koh, A., & Kenway, J. (2016). Introduction: Reading the dynamics of educational privilege through a spatial lens. In A. Koh & J. Kenway (Eds.), *Elite schools: Multiple geographies of privilege* (pp. 1–17). London: Routledge.

Loh, C. E. (2016). Elite schoolboys becoming global citizens: Examining the practice of habitus. In A. Koh & J. Kenway (Eds.), *Elite schools: Multiple geographies of privilege* (pp. 70–86). London: Routledge.

Lutz, C. (1988). *Unnatural emotions: Everyday sentiments on a Micronesia atoll and their challenge to Western theory*. Chicago: University of Chicago Press.

Maxwell, C., & Aggleton, P. (Eds.). (2016). *Elite education: International perspectives*. London: Routledge.

McIntosh, P. (1988). *White privilege and male privilege: A personal account of coming to see correspondences through work in women's studies* (Working Paper 189). Wellesley, MA: Wellesley College Center for Research on Women.

Osterman, K. F. (2000). Students' need for belonging in the school community. *Review of Educational Research, 70*(3), 323–367.

Penuel, W. R., & Wertsch, J. V. (1995). Vygotsky and identity formation: A sociocultural approach. *Educational Psychologist, 30*, 83–92.

Probyn, E. (1996). *Outside belongings*. New York: Routledge.

Seidman, I. (2006). *Interviewing as qualitative research: A guide for researchers in education and social sciences* (3rd ed.). New York: Teachers College Press.

Thompson, J. (1990). *Ideology and modern culture*. Stanford, CA: Stanford University Press.

Wexler, P. (1992). *Becoming somebody: Toward a social psychology of school*. London: Falmer Press.

Yuval-Davis, N. (2011). *The politics of belonging: Intersectional contestations*. Thousand Oaks, CA: Sage.

8

Spatial, Relational and Affective Understandings of Citizenship and Belonging for Young People Today: Towards a New Conceptual Framework

Bronwyn E. Wood and Rosalyn Black

Introduction

> Belonging is 'at once a feeling, a sense and a set of practices'. (Wright 2015, p. 392)

The past two decades have seen a growing focus within educational policy, practice and research on young people's citizenship and their role within the democratic project. More recently, we have also seen an emerging interest in belonging as a key aspect of young people's citizenship (Arnot and Swartz 2012; Harris 2015a; Mitchell and Parker 2008). This is not a new or surprising idea as citizenship is 'always tied up with

B. E. Wood (✉)
Victoria University of Wellington, Wellington, New Zealand
e-mail: Bronwyn.Wood@vuw.ac.nz

R. Black
Deakin University, Melbourne, VIC, Australia
e-mail: rosalyn.black@deakin.edu.au

© The Author(s) 2018
C. Halse (ed.), *Interrogating Belonging for Young People in Schools*,
https://doi.org/10.1007/978-3-319-75217-4_8

questions of belonging' (Abu El-Haj and Bonet 2011, p. 31) or, indeed, of not-belonging. What has changed, however, is how young people experience citizenship and belonging.

Increased global flows of both ideas and people, and the 'fluidity of membership' (Baumann 2016, p. 23) that now characterise many of the world's largest urban centres, have disrupted the traditional bonds between identity, citizenship and place. Traditionally, the grounds for inclusion as a citizen who belongs were predicated on a close sense of attachment to a territorial place and on static notions of space, territoriality and boundary-making associated with the nation-state. Thomas H. Marshall's (1950) historic analysis of citizenship defined this traditional notion of citizenship as the legal status and associated rights and duties of those who are full members of a community. His understanding rested upon the principle that all citizens are not only equal before the law, with equal access to opportunities for democratic participation and contribution, but that they feel that they belong—or have a place—within the democratic process. His understandings were also built on essentialist conceptions of the collective and the duties and responsibilities associated with that collective.

More recently, however, this Marshallian notion of citizenship has been subject to extensive criticism, especially for its lack of consideration for gender, race, socio-economic status and transnational affinities. Put simply, his thesis has been critiqued for failing to capture the complex and multidimensional experience of being a citizen and of belonging in society in the twenty-first century. While the old notions and configurations of citizenship remain strongly entrenched in the practices and operation of the nation-state and its institutions, these need to be expanded to include more flexible and expansive understandings of who is a citizen that consider, for example, those who cannot contribute to work, taxation or military service, such as the unemployed, the disabled, children and migrant workers (Lister 2007), as well as those whose sense of citizenship is no longer tied exclusively to the nation-state. These new notions of citizenship are needed to encompass the intensified social relations and new affinities, identifications, loyalties and animosities (Isin 2008) that now occur not only *within* the nation-state, but also *beyond* the nation-state as a result of changes associated with new communication and transport technologies, which have enabled global flows of capital, labour and people.

These shifting configurations of time, space and mobility, as a result of globalisation, have significant implications for how we conceptualise belonging and citizenship today and hold particular implications for young people whose identities are forged in such contexts. Young people today grow up with more-than-local politics (Mitchell and Parker 2008), but are still heavily influenced by policies and practices associated with nations and communities. It is not that we can simply replace the national with the global and reproduce container-like models of political space—instead, we need much more dynamic and flexible notions of space itself, especially if citizenship identities and practices are relational (Hörschelmann and Refaie 2014). In particular, the changing social and spatial affinities enabled by globalising processes have destabilised traditional notions of citizenship and have thrust the affective and relational concept of belonging much more overtly onto centre stage.

Citizenship and belonging are often used in interchangeable ways—as Marco Antonsich notes, 'belonging is used as a synonym of or in association with the notion of citizenship' (2010, p. 645)—but very little work has untangled the closely woven associations between these two terms or considered what this might mean for how we understand young citizens today. Citizenship has, in fact, been characterised as subject to an 'exclusionary impasse' in relation to belonging (Deiana 2013, p. 184), serving as a marker of exclusion as much as inclusion. The need for much more expansive understandings of citizenship and belonging, and for a greater understanding of citizenship as belonging, is evident from a range of recent analyses (e.g., Abu El-Haj 2015; Harris 2010; Isin 2008; Kallio and Mitchell 2016; Youkhana 2015; Yuval-Davis 2006, 2007; Yuval-Davis et al. 2005).

This chapter presents a review of recent work which profiles new and broadened concepts of citizenship and belonging and which reflects the complex relations that young people have with others, circulating objects, artefacts and changing social, political and cultural landscapes. As a result, we propose a fresh examination of the spatial, relational and affective dimensions of citizenship and belonging and a reconsideration of what these dimensions mean for young people today. Our argument is structured around three propositions which emerge from the contemporary literature in this area.

The first proposition is that *space* matters. Citizenship, and the cultural, political and social affiliations and identifications that attend it, are neither geographically neutral nor free-floating but have always been 'formed through scalar configuration and engagement with place' (Desforges et al. 2005, p. 444). Michel Foucault's assertion that the present epoch would be 'above all the epoch of space' (1986, p. 22) has borne some ripe theoretical and empirical fruit. People's identification with multiple and differently scaled and situated communities, and affiliations with transnational networks and new public actors, means that a fixed and territorial-based definition of citizenship is no longer adequate (Kallio and Mitchel 2016). Crucially, the implications of these global and spatial shifts, and how they shape the relationship between space and the geographies of belonging and citizenship in globalised times, requires further development (Cuervo and Wyn 2014; Farrugia 2014; Gieryn 2000; Harris 2015b).

A second and closely related way in which we argue for a reinvigoration of the concepts of citizenship and belonging is through a focus on *relationships*. Experiences of belonging and citizenship are constituted at the intersection with others. They are a part of what Hannah Arendt refers to as the 'web of human relationships' (1958, p. 183). This proposition highlights the significance of young people's connections to other people—both adult and young peers, near and far—and how these relationships shape their experiences of citizenship and belonging.

A third and final dimension, and almost inseparable from a focus on relationships, is a much closer focus on the significance of *affect and emotion* in citizenship acts and dispositions (Arnot and Swartz 2012; Black 2017b; Bondi and Davidson 2011). While experiences of identity and belonging 'quiver with affective energy' (Thrift 2004, p. 57), the significance of emotion in citizenship has often been neglected. Yet, as Audrey Osler and Hugh Starkey (2005) argue, while citizenship is about status and practice, it is mostly first experienced as a *feeling*. Importantly, it may not always be a warm and fuzzy feeling of attachment. There is evidence that citizenship action can also happen as a result of feeling dislocated, angry or discontented—consider the many protest movements of recent years such as Occupy, the Arab Spring protests or the Spanish Indignados, for example. This dimension seeks to highlight the integral role of affect in citizenship and belonging and how this provides fresh insights into young citizens today.

The goal of this chapter, therefore, is to seed fresh understandings of citizenship and belonging that better recognise their spatial, relational and emotional dimensions for young people. The intended outcome is a more dynamic and expansive notion of citizenship and belonging as characterised by more flexible social membership (Isin and Turner 2007) in keeping with how young people actually live as citizens today. The chapter proceeds with an examination of the theoretical traditions which have informed contemporary shifts in understandings of citizenship and belonging. We combine this with an examination of recent literature which has drawn attention to the significance of spatial, relational and affective dimensions of citizenship and belonging for young people. While we present these as three separate dimensions, we recognise that much of the literature collapses them together, whether by examining relational and affective or spatial and affective aspects of belonging and citizenship simultaneously. We have, somewhat artificially, drawn them out as separate dimensions for the purpose of developing this conceptual framework, although our empirical examples show that these ideas often intersect. We conclude by considering the implications of this approach and highlight the growing significance of belonging as an associated concept when studying youth citizenship in an increasingly globalised and transnational world.

Theoretical Origins

The move towards more spatial, relational and affective understandings of citizenship and belonging has not emerged as an isolated endeavour. Alongside the growth of transnationalism and globalisation, which has triggered a more fluid sense of citizenship, a set of broader shifts and theoretical turns have sparked new ways of seeing and knowing across many disciplines. Before we examine the evidence for fresh understandings of citizenship, we briefly review some of the broader theoretical shifts. In particular, we consider the influence of feminist and cultural studies on youth citizenship and the emergence of more everyday understandings of citizenship and belonging heralded by the affective turn (Bondi et al. 2005; Clough and Halley 2007).

Key critiques of fixed notions of citizenship stem from feminist and cultural studies which argue that we need understandings of citizenship which take into account the identities of those traditionally excluded from the public sphere—such as women, children, the disabled and minority groups (Deiana 2013; Dyck 2005; Lister 2007; Smith 1987). Ruth Lister's (2007) work, for example, interrogates citizenship's universalistic and normative claims from the perspective of marginalised groups and nation-state 'outsiders' in order to advance much more differentiated forms of citizenship. Drawing on the seminal work of Nancy Fraser (2003), Iris Marion Young (1990) and other feminist writers, Lister argues that a more inclusive and flexible notion of citizenship is needed which includes the ability for all members of society to participate equally and achieve social esteem or recognition and more explicitly recognise diversity of expressions and understandings of citizenship.

A further critique in feminist theorising has centred on traditional binaries which pay disproportionate attention to formal and public (male-dominated) expressions of social life, thus overlooking the 'hidden places' (Dyck 2005) of the domestic and the ordinary. Along with a number of other theoretical traditions (including from queer, Marxist, postcolonial, anti-racist, cultural and other critical theorists), such analyses have sought to bring to light the embodied, everyday and informal practices of traditionally disempowered people. A focus on the everyday also characterises wider traditions within sociology (Jacobsen 2009; Smith 1987), geography (Lefebvre 1971) and political studies (Fraser 2003) which seek to expose ways in which the state is enmeshed in the ordinary and to demonstrate the political possibility of such spaces (Staeheli et al. 2012). Attention to the everyday has, therefore, been a significant aspect of recent work on children and young people's citizenship practices. It has drawn attention to how everyday actions that previously went under the radar could be considered 'political' (Kallio and Häkli 2011; Lister 2003; Wood 2012, 2015b). In so doing, it has contributed to a re-working of the notion of the political and of citizenship.

A further and associated theoretical area which has influenced how we understand citizenship and belonging can be described as the 'affective turn' (Clough and Halley 2007). While emotional studies have long been the focus of psychologists, this turn has drawn attention to aspects of emotion and affect from across the disciplines (Bondi 2005). Such studies have critiqued Cartesian duality and previous understandings of emotion as separate from actions or rational thought—a point also reinforced by feminist authors (Boler 1999). They are associated with a scholarly focus on embodiment, performativity (Butler 1990) and an integrated understanding of mind, body, feelings and actions which occur with almost seamless feedback (Wetherell 2015).

The theoretical implications for citizenship and belonging are twofold: firstly, that feelings of belonging (or not belonging) are inseparable from the experience of being a citizen (Mitchell and Parker 2008; Osler and Starkey 2005); and, secondly, that these feelings need to be understood within the context of specific emotional geographies and locations (Bondi et al. 2005; Wright 2015). Such ideas have shifted our thinking about citizenship away from something that is constituted through status, rights and responsibilities and towards something that includes and occurs through geographically embedded practices at the intersection of social relationships (Hörschelmann and Refaie 2014; Kallio and Mitchell 2016). We proceed by tracing some of the seminal literature that has responded to these broader theoretical shifts and contributed to the advancement of more spatial, relational and affective understandings of young people's citizenship and belonging.

Place, Citizenship and Belonging

There is a large corpus of scholarship which understands belonging as 'an inherently geographical concept' (Mee and Wright 2009, p. 772) and which seeks to highlight the complexity and nuance of individuals' relationships and experiences of citizenship and belonging within specific geographical places. Within the sociology of youth scholarship, for example, there is a growing awareness of the importance of place for young people and a growing use of spatial analyses (Cuervo and Wyn 2014;

Farrugia 2014). This shift addresses what David Farrugia describes as 'the invisibility of spatial processes in young people's lives' (Farrugia 2014, p. 293). It has been spearheaded by emerging research evidence which carefully traces the close links between space and citizenship experiences or practices and how these links have changed in recent times.

One key component of this examination of place characterises the impact of an increasingly globalised world upon traditional notions of the individual and the state. Increased movements and flows of people have contributed to the prospect of 'living permanently with variety and difference' (Bauman 2016, p. 24). New flows of data, images, media, goods, information and people have contributed to a growing interest in the 'cosmopolitanisation' of citizenship which Ulrich Beck defines as the 'erosion of distinct boundaries dividing markets, states, civilisations, cultures, and not least of all the lifeworlds of different peoples' (2007, p. 1). This draws into question the bonds between identity and citizenship, individual and place, neighbourhood and belonging. It prompts a more global and layered understanding of citizenship that is characterised by flexible and multiple notions of identity and rights beyond the nation-state (Beck 2007; Isin and Turner 2007; Osler and Starkey 2005; Ronkainen 2016).

Conversely, other studies have led to the growing recognition that, despite the multiple mobilities of the globalised world, a sense of local connectedness still shapes young people's experiences of citizenship. As Anita Harris and Johanna Wyn (2009, p. 327) observe, it is within the 'micro-territories of the local that young people may form their strongest sense of belonging and citizenship'. Susan Goodwin and Alexandra Young's (2013) study of social housing neighbourhoods in urban Sydney, for example, found that children and young people had a deep knowledge of their local community and were concerned about how issues such as violence, homelessness, transport and employment affected it. Osler and Starkey (2003) similarly found strong affective ties amongst young people in culturally diverse Leicester. Young people appear strongly motivated to enact or practice their citizenship at the local level whether through established modes, such as volunteering, or through other modes, such as advocacy, protest or social change projects (Hart 2009; Wood 2012). These acts, and the desire for membership and recognition that attends them, are often founded upon everyday relational practices, a dimension of citizenship and belonging that we turn to next.

Relationships, Citizenship and Belonging

The previous section of our chapter highlighted how young people's citizen identities and actions are inseparable from specific geographic contexts. These sites are not 'flat', static 'landscapes' but are the product of complex interlocking and non-interlocking networks of relations at every scale (Massey 1992). Space is relational. Doreen Massey argues that we need to view space as the product of 'the simultaneous coexistence of social interrelations and interactions at all spatial scales, from the most local level to the most global' (p. 80). Citizenship and belonging need to be seen, therefore, as dynamic and inseparable products of both spatial and relational practice. They are 'experiences of being part of the social fabric' (Anthias 2006, p. 21).

A focus on the relational aspect of citizenship enables a more ecological and interconnected understanding of young people's experiences of citizenship and belonging within their communities and through their interrelationship with others. For many young people, citizenship and belonging is contingent on being made welcome within 'a community of membership' (Anthias 2006, p. 21). Even in urban communities characterised by high socioeconomic disadvantage, culturally diverse young people may describe a climate of 'cohesion, connection and belonging' that is made possible within their community precisely because of the diversity that characterises it (Harris 2015a, p. 7).

Alternately, they may describe experiences of 'unbelonging', such as those of recently arrived young Sudanese immigrants in a rural Australian school and community (Edgeworth 2014, p. 351). Kathryn Edgeworth describes how insider discourses construct rurality and belonging in very specific, hegemonic and historic ways that render Black students' bodies and cultures 'out of place' (2014, p. 362) in the places in which they seek to belong. More than this, Edgeworth argues, it is the place itself—the geography of the rural, with its attendant homogeneity, small population and located history—which intensifies the experience of exclusion for young people who are so easily seen as different. This research highlights the mutuality of spatial and social effects on citizenship experiences—and how they serve to reinforce a sense of un/belonging. It also highlights the way in which the characteristics of place may assert a reified notion of citizenship that is attached to a homogenous racial, linguistic and historical identity—one which excludes those who are not seen to be part of its legacy.

A relational perspective on citizenship enables us to grasp how the political sphere intersects closely with interpersonal relationships and connections (Hörschelmann and Refaie 2014). As global displacement escalates as a result of social, economic and cultural upheavals, young people often bear the brunt of such changes. In just one example of many, Anne Rios-Roja (2011) describes the efforts of young immigrants in Catalonia to find a place of belonging in a legal and discursive environment that is as likely to revile them as risky aliens as it is to welcome them as potential citizens. These and other accounts of the experience of particular young people in particular places and times highlight the contested and conditional nature of citizenship and belonging, not only for those young people but also for vast numbers of other young people forced to be 'out of place' in search of economic and social membership and security. Perceptions of young people as 'risky' results in limited social interaction and trust with others and, therefore, decreases meaningful connections and inclusion. Such experiences of lack of relationship also contribute to shaping young people's experiences of citizenship and belonging.

Relationships with adults are significant in our understandings of young people's citizenship and belonging. An intergenerational focus can show how adults can regulate and control the citizenship actions and sense of belonging of young people. Alison Baker, for example, describes the experience of young graffiti writers on the socioeconomically disadvantaged geographical peripheries of a large city (Melbourne) who find themselves caught between such categories as 'art or vandalism, professional or amateur, artist or criminal, and legitimate or illegitimate citizens' (2015, p. 997). On the one hand, these young people are part of a legal programme run by the local government, a programme which invites them to contribute to the creative identity of the local community and to have a legitimate presence within the local democratic process. On the other, they remain at risk of criminalisation and encounters with police under the state government's graffiti prevention legislation. Intergenerational spaces can also be supportive of children and young people's citizenship identities and actions.

In other examples of support within intergenerational spaces, Bronwyn Wood (2015a) found that the actions of teachers played a significant role in the type of active citizenship young people took within citizenship education programmes. Teachers supported or restricted young people's awareness of social issues and, in turn, the nature of the social action that they took to address that issue. As a result, teachers played a key role in shaping the locally or globally-focused citizenship identities and spatial orientations of their students. Similarly, Rosalyn Black (2015) has highlighted the importance of interpersonal relations in young people's education for citizenship, illustrating the challenges and risks faced by teachers who champion citizenship education programmes in the face of conflicting or competing education discourses and priorities.

Relational experiences also shape young people's mobility in ways that contribute to their acceptance and belonging as citizens in society. Sue Webb and her colleagues (2015) added a temporal dimension to their exploration of young people's belonging in low socioeconomic rural locations by looking at the role that such places play in shaping young people's future aspirations. Their interviews with young people in four Australian rural communities highlight the tensions that can exist between young people's desire to move to the city in pursuit of higher education and other positional opportunities, and the 'pull of home' that often sees them return to their rural town or village once they have completed their studies (Webb et al. 2015, p. 34). They suggest that, while rural young people find the attraction of education, work and travel to distant places very appealing, their sense of attachment to their local place, as well as the value of the close-knit relationships they experience within it, are ultimately more important and more seductive. In some instances, in fact, young rural people's grounded sense of their local places, and of the freedom, safety and social connectedness that they associate with those places, may preclude their willingness to explore the possibilities that urban spaces may have to offer (Farrugia 2014; Gill and Howard 2006). Bourdieu's (1977) notions of social and cultural capital are also strongly founded on relationships and illustrate the significance of family resources, assets and learned dispositions (habitus) in shaping practice.

Affect, Citizenship and Belonging

The final dimension that we argue requires attention for contemporary understandings of young people's citizenship and belonging is that of affect. As we propose in the introduction, traditional concepts of citizenship and belonging have a number of limitations when it comes to examining how young people feel about being part of a society. Irina Schmitt (2010), for example, describes how Turkish young people who were born in Germany and who held full status as German citizens felt that they would 'never be German' but would remain as 'foreigners' throughout their lives there.

This draws into question many studies of citizenship which assume that legal status constitutes citizenship belonging. Such approaches 'serve to naturalise socially produced, situational and contextual relations, converting them to taken-for-granted, absolute and fixed structures of social and personal life'. In so doing, they 'gloss over the fissures, the losses, the absences and the borders within them' (Anthias 2006, p. 21). Many of these experiences are felt more than seen. Attention to more affective dimensions of citizenship and belonging provide deeper insights about how young people feel about their experiences of being a citizen and their sense of attachment and connection to places and people.

An examination of emotion and affect provides a way of bringing together the other two dimensions of citizenship and belonging which we have presented in this chapter. In particular, a focus on affective and emotional connections to the geographies of place provides a powerful lens for examining young people's citizenship actions and dispositions. As discussed earlier, a sense of attachment to a specific space or place can be a powerful factor behind young people's acts of care towards that place, fuelled by a desire to protect, preserve and transform it (Bartos 2013; Black 2017a; Goodwin and Young 2013; Harris 2015b; Osler and Starkey 2003; Wood 2014).

Emotions of belonging to a place are not fixed or static but are a fluid and constantly re-forming spatial relationship, or in Anne Bartos' words, 'a process, one that is created through the coming and going of agents, through the repetition of norms, stories and experiences shared in place, and entangled in a web of socioeconomic and ecologic relationships spanning across both geographic space and time' (2013, p. 89). Moreover, affective dimensions are constituted within and between social relations and interactions and cannot be understood in isolation of these. Our second dimension of social relationships, therefore, is enhanced through the addition of an affective gaze which examines how affect is distributed: 'it is an in-between, relational phenomenon' (Wetherell 2015, p. 158). Thus, belonging can be understood as a reflection of not just deeply personal individual experiences, but of a form of 'collective identity or citizenship' (Antonsich 2010, p. 647).

An affective gaze also provides a way to understand the experience of many young people who find themselves holding affective affiliations to more than one nation or location. A number of recent studies of transnational young people illustrate collective and hybrid aspects of belonging—and young people, as a result, experience a high degree of flux, fluidity and conditionality in their citizenship and sense of belonging (or not belonging) (e.g., Abu El-Haj and Bonet 2011; Arnot and Swartz 2012; Yuval-Davis et al. 2005). Many transnational young people feel included as citizens—recognised and capable of action—within one aspect of a place or period of time but not another.

Such experiences relate closely to the emotional experience of inclusion and exclusion. For example, Thea Abu El Haj and Sally Bonet (2011) describe how young people from Muslim, transnational communities living in New York after 9/11 found themselves positioned as outsiders, even though they were legally Americans. This challenged their sense of belonging as the political conditions for substantive inclusion in American society were absent. However, the research also found that these same young people still actively worked to challenge and reshape US culture and politics, as well as forming affiliations and commitment to the global community of Muslims and other imagined communities. These ideas highlight the significance of studying affect as an integral dimension of citizenship and belonging, and holding much more flexible notions of citizenship which match the range of ways which young people experience being citizens.

Conclusion

Recent refugee flows in the Middle East and Europe demonstrate the complexity of citizenship today where state systems continue to play an enduring role in controlling and regulating citizens' legal status, whilst at the same time struggling to cope with new forms of transnational citizenship, affiliations and belonging (Kallio and Mitchell 2016). At a time when global flows and flux are stripping away its traditional meanings, associations and promises, it may be time for a new language and a fresh understanding of citizenship. At the same time, we need understandings which recognise that old configurations of citizenship formation *among young people* still exist alongside the new.

In this chapter, we have argued that such new understandings should be strongly shaped by spatial, relational and affective dimensions and that a focus on these dimensions offers an opportunity to embrace more flexible, hybrid and inclusive aspects of citizenship and belonging. Our argument began from a geographic starting point by highlighting how globalising and transnational practices and processes have impacted upon traditional conceptions of space, and therefore upon citizenship, identity and belonging. In particular, we have suggested that shifts in spatial flows and social interactions have enabled a much more fluid form of citizenship in which 'the state and national polity no longer appear as the self-evident loci of citizenship' (Kallio and Mitchell 2016, p. 259). We have argued that a new vocabulary of citizenship is needed to explain these new times, and suggested that an integrated framework of spatial, relational and emotional dimensions of citizenship and belonging could provide this.

Through a spatial, relational and emotional analysis of youth citizenship, *belonging* has emerged as an indispensable dimension of citizenship in contemporary times—and arguably as a 'thicker' concept than citizenship (Yuval-Davis et al. 2005, p. 526). By focusing on belonging alongside citizenship, we gain a richer and more insightful way of thinking about young people's role in contemporary society that goes beyond ideas of membership, rights and duties, and beyond forms of identification with other people (Anthias 2006). We also gain a way of thinking about the everyday social places in which citizenship is lived, 'along with the feelings of being part of a larger whole and with the emotional and social bonds that are related to such places' (Anthias 2006, p. 20).

This does not mean, however, that citizenship no longer has value as an analytical tool. Citizenship has always been 'a mark of belonging and commitment to a specific place' (Desforges et al. 2005, p. 440), 'a set of relationships by which membership is constructed through physical and metaphorical boundaries and in the sites and practices that give it meaning' (Staeheli 2011, p. 394). We have argued that the affective and relational aspects of young people's relationship to place may be as powerful in shaping their experience of citizenship as the nature of the places themselves.

Eva Youkhana (2015, p. 20) articulates the importance of 'approaching belonging from what is performed as belonging and how it is enacted in certain situations'. We would like to extend this contention and suggest that, especially in complex socio-geographic contexts, young people's belonging should be understood in terms of what is experienced and performed as belonging (*affective*); how such emotions arise and flow between people (Bondi 2005) and create the conditions for citizenship and belonging (*relational*); and how this is enacted in specific places (*spatial*). Just as 'notions of belonging are often based on an inside/outside dichotomy' (Youkhana 2014, p. 172), so notions of place are often based on a here/there (or here/not here) dichotomy. Both of these dichotomies conceal the nuances of young people's feelings and experiences of local belonging and citizenship.

The normative conception of citizenship, which characterises most education policy and practice, reflects and perpetuates 'an abstract notion of belonging' (Kennelly and Dillabough 2008, p. 494) that does little to reflect the ways in which citizenship and belonging are experienced by specific young people in particular places. We need to promote a better understanding of the multidimensional nature of young people's citizenship and belonging as an experience that is situated, relational and conditional, 'one that is both spatially and temporally precarious and subject to change depending on the context in which the individual finds him or herself' (Wood and Black 2014, p. 63). We also need to promote a better understanding of it as an ensemble experience that is 'always in a process of becoming, rather than an end state' (Staeheli 2005, p. 198). The fluidity and transnationalism of contemporary times and space mean that the changing spatial, relational and affective nature of young people's citizenship and belonging needs to be reflected not only in our current understandings of youth but also in educational policy, practice and research.

References

Abu El-Haj, T. R. (2015). Belonging in troubling times: Considerations from the vantage point of Arab American immigrant youth. In J. Wyn & H. Cahill (Eds.), *Handbook of children and youth studies* (pp. 433–445). Singapore: Springer.

Abu El-Haj, T. R., & Bonet, S. W. (2011). Education, citizenship, and the politics of belonging: Youth from muslim transnational communities and the "war on terror". *Review of Research in Education, 35*(1), 29–59. https://doi.org/10.3102/0091732x10383209.

Anthias, F. (2006). Belongings in a globalising and unequal world: Rethinking translocations. In N. Yuval-Davis, K. Kannabiran, & U. Vieten (Eds.), *The situated politics of belonging* (pp. 17–32). London: Sage.

Antonsich, M. (2010). Searching for belonging – An analytical framework. *Geography Compass, 4*(6), 644–659. https://doi.org/10.1111/j.1749-8198.2009.00317.x.

Arendt, H. (1958). *The human condition.* Chicago: The University of Chicago Press.

Arnot, M., & Swartz, S. (2012). Youth citizenship and the politics of belonging: Introducing contexts, voices and imaginaries. *Comparative Education, 48*(1), 1–10.

Baker, A. M. (2015). Constructing citizenship at the margins: The case of young graffiti writers in Melbourne. *Journal of Youth Studies, 18*(8), 997–1014. https://doi.org/10.1080/13676261.2015.1020936.

Bartos, A. E. (2013). Children sensing place. *Emotion, Space and Society, 9,* 89–98.

Bauman, Z. (2016). Living in an age of migration and diasporas. In P. Ahponen, P. Harinen, & V.-S. Haverinen (Eds.), *Dislocations of civic and cultural borderlines* (pp. 21–32). Switzerland: Springer.

Beck, U. (2007). A new cosmopolitanism is in the air. *Literaturen*, November 2007.

Black, R. (2015). Between policy and a hard pedagogical place: The emotional geographies of teaching for citizenship in low socioeconomic schools. *Pedagogy, Culture & Society, 23*(3), 369–388. https://doi.org/10.1080/14681 366.2014.994664.

Black, R. (2017a). Active citizenship in Australian schools. In A. Peterson & L. Tudball (Eds.), *Civics and citizenship education in Australia: Challenges, practices and international perspectives*. London: Bloomsbury.

Black, R. (2017b). Making the hopeful citizen in precarious times. In P. Campbell, C. Hickey, & P. Kelly (Eds.), *Young people and the politics of outrage and hope*. Amsterdam: Brill.

Boler, M. (1999). *Feeling power: Emotion and education*. New York: Routledge.

Bondi, L. (2005). Making connections and thinking through emotions: Between geography and psychotherapy. *Transactions of the Institute of British Geographers, 30*(4), 433–448.

Bondi, L., & Davidson, J. (2011). Lost in translation. *Transactions of the Institute of British Geographers, 36*(4), 595–598.

Bondi, L., Davidson, J., & Smith, M. (2005). Introduction. In J. Davidson, L. Bondi, & M. Smith (Eds.), *Emotional geographies* (pp. 1–16). Aldershot/ Burlington: Ashgate.

Bourdieu, P. (1977). *Outline of a theory of practice*. (R. Nice, Trans.) Cambridge: Cambridge University Press.

Butler, J. (1990). *Gender trouble: Feminism and the subversion of identity*. London: Routledge.

Clough, P., & Halley, J. (2007). *The affective turn*. Durham, NC: Duke University Press.

Cuervo, H., & Wyn, J. (2014). Reflections on the use of spatial and relational metaphors in youth studies. *Journal of Youth Studies, 17*(7), 901–915. https:// doi.org/10.1080/13676261.2013.878796.

Deiana, M.-A. (2013). Citizenship as (not) belonging? Contesting the replication of gendered and ethnicised exclusions in post-Dayton Bosnia-Herzegovina. In S. Roseneil (Ed.), *Beyond citizenship? Feminism and the transformation of belonging* (pp. 184–210). London: Palgrave Macmillan.

Desforges, L., Jones, R., & Woods, M. (2005). New geographies of citizenship. *Citizenship Studies, 9*(5), 439–451.

Dyck, I. (2005). Feminist geography, the 'everyday', and local-global relations: Hidden spaces of place-making. *The Canadian Geographer, 49*(3), 233–243.

Edgeworth, K. (2014). Black bodies, White rural spaces: Disturbing practices of unbelonging for 'refugee' students. *Critical Studies in Education, 56*(3), 351–365.

Farrugia, D. (2014). Towards a spatialised youth sociology: The rural and the urban in times of change. *Journal of Youth Studies, 17*(3), 293–307. https://doi.org/10.1080/13676261.2013.830700.

Foucault, M. (1986). Of other spaces: Utopias and heretopias. *Diatritics, 16*(1), 22–27.

Fraser, N. (2003). Social justice in the age of identity politics: Redistribution, recognition and participation. In N. Fraser & A. Honneth (Eds.), *Redistribution and recognition? A political-philosophical exchange.* Verso: London and New York.

Gieryn, T. F. (2000). A space for place in sociology. *Annual Review of Sociology, 26*(1), 463–496. https://doi.org/10.1146/annurev.soc.26.1.463.

Gill, J., & Howard, S. (2006). Revisioning the social: Young Australians and the rural/urban divide. *Citizenship Teaching and Learning, 2*(1), 66–78.

Goodwin, S., & Young, A. (2013). Ensuring children and young people have a voice in neighbourhood community development. *Australian Social Work, 66*(3), 344–357.

Harris, A. (2010). Young people, everyday civic life and the limits of social cohesion. *Journal of Intercultural Studies, 31*(5), 573–589. https://doi.org/10.1080/07256868.2010.513424.

Harris, A. (2015a). Belonging and the uses of difference: Young people in Australian urban multiculture. *Social Identities*, 1–17.

Harris, A. (2015b). Transitions, cultures and citizenship: Interrogating and integrating youth studies in new times. In D. Woodman & A. Bennett (Eds.), *Youth cultures, transitions and gernations: Bridging the gap in youth research* (pp. 84–98). Houndshill and New York: Palgrave Macmillan.

Harris, A., & Wyn, J. (2009). Young people's politics and the micro-territories of the local. *Australian Journal of Political Science, 44*(2), 327–344.

Hart, S. (2009). The 'problem' with youth: Young people, citizenship and the community. *Citizenship Studies, 13*(6), 641–657. https://doi.org/10.1080/13621020903309656.

Hörschelmann, K., & Refaie, E. E. (2014). Transnational citizenship, dissent and the political geographies of youth. *Transactions of the Institute of British Geographers, 39*(3), 444–456. https://doi.org/10.1111/tran.12033.

Isin, E. (2008). Theorising acts of citizenship. In E. Isin & G. M. Nielsen (Eds.), *Acts of citizenship* (pp. 15–43). London and New York: Palgrave Macmillan.

Isin, E., & Turner, B. (2007). Investigating citizenship: An agenda for citizenship studies. *Citizenship Studies, 11*(1), 5–17.

Jacobsen, M. (2009). Introduction: The everyday: An introduction to an introduction. In M. Jacobsen (Ed.), *Encountering the everyday: An introduction to the sociologies of the unnoticed* (pp. 1–42). Houndsmill: Palgrave Macmillan.

Kallio, K. P., & Häkli, J. (2011). Tracing children's politics. *Political Geography, 30*, 99–109.

Kallio, K. P., & Mitchell, K. (2016). Introduction to the special issue on transnational lived citizenship. *Global Networks, 16(3).* https://doi.org/10.1111/glob.12113.

Kennelly, J., & Dillabough, J. A. (2008). Young people mobilizing the language of citizenship: Struggles for classification and new meaning in an uncertain world. *British Journal of Sociology of Education, 29*(5), 493–508.

Lefebvre, H. (1971). *Everyday life in the modern world.* London: The Athlone Press.

Lister, R. (2003). *Citizenship: Feminist perspectives* (2nd ed.). London: Macmillan.

Lister, R. (2007). Inclusive citizenship: Realising the potential. *Citizenship Studies, 11*(1), 49–61.

Marshall, T. H. (1950). *Citizenship and social class.* Cambridge: Cambridge University Press.

Massey, D. (1992). Politics and space/time. *New Left Review, 196*, 65–84.

Mee, K., & Wright, S. (2009). Geographies of belonging. *Environment and Planning A, 41*(4), 772–779. Retrieved from http://www.envplan.com/abstract.cgi?id=a41364.

Mitchell, K., & Parker, W. C. (2008). I pledge allegiance to … Flexible citizenship and shifting scales of belonging. *Teachers College Record, 110*(4), 775–804.

Osler, A., & Starkey, H. (2003). Learning for cosmopolitan citizenship: Theoretical debates and young people's experiences. *Educational Review, 55*(3), 243–254.

Osler, A., & Starkey, H. (2005). *Changing citizenship: Democracy and inclusion in education.* Maidenhead: Open University Press.

Ríos-Rojas, A. (2011). Beyond delinquent citizenships: Immigrant youth's (re)visions of citizenship and belonging in a globalized world. *Harvard Educational Review, 81*(1), 64–94.

Ronkainen, J. (2016). Contents of citizenship? Multiple citizens' orientations towards nationality and different forms of citizenship. In P. Ahponen, P. Harinen, & V.-S. Haverinen (Eds.), *Dislocations of civic cultural borderlines* (pp. 33–56). Switzerland: Springer.

Schmitt, I. (2010). 'Normally I should belong to the others': Young people's gendered transcultural competences in creating belonging in Germany and Canada. *Childhood, 17*(2), 163–180. https://doi.org/10.1177/0907568210365643.

Smith, D. E. (1987). *The everyday world as problematic: A feminist sociology.* Boston: Northeastern University Press.

Staeheli, L. A. (2005). Editorial: Can American cities be sites of citizenship? What can we do about it? *Urban Geography, 26*(3), 197–199. https://doi.org/10.2747/0272-3638.26.3.197.

Staeheli, L. A. (2011). Political geography: Where's citizenship? *Progress in Human Geography, 35*(3), 393–400. https://doi.org/10.1177/0309132510370671.

Staeheli, L. A., Ehrkamp, P., Leitner, H., & Nagel, C. R. (2012). Dreaming the ordinary: Daily life and the complex geographies of citizenship. *Progress in Human Geography, 36*(5), 628–644. https://doi.org/10.1177/0309132511435001.

Thrift, N. (2004). Intensities of feeling: Towards a spatial politics of affect. *Geografiska Annaler, 86B*(1), 57–78.

Webb, S., Black, R., Morton, R., Plowright, S., & Roy, R. (2015). *Geographical and place dimensions of post-school participation in education and work.* Retrieved from http://files.eric.ed.gov/fulltext/ED561405.pdf.

Wetherell, M. (2015). Trends in the turn to affect: A social psychological critique. *Body & Society, 21*(2), 139–166. https://doi.org/10.1177/1357034x14539020.

Wood, B. E. (2012). Crafted within liminal places: Young people's everyday politics. *Political Geography, 31*(6), 337–346. https://doi.org/10.1016/j.polgeo.2012.05.003.

Wood, B. E. (2014). Researching the everyday: Young people's experiences and expressions of citizenship. *International Journal of Qualitative Studies in Education, 27*(2), 214–232. https://doi.org/10.1080/09518398.2012.737047.

Wood, B. E. (2015a). Participating as young citizens in diverse communities. In J. Wyn & H. Cahill (Eds.), *Handbook of children and youth studies* (pp. 405–417). Singapore: Springer.

Wood, B. E. (2015b). A genealogy of the 'everyday' within young people's citizenship studies. In K. P. Kallio & S. Mills (Eds.), *Politics, citizenship and rights volume 7 of Skelton, T. (Editor-in-Chief) Geographies of children and young people* (Vol. 7, pp. 1–14). Singapore: Springer.

Wood, B. E., & Black, R. (2014). Performing citizenship down under: Educating the active citizen. *Journal of Social Science Education, 13*(4), 56–65. https://doi.org/10.2390/jsse-v13-i4-1413.

Wright, S. (2015). More-than-human, emergent belongings: A weak theory approach. *Progress in Human Geography, 39*(4), 391–411. https://doi.org/10.1177/0309132514537132.

Youkhana, E. (2014). Creative activism and art against urban renaissance and social exclusion–space sensitive approaches to the study of collective action and belonging. *Sociology Compass, 8*(2), 172–186.

Youkhana, E. (2015). A conceptual shift in studies of belonging and the politics of belonging. *Social Inclusion, 3*(4). https://doi.org/10.17645/si.v3i4.150.

Young, I. M. (1990). *Inclusion and democracy.* Oxford: Oxford University Press.

Yuval-Davis, N. (2006). Belonging and the politics of belonging. *Patterns of Prejudice, 40*(3), 197–214.

Yuval-Davis, N. (2007). Intersectionality, citizenship and contemporary politics of belonging. *Critical Review of International Social and Political Philosophy, 10*(4), 561–574. https://doi.org/10.1080/13698230701660220.

Yuval-Davis, N., Anthias, F., & Kofman, E. (2005). Secure borders and safe haven and the gendered politics of belonging: Beyond social cohesion. *Ethnic and Racial Studies, 28*(3), 513–535. https://doi.org/10.1080/0141987042000337867.

9

Equality, Citizenship and Belonging: Why Is Developing an Inclusive and Caring Society So Hard?

Kerry J. Kennedy

I have read these chapters interspersed with alerts from *CNN*, *The Guardian* and *The Sydney Morning Herald*. There has been a significant interaction between the academic texts and the public texts. The latter paint public life on a broad canvass where populism dominates the discourse, where there appears to be a retreat from liberal democratic values and where racism, intolerance and nationalism are increasingly normalised even by the liberal media. The academic texts offer nuanced insights into the broader public discourses—they act as a kind of brake on what at times seems like a world out of control. Of course, these academic texts also stand out as fine contributions to theorising, concept building and deep understanding of complex social practices. Yet, I am very impressed with their insights into public issues and their potential to shed light on the darkness that seems to be enveloping our public life. Academic work might well be conceived inside the academy, but its potential to impact on the world outside may be its most significant

K. J. Kennedy (✉)
The Education University of Hong Kong, Hong Kong, China
e-mail: kerryk@eduhk.hk

© The Author(s) 2018
C. Halse (ed.), *Interrogating Belonging for Young People in Schools*,
https://doi.org/10.1007/978-3-319-75217-4_9

contribution to knowledge building and development. This is a theme I would like to develop in my response to these chapters.

Initially, however, I would like to highlight what I think are the main ideas and issues in each chapter; reconstructing them as I have come to understand them through my own personal lenses. I shall insert some of my own views into this reconstruction process and say a little about what, together, the chapters have conveyed. At this point, I shall return to the public nature of the issues raised by these chapters in an attempt to articulate the role of academic work in supporting and giving direction to important public issues. I shall then examine these issues using an alternative theoretical lens to that used by the authors in their chapters: I want to move from a poststructuralist to a neo-institutionalist perspective. This is not because I am necessarily averse to poststructural explanations of events and actions. Rather, I think the events and actions described in these chapters are so complex that multiple perspectives may be able to shed new light and new insights if we are truly to understand them more fully.

The Chapters, Their Messages and Their Meanings—Reconstructions

Korea's Multiculturalism

Jessica Walton introduces us to a number of Korean primary school children. It is not clear whether these children are representative in any way but it really does not matter. She selected these children as part of her study because they allowed her to compare and contrast different ethnicities that are present in modern day Korea—multiethnic students who have at least one parent who was not born in Korea and monoethnic students both of whose parents were born in Korea. The latter are by far the dominant group in Korea and it is for this reason that the Korean government introduced a policy supporting multiculturalism. This was done not so much out of a commitment to diversity and multicultural values but rather to ensure that social harmony might not be endangered by the small degree of diversity that was introduced, largely, to meet economic purposes and objectives. You might call this 'pragmatic multiculturalism' rather than 'liberal multiculturalism'—it is instrumental in nature designed to ensure a cohesive society with an emphasis on integration. This idea might seem somewhat jarring to Western sensibilities. Yet, Kymlicka and He (2005) have shown that multiculturalism in Asia has distinctive characteristics in terms of both its foundation principles and its practices. This is not to downplay the importance of Western multicultural values but, when they are not faithfully replicated in other cultures and countries, we should not be surprised.

What shines through in this chapter are the voices of children. In an important sense, these voices bounce off the policy framework that the chapter articulates so well. Despite the relatively young age of the students, they seemed to have such well-developed views. One monoethnic student was very clear that he had no problems with multiethnic students as long as they adopted local values and worked hard! In the same way, multiethnic students did not see themselves any differently from monoethnic students except for the sense of exclusion they experienced. These students, for the most part, were born in Korea, spoke Korean and saw themselves as Korean: they did not like to be labelled as 'multicultural'. And apart from having one non-Korean parent, they are not. This led to a very disturbing conclusion, for these students personally and for Korean society generally.

Given the language proficiency of multiethnic students, their integration into the local education system and their apparent acceptance of local values, what accounts for social exclusion and lack of a sense of belonging on the part of these students? In the context of the study reported here, these can only be attributed to skin colour and the differences represented by physical characteristics. Perhaps this is why the Korean government recognised the need for a policy on multiculturalism. Yet, based on the results of this study, that policy has been dismally unsuccessful, and unsuccessful in more ways than one.

For monoethnic students, the policy did not prevent them from adopting racist attitudes and the multiethnic students in the study did not see any benefits flowing from the policy. They did not want to be constructed as 'multicultural' or 'multiethnic' citizens—they saw themselves as Korean. This contrasts significantly with the way many minority students in Western countries see themselves. For the multiethnic students in this study, 'being Korean' appears to be more important than 'being multicultural'. The main lesson from this study, however, is that no matter how much these students yearn to belong, they are so often rejected because 'being Korean' is more about how they look rather than their values, language and commitments.

Humanitarianism and Refugees

Christine Halse et al.'s chapter takes us to Australia, where issues to do with asylum seekers are rarely far from public view. The children and young people in this study are, on average, somewhat older than those in Walton's study. The voices of both primary and junior secondary students can be heard on a range of issues. Yet, unlike their Korean peers, these Australian students are not responding to or about their own personal experiences with asylum seekers. Australian government policy is designed to prevent asylum seekers from landing on Australian soil by detaining them in 'offshore processing centres'. Thus, it seems that the students in this study were responding to images of asylum seekers—images constructed by the Commonwealth Government, the media, their families, peers and public discourse in general. What becomes clear is that even though they appear to have no personal experiences of asylum seekers, they certainly have very strong views.

These views, however, are not consistent. Some students are for the total exclusion of asylum seekers from Australia, others for segregation within Australia and yet others show a more caring attitude, drawing on well-known liberal values. Anyone who follows the Australian media will not be surprised by these diverse responses because you can read about them or hear about them on a daily basis. Similar views are reflected in different political parties from the far right to the moderate left. The question for me is: how do young people of primary and junior secondary age develop such values and attitudes? Australia is known internationally for its positive multiculturalism and schools, in general, are supportive of liberal and inclusive values towards all groups in the community. Yet, for some students whose views are reflected in this chapter, this broader context seems not to have made a difference. Why?

For me, there are two possible answers to this question. Perhaps we have underestimated the toxicity of Australia's social environment when it comes to the issue of asylum seekers. These people have been excluded from Australia through legislative fiat that has been debated and eventually endorsed by the High Court. Daily, the right wing media, both locally and internationally, rail against the intrusion of asylum seekers into national spaces. Social media— unregulated, uncontrolled and open to all—can spread 'fake news' at a pace that can barely be conceived by those used to getting their news input from a daily newspaper or television news channel. Young people are embedded in this social environment, active and engaged in social media and therefore cannot fail to be influenced by these contexts. Even though they may hear 'both' sides of the story—the loudest clanging noises are usually from the political right.

The second possible answer as to why has to do with the certainty and fearlessness with which the students in the study expressed their views. These are no shrinking violets! We perhaps underestimate the capacity of young people to develop and hold views on current social issues but it is clear from this study that they do. It may be that they are influenced by their social environment as described above, or they may come from families or peer groups where issues are debated and discussed backwards and forwards. What stands out for many of these students, although by no means all, is that schools and their values may not be overly influential. We should expect schools to foster tolerance, care and compassion for all individuals and groups irrespective of their origin or race or gender and so forth. Some of the students in this study reflected these values but others clearly did not. This suggests that the 'hearts and minds' of students are at stake in the toxic social environment that creates asylum seekers as outside the bounds of decent human action and normalises exclusion as a twenty-first century value.

New Ways to Conceptualize Citizenship

Bronwyn Wood and Rosalyn Black's chapter examines issues of citizenship and belonging and concludes that, in its present form and particularly in the current context, citizenship acts to exclude rather than include and therefore does not meet the needs of a twenty-first century world. There is a certain logic to the argument when the plight of asylum seekers is considered. Their aim is to remove one set of boundaries that they find constraining and even harmful, and embrace a new set of boundaries (hence the appropriateness of the title of Halse et al.'s chapter) where they hope for a better life. Yet, the structures of a modern world do not make this an easy transition. A 'boundary-less' world exists only for globalisation's commerce, business and technology; not for citizens wishing to take advantage of what globalisation has created. Citizens are bounded by nation-states, their rules, laws and regulations. The impetus to change boundary locations may be pressing, often resulting from severe oppression and physical harm: but these conditions do not open up other boundaries that, for many, will remain closed. Even if opened, they may have the potential to be equally as harmful as existing boundaries. What can be done to make citizenship more accommodating?

The chapter argues that a more caring citizenship is needed, whereby citizens should be able to reach out to non-citizens and help them to feel included. It takes me back to T.H. Marshall's original essay on citizenship, formulated in the United Kingdom in the 1950s (Marshall 1950). The essay was designed to transition that country from its elitist political roots to a democratic and open society, especially given that the Second World War had been fought to support that end. For Marshall, full democracy was not achieved until citizenship was extended from its historical concerns with civil and political rights to embrace social rights. These rights were designed to address the massive economic inequalities of British society by providing access to the nation's benefits. Partha Dasgupta (1993, p. 104) put it this way: 'the right to a certain share of resources, the right to share to the full in the social heritage, and to live the life of a civilized being commensurate with the standards prevailing in the society in question'. These social rights form the basis of labour laws, social security, health welfare and education. Such rights have come under attack by neoliberals who have fought strongly to roll back the benefits of the welfare state. Yet, in so many ways, these rights have benefited men, women and children and all groups in society irrespective of their religion, ethnicity, sexual orientation or economic status. In terms of the discussed chapter, there was a limitation on this extension of citizenship equality.

Marshall (1950, pp. 28–29) noted 'citizenship is a status bestowed on those who are full members of a community. All who possess the status are equal with respect to the rights and duties with which the status is endowed'. This is the exclusive nature of citizenship so ably described in this chapter. Citizenship and its rights are contained within arbitrarily drawn national boundaries—there is geography to citizenship. Immigrants to new countries can surrender their original citizenship and apply for the citizenship of their new country—it is rarely given away easily. In some cases, citizens may have dual citizenships, but this is the exception. Citizenship is a national marker and it is not transferrable. But does it have to be? Does the twenty-first century require new ways of thinking about citizenship as argued in this chapter?

Some have argued for a move to 'global citizenship' or more cosmopolitan notions of citizenship that do not depend on the nation state. Metaphorically, this makes a lot of sense and is complemented by the idea of universal human rights meaning all citizens are entitled to such rights irrespective of national jurisdictions and frameworks. We have also seen the emergence of regional conceptions of citizenship in entities such as the European Union and stronger regional identities in organisations such as the Association of South East Asian Nations (ASEAN) (Kennedy and Brunold 2016). Yet, none of this has been accompanied by the transfer of responsibilities from the nation state to other entities. Citizenship confers status on the individual while at the same time conferring power on the state that controls who does and does not have access to the rights and benefits that accompany citizenship. The metaphoric appeal of 'global citizenship', therefore, is unlikely to replace the *realpolitik* of national citizenship and the power associated with it.

Finally, this chapter makes reference to the increased international mobility that has accompanied globalisation in the past decades. It is now well accepted that movement across borders is a common feature of the international landscape and, in places like the European Union, this can often be done without passports, barriers and intrusive boundaries. The irony is that such mobility is not available to asylum seekers. They can flee their countries by any means available, make their way across sea and land as far as they can before the barriers go up, national police act to 'protect' boundaries and the pathways ahead diminish. There are those few countries where asylum seekers are welcomed, where refugee status can be conferred and where a future can be created. But such decisions are in the hands of nation states that continue to wield extraordinary, and often inhumane, power over the globe's most vulnerable citizens. The fault in all this is not globalisation's: it is the fault of war, terrorism and contested power structures in an increasingly destabilised world.

Privilege as Belonging

Adam Howard and Hoa Nguyen take us inside the bubble of an elite school in the Middle East. It is a long way from the life of the Korean minorities and Australia's refugees. It is a world of privilege which is reproduced as an explicit objective of the school, its teachers and its students. Privilege is not a part of any hidden curriculum in this school; rather it infuses the curriculum pedagogies, extra-curriculum activities and even arrangements for eating together. What is more, the students are as aware of it as the staff: they sense the need for solidarity as they make their way along a predefined pathway to power and all of its rewards. They are neither apologetic nor embarrassed by their privilege since it is simply what they expect, on account of their status and on account of the way the school grooms them for the future.

Yet, privilege at this school is not so much about resources or about the material things the schools provides or that the students own. Privilege is about who these students are, who they see themselves to be and what they see themselves becoming. Clearly, they come from wealthy backgrounds, even though the school provides tuition support for some students. But privilege is about more than wealth. Privilege as portrayed here is about a way of being. It is about how the students understand themselves and their collective identity as privileged. It is about the way the school organises itself to develop a solidarity in privilege, perhaps even to the point of putting the group above themselves as individuals. Privilege has to be protected and this is what the process of schooling is about for these elite students.

There is an exchange reported in the chapter between students and the interviewer about classroom pedagogies. The students exult in the fact that they are encouraged to participate, interact, disagree with each other and disagree with teachers. Yet, what comes across is not so much the triumph of progressivist pedagogy as the triumph of privilege in these pedagogical exchanges. The students' views in these scenarios are as good as the teachers' and what the students seem to be implying is that this is the natural order of things. Privilege is theirs and they will not be cowed by authority of any kind. It is a revealing exchange and one which consolidates the general tone of the chapter about the power of privilege to create a class or group being prepared for their destiny. It is privilege that creates a sense of belonging for these students—the privilege of class with its shared purposes, shared destinations and shared futures.

It is not possible to read this chapter without reflecting on the other chapters in this section. It is social fragmentation that can be sensed in the discussion of Korean minorities, refugees and the exclusive nature of citizenship. These chapters represent a search for bringing societies together, for eliminating barriers, for respecting human dignity. Howard and Nguyen's chapter, however, demonstrates all too well that some groups in society are more concerned at looking after themselves than looking after others. This came through particularly when students were talking about community service that was not mandatory. All students seemed to participate and the students did learn from it. Yet, what they learned seemed to be directed at consolidating their own privilege rather than alleviating the needs of others who were not so well off.

These chapters, overall, demonstrate major conundrums confronting societies in the twenty-first century. They also show how research can produce sensitive and nuanced responses to these conundrums, peeling back layers of mystery that often surround complex social issues and opening up a new dialogue about possible ways forward. Of course, these chapters are neither public texts nor policy texts. The challenge, then, is how academic work such as we read here can fulfil not just the standards required by the academy, but also the needs of societies confronted by complex and enduring problems. How can the academy speak to society? This is by no means a new question but the work reported here brings it to the fore—at least for me. What is more, the issues are too important to be left to politicians and policy makers—academics represent a 'third' voice and they need to be heard. This means that academics also need to recognise the social role they can play so that their work can meet multiple ends. A fantasy? I hope not.

Above all, we need solutions to the many problems in our societies and academics hold out some hope that they can provide deep insights to the chaos that surrounds us all.

The Long Shadow of Institutions

The research reported in these chapters focuses on individuals' values and attitudes. It is framed theoretically so that we 'see' only individuals with little attention paid to any relationship between them or to the broader societies in which they are embedded. Yet, students in Korea and Australia, and students in Jordan's elite school live in what Weldon (2006, p. 333) has called 'civic regimes' characterised by laws, regulations and policies that construct 'citizenship' within specific jurisdictions usually character-ised as nation-states. Weldon's argument, and that of institutionalists in general, is that the civic regime of a particular nation state exerts a strong influence on the values and attitudes of citizens. In particular, a civic regime can influence tolerance for difference and a society's capacity for inclusiveness. How influential is this institutional perspective in under-standing the chapters in this section?

South Korea's civic regime could be labelled as a 'collectivistic-ethnic type' (Weldon 2006, p. 334):

> The essential point from this perspective is that citizenship is inherently exclusive—it is a reflection of one's ethnic identity and self, not just mem-bership in a political community.

In South Korea, as in a number of other Asian (China, Japan and Thailand) and European (Austria, Switzerland and Belgium) countries, citizenship is determined by 'the *jus sanguinis* citizenship principle, which requires citizens to be of the same ethnic bloodline as the "native" population' (ibid.). Monoethnic South Korean students' attitudes to multiethnic students can be understood in the context of the civic regime that drives citizenship policy and that is the product of history, tradition and politics. Weldon's argument is that civic regimes of this type are less likely to encourage tolerance and inclusiveness, which is exactly what the multiethnic South Korean students experienced. The attitudes of these students were, in all likelihood, not just individual or random: they were very much a reflection of the civic regime in which these students were growing up and of which they were a part.

For the Australian students, the issues are somewhat different but institutions can still play an explanatory role. Australia's civic regime would be characterised as an 'individualistic civic regime' (Weldon 2006, p. 335). In such a regime, human individuality plays a greater role than ethnicity or culture. Multiculturalism is often promoted in such regimes as a means to establish equal rights, respect for diversity and cultural pluralism as core values. Clearly, these regime values do not appear to be the values of many of the students in Halse et al.'s study. There is, however, a confounding issue. The asylum seekers about whom the Australian students are expressing an opinion are not citizens. They are fleeing from one citizenship that, in all likelihood, is unable to protect them or guarantee their rights. As asylum seekers, however, they have yet to be given opportunities with a new Australian citizenship. In this sense, Australia's civic regime does not apply to asylum seekers and the views of many students reflected this.

In trying to understand the influence of institutions on individuals, the argument, historically, has not been that there is a deterministic relationship. Rather, the argument is that attitudes and values are most likely determined by a combination of individual values and institutional influences. Researchers such as Weldon (2006), using quantitative methods, seek to identify specifically what can be attributed to individual dispositions and what can be attributed to the influence of institutions when it comes to attitude formation. Conceptually, this is an attractive idea although the extent to which such matters can be subject to scientific measurement raises some concerns. Nevertheless, it does seem that institutions matter—just how much they matter is still open to debate. Ng and Kennedy (in press), for example, have recently shown that human agency can be a powerful force of resistance against the insistent press of institutions. In such a context, it seems that institutions do not so much determine values and attitudes as provide the environment in which values are formed, and these values may either support or resist the macro environment.

From this perspective, Wood and Black's chapter provides a challenge for citizenship by trying to domesticate it so that it meets new conditions and inserts itself into new struggles. Their argument is that citizenship should send signals about belonging and inclusion rather than exclusion. Yet, the civic regimes related to citizenship are inherently exclusive, including Australia's pluralistic approach. Seeking a more humane, more open and more tolerant citizenship represents an attempt to change the institution. As T. H. Marshall showed, civic institutions have changed over time and the direction in which they have changed has been to become more inclusive. What is regarded as citizenship today may not be so regarded tomorrow, and this is the point of their chapter—institutions need to change when they no longer serve their purpose.

For Jordan's elite students, the private school itself is the institution that facilitates their sense of belonging to a privileged class. This kind of school is a neoliberal institution designed for private purposes, isolated from society's common aspirations, producing global citizens above and beyond their individual nation states. Their stage is the world and their school prepares them for this stage by creating solidarity of purpose and privilege in direct antithesis to the notion of common schools for democratic living. Recall the student who had been at a public school before going to Olive Grove. She felt she had been ignorant in the public school but at Olive Grove had access to knowledge and understanding. Elites experience privilege and it becomes the shield that protects them, not only in school but throughout life.

Conclusion

I think these chapters are important and I hope I have not over-analysed them. I have tried to connect them to public issues and I have tried to reframe them with alternative theoretical perspectives. Looking at them in these different ways has not diminished their importance but rather enhanced it. At the end of this process, the issues raised by the chapters remain. They remain in the public domain and they remain in the public consciousness. But these chapters have inched us forward in understanding the challenges that confront us. We need more of this kind of work.

References

Dasgupta, P. (1993). *An inquiry into well-being and destitution.* Oxford: Clarendon Press.

Kennedy, K., & Brunold, A. (Eds.). (2016). *Regional contexts for citizenship education in Asia and Europe.* New York and London: Routledge.

Kymlicka, W., & He, B. (2005). *Multiculturalism in Asia.* Oxford: Oxford University Press.

Marshall, T. (1950). *Citizenship and social class and other essays.* Cambridge: Cambridge University Press.

Ng, H. Y., & Kennedy, K. (in press). Citizenship status and identity of ethnic minorities: Cases of Hong Kong Filipino youth. In J. Gube & F. Gao (Eds.), *Education, ethnicity and inequality in multilingual Asian contexts* (p. xxx). Dordrecht: Springer.

Weldon, S. (2006). The institutional context for of tolerance for ethnic minorities: A comparative, multilevel analysis of Western Europe. *American Journal of Political Science, 50*(2), 331–349.

Part III

Places and Spaces of Belonging

10

The Formation of a Sense of Belonging: An Analysis of Young People's Lives in Australian and Italian Rural Communities

Mauro Giardiello and Hernan Cuervo

Introduction

Studies on belonging usually apply a spatial interpretation and justification to the construction of belonging by individuals and collectivities. The last few decades, for instance, have seen considerable attention paid to place-attachment as a conceptual and empirical tool to explain patterns of belonging (Antonsich 2010; Lewicka 2011). In particular, the re-imagination of places and collectivities through the flow of migratory movements has been a topic of intense inquiry (e.g., Crowley 1999; Haukanes 2013; Ralph and Staeheli 2011). Other studies, like Mia Fallov et al. (2013),

M. Giardiello (✉)
University of Roma Tre, Rome, Italy
e-mail: mauro.giardiello@uniroma3.it

H. Cuervo
The University of Melbourne, Melbourne, VIC, Australia
e-mail: hicuervo@unimelb.edu.au

© The Author(s) 2018
C. Halse (ed.), *Interrogating Belonging for Young People in Schools*,
https://doi.org/10.1007/978-3-319-75217-4_10

have drawn more explicitly on the concepts of mobility and motility (that is, the potential for movement) to understand procedural relationships between people and place. Sometimes viewed as a relational concept that generates affiliations through sharing generational exposure to global risks (Beck and Levy 2013), cosmopolitanism is another important conceptual tool for rethinking the usefulness of spatial boundaries and binaries such as local/global or urban/rural. In other instances, in particular within youth studies literature, cosmopolitanism is understood as a resource that shapes and reconfigures the intersection between biographies and places (Skrbis et al. 2014; Thomson and Taylor 2005).

This paper contributes to this burgeoning literature and argues that a sense of belonging is not merely defined by place but relies particularly on the quality of the relationships constructed through the reflexive rituals and practices in different domains of life. The performance of these everyday practices gives meaning and value to the identities of subjects and places. We support our theoretical understanding through an analysis of a longitudinal mixed-methods research project with young Australians in rural settings and a quantitative study with young people in a rural community in Southern Italy.

The Australian study draws on the concept of belonging to gain an insight into the heterogeneous experiences and transitions of individuals in rural settings. It contributes, through a relational approach, to the field of youth studies by moving beyond a framework based on pathways and indicators of normative progress, to a focus on the quality of cultural, economic, social and ecological relationships that support young people's everyday lives. The interpretation of the results of the Italian research, using the framework generated in the Australian study, shows that belonging among young people can no longer be attributed to ascribed factors, such as fixed assets, but appears as a continuous process where affective and cultural practices sediment over time as the result of daily rituals that are structured in specific social relations and give meaning and value to young people's identity and to the places where they live. In this chapter, we elaborate on the social mechanisms through which these relational processes construct sense of belonging among young people in two different rural realities, both of which are characterised by uncertainty, fluidity and social fragmentation.

Theoretical Background

In a globalised, fluid and fragmented world, belonging remains a fundamental resource that defines the quality of the life of future generations. Although the prevailing representation is to portray young people as disembodied from place, a sense of belonging to place continues to be a fundamental interpretative key to understanding their lives and worldview.

This chapter reflects on the construction of belonging among new generations in rural Australian and Italian realities. Although these are very different realities in terms of territoriality and life/age cycles, belonging is a dynamic and central relation between subjects and place in each (Cuervo and Wyn 2014; Hopkins 2010). Our research shows that, in both Australian and Italian rural environments, belonging is multifaceted and comprises interconnected dimensions that generate the cultural, emotional and educational resources through which young people reconstruct their relationship with life in different aspects of their community. This is particularly evident in rural areas. These are often considered marginal, static, un-innovative and opposed to modernity. Yet, in these contexts, the belonging of future generations formulates new visions of late modernity with rurality at its core.

Our Australian research provides the starting point of our theoretical and empirical analysis. We use it to deepen our understanding of the sense of belonging, and its social and educational value, among young people in a small rural community in the South of Italy. This community is strongly marked by migration dynamics and social and cultural transformations. The use of qualitative analysis, which emphasises the subjective construction of a sense of belonging and reflects on the affective nature of links with place, allows us to form a theoretical framework of interpretation that is highly generalisable.

A Longitudinal Analysis of Young People's Lives in Rural Victoria, Australia

In Australia, as internationally, there is a longstanding perception of rural spaces as located simply 'out there' on the social and economic periphery, offering young people more educational and employment challenges than opportunities (HREOC 2000; Kenway et al. 2006). Against this discourse of disadvantaged rural life—often bordering on a trope (Wyn 2015)—the Australian longitudinal study entitled *Life Patterns*, follows two cohorts of Australians who left school in 1991 and 2006, respectively, and has provided evidence of the rich nature and quality of young people's lives in rural spaces (e.g., Cuervo and Wyn 2014; Wyn 1998). This chapter focuses on the older cohort. Its aim is to provide a retrospective view of rural young people's pathways over the last 25 years, during a time of radical changes in rural life (Cuervo 2016).

The *Life Patterns* study began in 1991, surveying 29,000 young people in Victoria in their last year of secondary schooling and about to transition to tertiary studies and work. In 1996, in its fourth wave, the sample of the study was reduced to a more manageable size of 2000 participants, with more women (66%) than men and more urban (65%) than non-urban people. Participants were originally surveyed every year during the 1990s and every two years after 2000, while a subset of 30–50 participants were interviewed every two years until 2005, and every three years since. Over the two decades, participants were asked questions regarding their studies, current work, living arrangements and life goals and future aspirations. The current sample has 277 participants of whom 18% live in rural places. In 2011, in-depth interviews were conducted with 19 participants living in rural Victoria to explore their decisions since their schooling days, to stay in their rural communities.

Participants were very aware of their status as 'other' in public discourses and went to a great length to explain their decisions to stay or return to their rural communities after a period of study or work elsewhere, despite the apparent plethora of educational, work and lifestyle choices in urban areas.

Yet, over two decades, two life goals have remained the constant, top priorities for young people. The first life goal was 'to have a special relationship with someone'; the second is 'job security'. Across both the 1991 and 2006 cohorts, at least 80% of participants continuously rated these life goals as a 'very high' or 'high' priority in their lives.

While policy on young people's transitions places the emphasis on moving out of the family home and achieving an autonomous lifestyle (Wyn et al. 2012), the *Life Patterns* survey and interview showed that rural participants give a central role to family and significant others in their quest to build a life in spaces undergoing radical social and economic changes. It is here that the idea of belonging becomes a useful concept to escape the limitations of binaries that frame rural young people's transitions, such as local/global, mobile/stuck, transitioning/at-risk. Further, contrary to current normative policies fixated on markers of adulthood (e.g., leaving school and getting a job), which tend to provide a smooth and direct relationship between each, we believe that focusing on belonging and individuals' emotional and social relationships to people, places and ways of being, offers a more nuanced insight into young people's decisions (Hall et al. 2009; May 2013).

Belonging, with its relational focus, renders visible the processes and steps that construct the different stages of life, such as attending tertiary education, achieving full-time work, forming a family. For example, several interview participants discussed the need to strategically follow an education and employment pathway that would increase their chances of remaining connected to their local communities. Among the rural participants who moved to urban centres to study, women concentrated their career choices in vocational degrees (e.g., teaching or nursing) while men focused on agricultural studies and 'hands-on' courses (e.g., electrician or plumbing) because these occupations would enable them to pursue employment trajectories in their local or other rural communities. Furthermore, this pattern is consistent across the rural participants in both cohorts of the *Life Patterns* study.

Interestingly, we found that, for young people migrating to the city to study at university, keeping in contact with other 'country minded' people was essential for a sense of belonging and that this was constructed as a result of cultural familiarity and their shared experiences of rural life. As one participant in the 2011 interview wave explained in looking back on her immediate post-school experiences at university: 'when I went to uni, I hung out with those other college kids, which were country kids ... we'd been to small community-type schools—lived in small community-type towns, and when we came to college, that college community provided somewhat of a surrogate for that small-town feeling'. This and similar life experiences equipped rural participants with a habitus—a set of predispositions oriented towards a certain (rural) way of being and viewing the social world—that they carried with them beyond the geographical boundaries of their home-community. While habitus is not a strictly a synonym of belonging, Pierre Bourdieu's (1980) concept is useful for explaining and accounting for some of the different practices of belonging, such as sharing university accommodation, that resulted from participants' shared understanding of a common rural life.

Predispositions towards a rural way of being were also sustained through the intersection of biography and place. For some participants, it was the landscape which provided an anchor to their identity: '[belonging] is not just a connection to the people, but it's a connection to the actual landscape, to the environment as well'. This might mean always living close to the beach. As one participant said in the interviews in 2011, registers of meaning were based on 'knowing the soil, the trees'. Most importantly, however, participants reported belonging as an ongoing process constituted through emotional and relational connectedness.

Drawing on the work of Judith Butler (1997) and Vikki Bell (1999), belonging is also an ongoing process that refers, in many instances, to a performance involving repeated rituals and everyday practices (such as caring for others or sharing activities). In the following section, we problematise the concept of belonging through Butler's notion of performativity as recurrent, ritual performance of particular practices. We do this through the story of one participant living in a small rural town in Victoria. While the data in this section and the next is not confined to school experiences of social inclusion/exclusion, it highlights the dynamic, complex and performative nature of belonging.

Problematising Belonging

Claire has lived her whole life in the same small, rural, farming community in central Victoria. Her parents always encouraged her to study hard. Data from the survey wave in 1995 reveals that she enjoyed schooling and that the two main positive influences in her life, beyond her parents, had been her school teachers and work colleagues. Reflecting on her school days, she said: 'I mean I loved school, I loved that whole environment, things like that.' Her views about her schooling days resonate with the close-knit community feeling, sustained by strong student-teacher relationships that transpire in much of the rural education literature (see Cuervo 2016). She affirms that 'I was good at school and got good marks, I could have gone on to primary school teaching but finance was always a problem with my family and they couldn't afford to send me anywhere'. Claire added that 'further education is so expensive and it could all pan out to nothing, but again life is full of risks so I guess you've just got to do what you feel is right'. For many of the *Life Patterns* participants in the 1990s, a lack of rural and regional tertiary education institutions meant they had to migrate to metropolitan centres, with all the financial and emotional implications, if they wanted to continue studying (Wyn 1998). This scarcity of rural tertiary education institutions has been one of the biggest push factors moving young people out of rural communities and generating the need to start their construction of spaces of belonging anew.

Unable to afford to move and attend a tertiary institution, Claire spent one year 'picking up odd jobs' before finding work in the local printer as a receptionist, where she has continued working until now. While Claire has lived her whole life in the same community, she feels that she does not belong to the community that, like other rural places, discriminates between farming and non-farming members (see Bryant and Pini 2009).

Further, a few years ago the community received recently arrived migrants from Iraq: 'There's quite a big Iraqi population and when I was like in primary school age you wouldn't ever see that'. She feels this social group is being unfairly treated in the community: 'I still think they're a bit outcast, which I find a little bit disturbing ... they sort of got a bit of a stigma attached to them or something, a lot of people feel. I think they worry that they get special treatment and a lot of people don't like that. I guess they're not used to a different type of person and maybe that's why they're a bit wary of them, but I think everyone deserves a chance.' This process of social exclusion goes against Claire's values: 'I think it's good to have a multicultural society though, I think you can learn from them and things like that.'

Claire's belonging is sustained through her daily work in the same workplace over two decades and particularly by her relationship with her grandmother for whom she has cared for more than a decade. As she puts it,

'Well, get up and go to work, come home. It doesn't sound very exciting, does it?' And then continues to share the significance of caring for her grandmother: 'I suppose you feel like you belong if your family is here … you feel a sense of belonging if you've got people around that you care about'. Thus, belonging is created through the performance and the experience of ritualised, everyday practices such as dwelling, working, socialising and caring in familiar spaces that creates a thick rural place and identity (Edensor 2006). Further, these secular rituals of caring denote the affective dimension of belonging (Probyn 1996), providing individuals with an anchor in a particular social context. This needs to be understood not just as 'place-attachment', but as coming into being through daily deliberate performances and through unreflexive practices of performativity (Butler 1997). It is the repetitive practice of caring for her grandmother and their consequent bond, for example, that generates the feeling of belonging for Claire. As Bell (1999) puts it in her interrogation of the relationship between performativity and belonging: it makes us who we are in a particular context and deeply shapes Claire's production of the self (see Bell 1999; May 2013). These repetitive practices help to construct emotional belongings to a particular place that might otherwise be experienced as hostile to the ideas of social inclusion and multiculturalism that Claire values. Thus, 'one does not "ontologically" belong to the world or any group within it' (Bell 1999, p. 2) but achieves it, in this case, through affective practices of caring.

While this example is not specifically confined to the space of schooling (as is our Italian example that follows), we argue that examining people's lives through a longitudinal view enables researchers to better understand social patterns of continuity and change. A sense of belonging once experienced in her childhood and youth at school has been replaced by what Claire sees as 'disturbing' behaviour by some community members towards migrants and those that do not share an occupational activity (that is, agriculture) deemed the traditional core practice of the place. The apparent contradiction of feeling socially excluded by the wider community but included through her relationship with her grandmother should be seen as an example of the multifaceted nature of belonging, rather than a contradiction in itself. For many members of society who do not belong to the mainstream population, this might be a common practice of feeling an 'outcast' in some spheres of their (public) lives (e.g., school, workplace) and finding refuge in the private and intimate space of their family and close relationships. Finally, Claire's story also shows the dynamic and changing nature of belonging from social inclusion in school to exclusion in the community, and the efforts individuals might have to go through to generate spaces of belonging.

We turn now to the Italian study to examine how these conceptualisations of belonging contribute to understanding young people's lives in a community far from rural Victoria.

A Small Rural Community in Southern Italy

A qualitative and quantitative research study was carried out on young Italians aged 11–14 at the middle school of the community of San Leucio del Sannio, in the province of Benevento, during the school year 2010–2011. In the first phase, the research used focus groups with young people enrolled in the middle school of San Leucio del Sannio. The focus groups gave rise to the theoretical reflections, the research hypotheses and the formulation of a semi structured questionnaire (Krueger and Casey 2009). In the second stage, a semi-structured questionnaire was administered to a sample of 101 students, chosen at random, in one section of the school of San Leucio del Sannio. The questionnaire consists of 47 variables but only three of them have been analysed in the present work: (1) *What does 'community' mean to you?*; (2) *In your opinion what is the sense of belonging to a community based on?*; and (3) *How does belonging tie you to your community?* The students selected in the sample are, on average, 13 years old and their parents rank medium-to-low in terms of education and socio-economic status. A Multiple Correspondence Analysis has been used because the questions asked for qualitative responses.

The context of rural Italian realities reflects an intersection of social, economic and cultural elements that create a complex social, economic and cultural framework that no longer can be represented by an anachronistic dichotomy of rural versus urban or rural versus modern. This is echoed by the international literature with the idea that rurality is a multidimensional concept, symbolically constructed and historically and culturally conditioned (Bourke and Lockie 2001, p. 9). Within the multifaceted archipelago that forms rural realities, the concept of community 'has a long history as a unit of analysis in studies of rural societies' (Panelli 2006, p. 68). This is central, especially in Italy, because communities have always represented important historical, economic and social realities. In particular, San Leucio del Sannio, where the process of formation of the sense of belonging among young people was analysed, fits into the context of Italian society as one of 5627 small municipalities, none of which exceed 5000 inhabitants, and which account for 69.9% of administrations in Italy (IFEL 2015, p. 5). These settlements are not homogeneous but very different and have different dynamics, both evolutive and involutive, in the social, demographic, economic, financial and institutional fields.

From this point of view, the village of San Leucio is among those rural areas of southern Italy that experienced a crisis in their primary sector (mainly as a result of the decline in the tobacco market). This community is one of the settlements assessed as an 'intermediate peripheral area' (IFEL 2015, pp. 58–59), characterised by a constant process of demographic depopulation and economic decline. This is attributed to the primary sector's failure to secure a footing in high quality market niches and sectors, and to the withdrawal of the public sector as a result of free market policies. This resembles similar social, political and economic processes identified in Hernan Cuervo and Johanna Wyn's (2012) research in rural areas in Victoria, Australia.

The Sense of Belonging in the Community

Most importantly, rather than reducing what it means to be and live rural to quantitative criteria, we interpret the community as a place of social relations based on a shared sense of belonging built with practices deriving from the action by both individuals and social actors.

In general terms, we can argue that the Italian research, based on the analysis of the relative frequency of the sense of belonging expressed by young people, confirms the formation of belonging outlined by the theoretical framework drawn up on the basis of the results of the qualitative research in Australia. Although this takes different shapes and shades, depending on the specific territorial location, the relationship between place and sense of belonging among Italian young people shows that the formation mechanism of belonging is performative. It operates across different domains and is exercised through different forms 'of doing' that are stylised and routinised over time in any given location. More specifically, the comparison of data on the sense of belonging of young people in the rural community of San Leucio del Sannio and the life stories analysed by Cuervo and Wyn (2012, 2014) highlights how, in both realities, the sense of belonging to place 'is built through conscious and non-conscious performances characterised by affective practices, stuck and relational' (Edensor 2006, p. 44).

Faced with these considerations, the young people of the rural Italian community, responding to the survey question, 'In your opinion, what is the sense of belonging to a community based on?', were least likely to agree that belonging meant 'to live in a certain place' or 'to be born in a certain place'. In this case, it is clear that the place itself does not confer a sense of belonging relative to the relationships that give meaning and identity to it (Giardiello 2015).

Belonging and Community: Elective, Educational and Emotional Resource

Although the relationship between place (community) and biography is common across both young Australians and Italian young people, focusing on the concept of community allows us to articulate the complex relationship that develops between place and belonging and to identify, more precisely, the specificity of the Italian reality. In this case, the community, considered through the category of performativity, is configured not so much as a predefined reality as a process that is built on the basis of a set of performative acts. In the contemporary conditions characterised by the dissolution of the traditional social structures that were the basis on which communities were formed, it appears that the formative mechanisms of belonging constitute a generative grammar, whereby young people define the contours and meaning of their lives and community.

From this perspective, the representation of the community presented and experienced by young people is also the expression of the sense of belonging that is built and practiced in their daily lives.

However, the analysis would be deficient if we considered this the only distinguishing factor for the Italian reality. The relationship between place and belonging among new generations (including young Australians) is no longer defined by ascribed factors. Increasingly, this relationship presents as a continuous process that, through relational and emotional practices, builds a habitus where the subject feels at one with the environment. Despite seeking a common interpretation of the interesting convergence between the two realities, an articulated framework emerges from the Italian young people in which belonging associated to cultural identity is central in building their sense of community.

In line with these reflections, we analysed the relationship between belonging and community by applying the statistical method of multiple correspondence analysis to the variables 'What does "community" mean to you?' and 'In your opinion, what is the sense of belonging to a community based on?' Figure 10.1, below, shows three areas of similarities. In the second quadrant, we can observe a situation where, together with a sense of belonging to the community based on 'to share the same interests irrespective of where you live', 'to feel to have a common future' and 'to be born in a certain place', an idea of community of 'spirit' (Tönnies 1957) or friendship comes out.

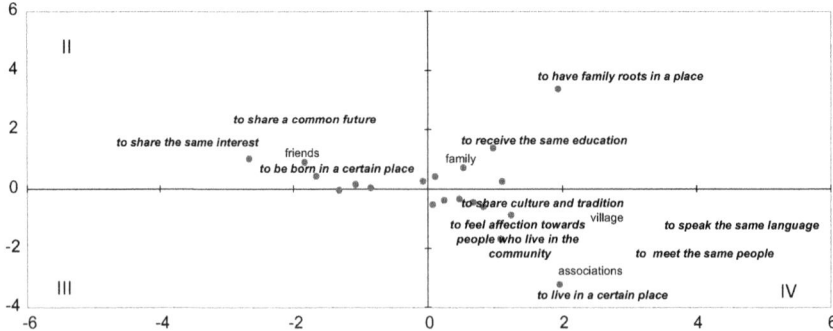

Fig. 10.1 Multiple correspondence analysis applied to the variables 'What does 'community' mean to you?' and 'In your opinion what is the sense of belonging to a community based on?'

This quadrant shows a positive association between biography and place because the meaning of the belonging, although linked to a specific place, is the product of both a shared common vision or generational belonging that is the consequence of informed, rather than random, choice. In summary, this is a form of 'elective belonging' that is embodied within the local.

The link between elective belonging and physical, local place plays a crucial role in forming a sense of belonging to a global world, even though the local places incorporate 'historical residues [that are] defensively constructed in opposition to global process' (Savage et al. 2005, p. 53). This generates a specific vision of the community wherein belonging is understood as performative practice. It may be noted, then, that the conception of community is directly proportional to the quality and type of belonging produced. More specifically, an elective belonging corresponds to the formation of a community of spirit or friendship, considered by Ferdinand Tönnies (1957) to be the properly human and more elevated form of community.

Continuing the analysis, Quadrant I on the upper right side of the factorial plane illustrates that a sense of belonging is described by the modalities 'to have the family roots in a place' and 'to receive the same education' and that these are linked to a concept of community structured around the family. Thus, one of the central sources through which young people build their sense of belonging is through education produced, reproduced and transmitted by the family, rooted in a specific place.

Additionally, then, belonging stimulates the construction of a common vision, thanks to the performative action of the family. Relations with the family are always the most important. When young people consider family as the resource that defines their sense of belonging, it is still part of the territorial context (this was apparent also among the young people in Australia). Thus, the relationship with the family not only constitutes a sense of place but is also able to reproduce a moral principle (educational resource) through which wider social and civic solidarities are formed. This educational and moral resource, found through this specific sense of belonging, represents the embryo of the community. This finding is noteworthy because it is clear that, for these young people, parental ties, as the most significant in the family, form the basis of the community.

In quadrant IV (lower quadrant on the right), a pattern emerges of territorial community defined through cultural, relational and affective practices, ritualised and embodied in a certain place. This appears as a semantic area in which the presence of modalities that define a community sense of belonging—'to share culture and tradition', 'to speak the same language', 'to feel affection toward people who are part of a community', 'to meet the same people' and 'to live in a certain place'—is associated with an idea of community intended both as a 'village' and as 'associations'. Thus, the analysis reveals the close, interdependent relationship between community and belonging. The type and quality of the sense of belonging are not only predictive but also generative of a specific community structure. From this point of view, the three forms of community outlined by the analysis, defined as 'spirit or friendship', 'parental' and 'local community', represent the results of the different performative actions involved in the construction of belonging.

From this perspective, for the young people in Italy (as in Australia), belonging represents a central resource in the construction and meaning of their life contexts. It is clear that stability, sense of place or integration is not so much determined by a generic formal and territorial belonging, mechanically produced, but from the quality of the resources it generated.

The Generative Belonging of Ties: School, Grandparents, Family and Places

Belonging is emerging as a fundamental key to understand not only social processes but also the similarities that link young Australian and Italian young people and their roles as the actors in their communities. If belonging is configured as a performative act, which draws on affective, interpersonal and cultural resources (Bourdieu 2001), then these same mechanisms are the foundation for the social bonds developed among both young Australians and Italian teenagers. Let us assume the precept of community as a social project whose implementation is tied to the performance of the different social actors who operate in it. The capacities and contributions of the actors form an orientation for the activation of belonging. This belonging is strategic, being necessary to form and redefine the network of social links representing the dynamic backbone of the community.

To get a clearer picture of the role played by belonging in generating social ties, this hypothesis has undergone an in-depth analysis through multiple correspondence analyses. Figure 10.2, below, shows the factorial axes obtained by analysing the variables, 'In your opinion what is the sense of belonging to a community based on?' and 'What does it tie you more to in your community'. More precisely, on the left of the factorial plane, there is an area of similarity in which there is an association between a sense of cultural belonging, based on 'to share culture and tra- dition' (v5 in the plot), 'to speak the same language' (v3 in the plot), 'to receive the same education' (v4 in the plot), and the presence of a very important link with the school, the church, grandparents and the park. This supports the fundamental consideration about the generative role of belonging in not only building social bonds but also enriching their meaning by giving subjects a sense of orientation.

This is a most important point. Membership is designed as a dynamic cultural resource. It is not abstract. It is able to target links which make it manifest through specific and practical functions. The linkages identified in both secular and religious social institutions, like the school and the

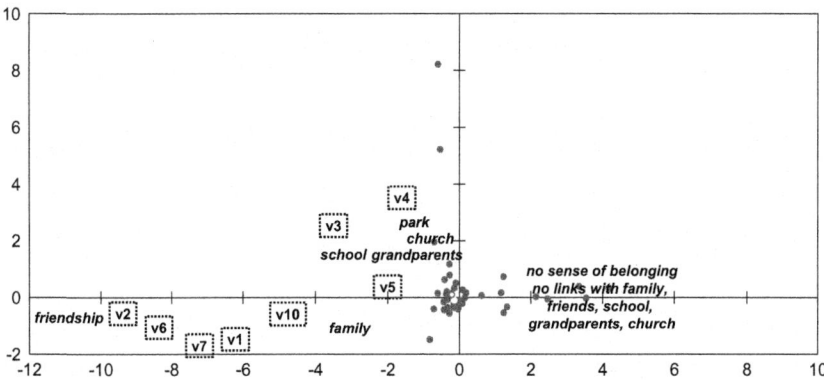

Fig. 10.2 Multiple correspondence analysis applied to the variables 'In your opin- ion what is the sense of belonging to a community based on?' and 'What does it tie you more to in your community'

Church, and in intergenerational and informal places, such as grandparents and parks, are a clear example of the reconstruction of cultural heritage in a single framework of meanings that recomposes the past, the present and the future. As shown in the Australian study, education and significant places shape the formation of belonging.

On the bottom left of the factorial plane, a second semantic area is observed in which the modalities that make up the sense of belonging are placed in the central part of the quadrant. This nucleus consists of the modalities 'to share the same interests irrespective of where you live' (v2 in the plot), 'to be born in a certain place' (v6 in the plot), 'to feel affection toward people who are part of that community' (v7 in the plot), 'to often meet the same people' (v1 in the plot), 'to have the family roots in a certain place' (v10 in the plot). There are two extreme points, placed to the left and to the right respectively, where the modalities of the concept of elective membership are placed on one side and those of family-emotional on the other. Each of these two points identifies a specific link: the first, on the left, 'to share the same interests regardless of where you live' produces an elective, weak link (Granovetter 1985) and is structured around friendship; the second 'to have family that has its roots in a certain place' generates a strong or bonding link (Putnam 2000) because it is identified with the family.

Finally, the last two areas of similarity, in the upper and lower right quadrants, represent a broader semantic area where the absence of a sense of belonging corresponds to an absolute lack of ties. This produces an uncomfortable situation of social and individual anomie. These reflections clearly indicate that the quality of life and the perception of belonging takes on a role and a central function in building the life of young people determined, in a decisive manner, by their relationships, relations and life practices.

Conceiving of belonging as the product of 'doing' and 'the stylized production of acts' over time (Butler 1999, p. 179) 'allows us to move beyond traditional conceptualisations of the term as place-attachment' (Antonsich 2010). This conceptual move was evident from our research in both Australia and Italy. The Australian research demonstrates how the thickness of belonging to a place is not the product of formal acts but the result of affective and care practices, and the sharing of a way of life. The Italian research shows how the young people of the Italian community have given the most significant consensus to the items 'to share the same interests beyond the place where you live', 'culture and tradition' and 'to frequently meet the same persons' that represent relational practices, reflective or ritualised, providing further confirmation of how the sense of belonging is built on different relational records, including shared practices and commonality of cultural identifications or lifestyle. This was demonstrated in the analysis of responses to the items 'to share the same interests irrespective of where you live' and 'to share culture and tradition' which participants related to most. It is also useful to note the revealing agreement with the item 'to often meet the same people'. This shows how belonging is built in compliance with the daily rituals that are structured through specific social relations. The Italian data also reveals a similar process in the construction of belonging based on a performance, conscious and unconscious, gradual and continuous, which gives, in terms of relationships, meaning and value to identity and to the places where the subject lives.

Concluding Remarks

Bringing these two studies together has revealed how, despite geographical distance and socio-economic differences, belonging is an increasingly important concept to make meaning of during this time of rapid social change for young people. In particular, the concept of community is viewed not merely as a space delimited by precise boundaries, static and unchanging. Rather, it is a relational place. More than a simple relationship between tangible and intangible dimensions, it is determined by the constant performative action of social actors. Community, and what it means to belong to it, refers firstly to the concept of habitus, in accordance with Bourdieu (1980), made of practices and disposals rooted within a determined setting as 'interactions between individuals and their environment' (Cuervo and Wyn 2012, p. 127). Secondly, it refers to the post-structural theory by Butler (1999) where, rather than developing the concept of identity as fixed property of the individual, it is regarded as the result of continuous performative actions ritualised over time. These approaches offer the possibility to conceptualise community as a habitus which does not consist in *opus operatum* (a cognitive closed structure) but as a *modus operandi* where the performative action acts (Swartz 1997). In this case, it is clear that communities are open projects that, however rooted in certain territories with social and institutional organisation and cultural backgrounds, are always subjected to a process of constant re-meaning by the social subjects.

This work explores the link between place, sense of belonging and biography. Focusing on rural places, it shows them as no longer marginal but as contexts in which subjects, activating affective and educational resources, generate unprecedented social relationships and build a new sense of belonging, thus making significant and domestic what might otherwise be seen as an empty and increasingly fragmented space.

We have utilised an interpretative model to analyse the formation of new forms of belonging in rural areas. We have explored what can be considered the basic mechanisms by which young people in Australia and Italy build their sense of belonging. The most significant mechanisms identified are:

1. The educational relation to rural life constructed by a generation of young Australians. This construction utilised post-school qualifications to achieve the young people's goals of remaining close to people and places that matter to them.

2. The performative aspect of belonging in multiple domains of life. This offered a starting point to analyse how young people build their sense of belonging through the formation of connections with people and places, over time, in an increasingly fluid, unstable and mobile context.

3. Belonging as habitus as a structure for understanding and meaning. Through social, cultural, emotional and relational practices, on a daily basis, the performative properties of subjects build their identity and relationship with places. Belonging is conceived not as an ascribed factor or a fixed property but as an ongoing process which results in a more general sense of community.

4. The multifaceted character of belonging. Based on the presence of multiple, interconnected dimensions that combine themselves in different ways, several configurations of belonging are generated. From these, the structure of social bonds that make up the plot of the life context of young people takes shape.

5. The sense of belonging as a product of the intersection of biographical action and location. This outlines new strategies that use resources to counter individualisation processes and the fragmentation and social disorganisation processes that face local communities.

6. Rurality no longer as a marginal or residual area of modernity (Woods 2010). Rather, rurality is seen as a territory within which new forms and modes of meaning and appropriation of space and identity are defined. The focus on a rural place not only allows one to visualise this relationship but also to illuminate the explanatory value of membership.

All of this leads us to a preliminary synthesis which, despite the results, cannot be generalised since it is linked to specific local contexts. However, both research projects invite important reflections. Both the qualitative and quantitative data show the emergence of a common base between Australia and Italy, with local variations linked to these places where belonging presents with a multifaceted character (constituted of a plurality of interconnected dimensions). The reflective and ritual practices lived in different domains generate cultural, emotional and educational resources through which young people rebuild their relationships with the various contexts of life that make up their local community. Thus, the chapter highlights the role of affectivity and also of education as drivers behind individuals' exertions to construct links between the self and community. Education, in particular, is a resource that, together with social, relational and affective resources, forms a specific capital. Promoted and enabled by the subjects through performative practices, it equips them to respond to hazardous processes of expropriation and social fragmentation. Education and the link with the educational institution express an essential element of rural life for young Australians and Italian young people, representing a fundamental integrative mechanism. This is not only symbolic and relational but also functional, with the local context considered important as a place of emotional, cultural and relational investment. These reflections clearly show how the quality of their experience of the sense of belonging takes a central role in building the lives of young people, resulting in the relationships and life practices that new generations develop and carry forward into their future lives.

References

Antonsich, M. (2010). Searching for belonging – An analytical framework. *Geography Compass, 4*(6), 644–659.

Beck, U., & Levy, D. (2013). Cosmopolitanized nations: Re-imaging collectivity in world risk society. *Theory, Culture & Society, 30*(2), 3–31.

Bell, V. (1999). Performativity and belonging: An introduction. *Theory Culture & Society, 16*(2), 1–10.

Bourdieu, P. (1980). *Lesens pratique*. Paris: Les Editions de Minuit.

Bourdieu, P. (2001). The forms of capital. In A. Halsey, H. Lauder, P. Brown, & A. Stuart Wells (Eds.), *Education, culture, economy & society*. Oxford: Oxford University Press.

Bourke, L., & Lockie, S. (2001). Rural Australia: An introduction. In S. Lockie & L. Bourke (Eds.), *Rurality bites* (pp. 1–13). Annandale: Pluto Press.

Bryant, L., & Pini, B. (2009). Gender, class and rurality: Australian case studies. *Journal of Rural Studies, 25*, 48–57.

Butler, J. (1997). *Excitable speech: The politics of the performative*. New York: Routledge.

Butler, J. (1999). *Gender trouble: feminism and the subversion of identity*. New York: Routledge.

Crowley, J. (1999). The politics of belonging: Some theoretical considerations. In A. Geddes & A. Favell (Eds.), *The politics of belonging: Migrants and minorities in contemporary Europe* (pp. 15–41). Aldershot: Ashgate.

Cuervo, H. (2016). *Understanding social justice in rural education*. New York: Palgrave.

Cuervo, H., & Wyn, J. (2012). *Young people making it work: Continuity and change in rural places*. Melbourne: Melbourne University Press.

Cuervo, H., & Wyn, J. (2014). Reflections on the use of spatial and relational metaphors in young people studies. *Journal of Young People Studies, 17*(7), 901–915.

Edensor, T. (2006). Performing rurality. In P. Cloke, T. Marsden, & P. Mooney (Eds.), *Handbook of rural studies* (pp. 484–495). London: Thousand Oaks.

Fallov, M., Jørgensen, A., & Knudsen, L. B. (2013). Mobile forms of belonging. *Mobilities, 8*(4), 467–486.

Giardiello, M. (2015). Is the sense of belonging a strategic resource for adolescent identity? *European Scientific Journal, 1*, 129–138.

Granovetter, M. (1985). Economic action and social structure: The problem of embeddedness. *American Journal of Sociology, 91*(3), 481–510.

Hall, T., Coffey, A., & Lashua, B. (2009). Steps and stages: Rethinking transitions in young people and place. *Journal of Young People Studies, 12*(5), 547–561.

Haukanes, H. (2013). Belonging, mobility and the future: Representations of space in the life narratives of young rural Czechs. *Young, 21*(2), 193–210.

Hopkins, P. (2010). *Young people, place and identity.* Oxon: Routledge.

Human Rights and Equal Opportunity Commission (HREOC). (2000). *Emerging themes: National inquiry into rural and remote education.* Canberra: Commonwealth of Australia.

IFEL, Fondazione ANCI. (2015). *Atlante deiPiccoloComuniItaliani.* Roma: IFEL.

Kenway, J., Kraack, A., & Hickey-Moody, A. (2006). *Masculinities beyond the metropolis.* New York: Palgrave Macmillan.

Krueger, R. A., & Casey, M. A. (2009). *Focus groups: A practical guide for applied research.* London: Sage.

Lewicka, M. (2011). Place attachment: How far have we come in the last 40 years? *Journal of Environmental Psychology, 31,* 207–230.

May, V. (2013). Self, belonging and social change. *Sociology, 45*(3), 363–378.

Panelli, R. (2006). Rural society. In P. Cloke, T. Marsden, & P. Mooney (Eds.), *Handbook of rural studies* (pp. 63–90). London: Sage.

Probyn, E. (1996). *Outside belongings.* New York: Routledge.

Putnam, R. D. (2000). *Bowling alone: The collapse and revival of American community.* New York: Simon & Schuster.

Ralph, D., & Staeheli, L. (2011). Home and migration: Mobilities, belongings and identities. *Geography Compass, 5*(7), 517–530.

Savage, M., Bagnall, G., & Longhurst, B. J. (2005). *Globalization and belonging.* London: Sage.

Skrbis, Z., Woodward, I., & Bean, C. (2014). Seeds of cosmopolitan future? Young people and their aspirations for future mobility. *Journal of Young People Studies, 17*(5), 614–625.

Swartz, D. (1997). *Culture and power: The sociology of Pierre Bourdieu.* Chicago: The University of Chicago Press.

Thomson, R., & Taylor, R. (2005). Between cosmopolitanism and the locals: Mobility as a resource in the transition to adulthood. *Young, 13*(4), 327–342.

Tönnies, F. (1957). *Community and society (Gemeinschaft und gesellshaft).* East Lansing: Michigan State University Press.

Woods, M. (2010). *Rural geography: Processes, responses and experiences in rural restructuring.* London: Sage.

Wyn, J. (1998). *Young people living in rural Australia in the 1990s*. Research Report 16. Melbourne: Young People Research Centre.

Wyn, J. (2015). Young people and belonging in perspective. In A. Lange, H. Reiter, S. Schutter, & C. Steinter (Eds.), *Handbook of child and young people sociology*. Wiesbaden: Springer.

Wyn, J., Lantz, S., & Harris, A. (2012). Beyond the 'transitions' metaphor: Family relations and young people in late modernity. *Journal of Sociology, 48*(1), 1–20.

11

Exploring Spaces of Belonging Through Analogies of 'Family': Perspectives and Experiences of Disengaged Young People at an Alternative School

Aspa Baroutsis and Martin Mills

Introduction

In this chapter, belonging is theorised using spatial theories (Lefebvre 1991; Massey 1993a, 2005; Soja 1996). This approach explores the spatial elements of schooling that encourage and support belonging in an 'alternative' school community and, in many cases, how these spaces differ from 'mainstream' or 'conventional' schooling. Here, even the categorisation of a school using terminology such as 'alternative' or 'unconventional' identifies a binary logic that is associated with a socially produced space.

A. Baroutsis (✉)
Faculty of Education, The Queensland University of Technology, Brisbane, Queensland, Australia
e-mail: aspa.baroutsis@qut.edu.au

M. Mills
Centre for Research on Teachers and Teaching, University College London, Institute of Education (IOE), London, United Kingdom
e-mail: martin.mills@ucl.ac.uk

© The Author(s) 2018
C. Halse (ed.), *Interrogating Belonging for Young People in Schools*,
https://doi.org/10.1007/978-3-319-75217-4_11

The notion of 'spaces of belonging' provides an analytic framework for exploring the practices in school communities. This chapter explores young peoples' perspectives and experiences of belonging at an alternative school in Queensland, Australia.

Space is often associated with practices of inclusion and exclusion (Gulson and Symes 2007; Paechter 2004), When discussing belonging, we acknowledge that not all practices of inclusion are positive or favourable for young people, for example, belonging to a gang whilst also creating a sense of community, can have negative outcomes. Additionally, mandated practices of belonging, such as wearing a school uniform can be stifling and encourage conformity rather than individuality. Similarly, experiences of non-belonging can also be productive and constructive in that they offer opportunities to resist dominant and normative practices especially if these practices are unjust, for example, social movements against oppression. Additionally, individuals can belong and not belong to various groups and communities at the same time. As such, 'belonging is a puzzling term' (Wright 2015, p. 391).

Consequently, we acknowledge that these experiences of belonging and non-belonging are not the same for all the young people at alternative schools. However, the young people we spoke to experienced non-belonging negatively in their mainstream schools and belonging in more positive ways at their current alternative school. When speaking with young people at alternative school sites about their previous schooling experiences, they frequently cited feelings of alienation, marginalisation, and disengagement that affected their capacity to learn and placed them at risk of dropping out of schooling altogether. However, when discussing their current, alternative places of schooling, spaces of belonging were often framed through analogies of 'family' and discourse associated with a 'home'. The young people often linked this sense of belonging within their school community to improved outcomes such as increased satisfaction with their education experiences, reengagement with learning, and a desire to plan and work towards future careers goals; as well as feelings of safety and acceptance.

The Organisation for Economic Cooperation and Development (OECD) (2013, p. 51) identifies the importance of students' sense of belonging in school communities, suggesting 'students tend to thrive when they … feel part of a social group, and feel at ease at school'. If schooling does not engender a sense of belonging for all young people, this suggests a level of injustice as it does not enable a 'parity of participation' (Fraser 2009) in education for all young people; particularly those who are disengaged from schooling or already economically and educationally marginalised. When adopting a perspective that privileges space in an analysis of education practices, thereby subordinating time or history, we are also able to highlight what Edward Soja (2002) refers to as 'spatial justice'. This is not a new form of justice, rather, it suggests that new insights can be gained when the spatial aspects of familiar ideas are foregrounded (Soja 2000, 2002).

This chapter theorises the notion of space (Lefebvre 1991) and spatial justice (Soja 2002) by foregrounding several spatial elements at an alternative school. These elements are collectively identified as 'spaces of belonging' and incorporate relational, material and pedagogical spaces. That is, the types of learning environments, material and symbolic, that promote and support feelings of belonging to a place such as a school community.

Theorising Space

Typically, educational space is often seen as 'a "container" within which education simply "takes (its) place", with varying degrees of effectiveness and efficiency' (Green and Letts 2007, p. 57), instead of acknowledging the interplay of structures and environments, both inside and outside school spaces, that interact to enable learning. In acknowledging that space is socially constructed (Gulson and Symes 2007; Soja 1996), there is benefit to a spatial analysis of alternative schools.

Often, learning and education are seen only as temporal processes, that is, they are 'expected to take place and progress over and through time, even if sometimes in specific spaces and places' (Paechter 2004, p. 449). However, Soja (2002, p. 116) suggests 'everything in society is spatially and historically constituted. There are no spheres, realms, systems, perspectives, rationalities, relations, ideologies, identities, etc. that are aspatial'. These perspectives adopt a 'critical spatial thinking'. This implies that, while everything exists in time, socially produced spaces have a spatial element that is equally significant to the historical and social dimensions.

Henri Lefebvre (1991) conceptualised space using the perceived-conceived-lived triad, that is, social practice, representations of space, and representational spaces (Lefebvre 1991, p. 33). While not without limitations, Lefebvre (1991, p. 38) first intimates that 'the spatial practice of a society secretes that society's space; it propounds and presupposes it, in a dialectical interaction; it produces it slowly and surely as it masters and appropriates it'. Therefore, the spatial practices of a society can be identified through interpreting the material, 'mappable', and physical forms of space, often identified as the 'real' space (Soja 2002). These spatial practices—for example, the everyday act of schooling of children in purpose-built physical spaces—produce and reproduce social formations, and ensure continuity and cohesion in a society (Lefebvre 1991, p. 33). Secondly, while perceived space identifies the material forms, conceived space is an 'imagined' space that emphasises the 'mental or ideational representations' of those material forms (Soja 2002, p. 113). Conceived spaces are dominant spaces in a society and are linked to 'the relations of production and to the "order" which those relations impose, and hence to knowledge' (Lefebvre 1991, p. 33). For example, the spaces of knowledge accumulation and production of the schooling of children and young people is often derived from our thinking and ideas about children. Finally, Lefebvre (1991) also identified the lived or representational space, a combination of the 'real' and 'imagined', that is, 'the space of "inhabitants" and "users"' that is experienced through 'coherent systems of non-verbal symbols and signs' (Lefebvre 1991, p. 39). Soja (2002, pp. 56–57) explains:

> Everything comes together in Thirdspace: subjectivity and objectivity, the abstract and the concrete, the real and the imagined, the knowable and the unimaginable, the repetitive and the differential, structure and agency, mind and body, consciousness and the unconscious, the disciplined and the transdisciplinary, everyday life and unending history.

This is a constructed social space that seeks to address the inequalities and injustices of a society, rejecting the values and perceptions that these spaces were constituted by, instead seeking to develop new values based on equality and justice. For example, spaces that redress schooling practices of exclusion, marginalised and disengagement of children and young people. It could be argued that it is within this thirdspace that belonging can be explored.

Soja's (2002) notion of 'thirdspace' draws on Lefebvre's (1991) concept of 'lived space' and Foucault's (1986) observation of 'heterotopias'. Unlike 'utopias' that represent a 'perfected form' of society, 'heterotopias' are 'real places' in society (Foucault 1986, p. 24). These heterotopic spaces are:

> something like counter-sites, a kind of effectively enacted utopia in which the real sites, all the other real sites that can be found within the culture, are simultaneously represented, contested, and inverted. Places of this kind are outside of all places, even though it may be possible to indicate their location in reality. Because these places are absolutely different from all the sites that they reflect and speak about, I shall call them, by way of contrast to utopias, heterotopias. (Foucault 1986, p. 24)

When describing these heterotopic sites, Michel Foucault (1986, p. 26) presupposes 'a system of opening and closing that both isolates them and make them penetrable'. That is, entry may be compulsory as in the case of a school, but it also requires the individuals to submit to certain modes of conduct and behaviours, otherwise they may be suspended or excluded from the school. Foucault (1986, p. 26) adds that there are other sites that:

> seem to be pure and simple openings, but that generally hide curious exclusions. Everyone can enter into these heterotopic sites, but in fact that is only an illusion: we think we enter where we are, by the very fact that we enter, excluded.

Additionally, heterotopias function to 'create a space of illusion that exposes every real space … their role is to create a space that is other' (Foucault 1986, p. 27). This reasoning can be applied to alternative education settings that are discussed below, as 'other' spaces of education. Here, the very existence of these separate educational sites is an illusion; where young people are being excluded from mainstream education by their very inclusion in the alternative school.

Central to the discussion of heterotopic environments, Foucault (1984, p. 252) identifies a relationship between knowledge, power, and space, which suggest that 'space is fundamental in any exercise of power'. This is of interest when discussing schools and schooling as they are often sites of spatial regulation that draws on discipline to reproduce social control. Foucault (1995, p. 141) proposed that 'discipline proceeds from the distribution of individuals in space'. That is, schools utilise 'disciplinary technologies' to control space and time and govern the subject (Foucault 1995; Soja 1996). Here, alternative school spaces, briefly outlined below and described in the latter sections of this chapter, deliberately seek to disrupt the traditional strategies of spatial governmentality. Given this, the notion of 'spaces of belonging' in this chapter explores the types of learning environments, material and symbolic that promote and support feelings of belonging to a place such as a school community. In addition to belonging as place, Marco Antonsich (2010, p. 649) submits that analysis can be broadened to include the 'politics of belonging', that is, the 'discourses and practices of socio-spatial inclusion/exclusion'. These politics often utilise categorisations that construct boundaries separating 'us' from 'them', that is, the group that claims to belong and the group that grants belonging (Antonsich 2010), that also align with thirdspace.

Alternative Education Spaces

In moving beyond socio-territorial constructions of belonging, Ash Amin (2002, p. 974), suggests belonging is associated with a commitment to the continuation of a situation or a community, rather than one based on culture or ethnicity. Mobility disrupts this continuity and is increasingly identified as an axis of inequality in modernity (Bauman 2000; Urry 2000). The schooling of disenfranchised young people is often characterised by a high degree of movement in, out, and across different schools (cf. McGregor and Mills 2012). One example of movement is seen in drop-out rates, with a recent report by Stephen Lamb et al. (2015, p. vi) showing that 26% of young people do not complete Year 12 (high school) qualifications in Australia. This number is much higher for young people from remote (56.6%) and very remote (43.6%) communities and from low socio-economic backgrounds (40%) (Lamb et al. 2015, p. vi). In another example, disengaged and marginalised young people move through these school spaces. This is often initiated and/or controlled by a structures or actions within a system hierarchy, for example, practices of exclusion or expulsion from schooling. In the state of Queensland in 2015, 11% of students across the state were on a 1–5 or 6–20 day suspension while 0.51% were expelled or had their enrolments cancelled (DET 2015). These gaps and absences, due to the individual's absences from school, can affect a young person's access to learning and can create disjointed learning experiences.

These movements in and out of education spaces can also create groups of 'residual' and 'redundant' students whose behaviours, and sometimes their very existence, are viewed as unfavourable. Zygmunt Bauman (2004, p. 16) explains:

> To be 'redundant' means to be supernumerary, unneeded, of no use—whatever the needs and uses are that set the standard of usefulness and indispensability. The others do not need you; they can do as well, and better, without you. There is no self-evident reason for your being around and no obvious justification for your claim to the right to stay around. To be declared redundant means to have been disposed ... 'Redundancy' shares its semantic space with 'rejects', 'wastrels', 'garbage', 'refuse'—with waste.... The destination of waste is the waste-yard, the rubbish heap.

Drawing on this analogy of waste, Martin Mills, Peter Renshaw and Lew Zipin (2013, p. 13) describe the following situation, drawing on research site visits:

> In one instance we were told by a number of people in a regional town about a high school where the principal had stated an intention to keep 'the rubbish out' of his school. In another instance, teachers and youth workers in a school for young people who were struggling within the mainstream complained that many high schools were using them as a 'dumping ground' for unwanted students.

This raises the issue of injustices associated with reduced access and increased mobility within and across schools. There is unequal spatial distribution in that these young people are often required to move, more than other young people, to attain a schooling environment that is suited to their needs. Doreen Massey (1993b, p. 63) suggests mobility is also related to control in that some have more control over their own movement than others and this differentiation 'can weaken the leverage of the already weak'. While not intended as criticism of either mainstream or alternative schooling, this also raises the question, 'Are alternative school spaces, by their very existence, contributing to this student mobility?' This is taken up in the conclusion.

Given the turbulent nature of some young people's experiences with schooling (Lamb et al. 2015; Smyth et al. 2010) and their level of mobility, learning spaces that promote acceptance and belonging are advantageous and likely to encourage reengagement with learning (Te Riele 2006). Many of the young people in alternative schools have traumatic lives struggling with complex home lives, domestic issues, family circumstances, homelessness, unemployment, teenage pregnancy, substance abuse, bullying, or depression and other health-related issues (cf. Mills and McGregor 2014; Mills et al. 2015). Yuval-Davis (2006, p. 197) explains, 'belonging is about emotional attachment, about feeling "at home" … about feeling "safe"'. Marco Antonsich (2010) identifies this as 'place-belongingness' that associates an emotional feeling to a place. In this statement, 'home' does not refer to the 'domestic(ated) material space, which feminist authors have criticised for reproducing gendered and patriarchal relations of oppression, violence, and fear' (Antonsich 2010, p. 646). Rather, as bell hooks (2008, p. 203) proposes, 'a true home is the place—any place—where growth is nurtured, where there is constancy', that is, a symbolic place of safety, familiarity, stability, and comfort.

Similar to family, another spatial analogy is that of community. Bauman (2001) suggests that this is a 'feel good' word that perhaps refers to a space that is unavailable to most. Central to his description is the notion of safety:

> To start with, community is a 'warm' place, a cosy and comfortable place. It is like a roof under which we shelter in heavy rain, like a fireplace at which we warm our hands on a frosty day. Out there, in the street, all sorts of dangers lie in ambush; we have to be alert when we go out, watch whom we are talking to and who talks to us, be on the look-out every minute. In here, in the community, we can relax—we are safe, there are no dangers looming in dark corners. (Bauman 2001, pp. 1–2)

However, in problematising the concept of community, he indicates that for some, this is a space of 'non-belonging, a togetherness of loners' (Bauman 2001, p. 68). This is especially the case of some young people in schooling, whether mainstream or alternative. Additionally, Bauman (2001, p. 69) cautions that communities can be spaces of constraint and conformity, adding individuals should experience 'the joy of belonging without the discomfort of being bound'.

About the Study

Research was conducted over a six-month period at an alternative school in Queensland. Elysium College, a pseudonym, is a co-educational independent secondary school with an enrolment of up to 150 students in single-sex[1] classes, or 'studios'. The school, in partnership with The University of Queensland, Griffith University and Youth Affairs Network Queensland (YANQ), was involved in a documentary film-making project that identified young peoples' views about their alternative schooling experiences. A professional film-maker came into the school and worked with young people, demonstrating the facets of the film-making process. The project was titled, *Building Young People's Voices*. The young people who volunteered to participate in the project were taught skills in this area from script writing, selecting locations, conducting interviews and video and audio skills. Other students chose to participate as interviewees. Data gathered from this project included raw and edited video footage of interviews with young people and staff as part of the documentary production process, with the researchers as observers; additional semi-structured interviews with individual staff and students conducted by the researchers as an evaluation of the film-making process; researcher observations; school documentation and artefacts; and the final eight short videos (https://vimeo.com/user38278132). Throughout this chapter, the students are identified using pseudonyms. These data were analysed using a thematic analysis (Boyatzis 1998; Braun and Clarke 2006).

Relational Space

Massey (1994, p. 265) submits that space is dynamic and created from a 'complex web of relations'. At Elysium, the relational space supports and encourages emotional and social interactions. Many of the young people at this school contrasted their experiences with those in their former mainstream school. In this section, we provide an indication of the types of experiences that contributed to these young people's sense of exclusion from their previous schools and their inclusion at Elysium. Hannah, a student, recollects her experiences:

> I was in a relationship, and my boyfriend moved away. So he stopped going to school, so I kind of like lost it a bit there. That same year, my parents divorced and that was a bit confusing. And then my friends stopped talking to me, and then I started going down into the hole of depression. It's like really hard to get out of there. You try talking to someone … so you talk to your friends about it and they'd be like, 'Oh, ok. Oh well. I don't know how to handle it so I'll ignore you'. So they were ignoring me and then I lost motivation to keep going to school…. I searched for a job. I couldn't get a job. So I actually just sat on the couch at my mum's place and did nothing for six months. And that didn't help anything at all.

Hannah went on to say that her life turned around when she found Elysium and felt that she belonged. As well as their personal traumas, some young people also experienced trouble with mainstream schooling. Piper expressed her feelings of alienation:

> I left school in 2008 and that was because I couldn't work up the courage at all to go to school. I just felt completely out of place there. I felt no one understood or really spoke to me about it, or tried to help me. It didn't work out for me.

For other students, their disengagement resulted from their classroom interactions. For example, Johnny explains:

> At conventional school, I always seemed to do the wrong thing. I'd always get detentions and I started to get a bad reputation with the teachers. My first school that I went to I ended up getting expelled, then I went to

another school but I didn't end up going. I just stayed home and made excuses. I just didn't enjoy it. I don't know why I got into trouble a lot. I just got in trouble. At the start, I used to listen to the teachers, and then after a while, I don't know, I didn't really care anymore so I just stopped listening and gave up.

For some students, like Harry, this culminated in expulsion:

I'm not allowed back to any schools in Queensland because I've been kicked out and this is a second chance for me. I respect that they have given me this second chance. I'm quite grateful to be a student.

Peter Kraftl (2013, p. 90) indicates that the young people in his study on alternative schools were not 'anti-school', rather, they were 'critical of the kinds of spaces that contemporary mainstream schools had become'. Similarly, these young people's narratives at Elysium were, at times, critical of their mainstream schooling spaces for not listening to or accommodating their needs.

For many young people, their previous schooling experiences enabled them to fully appreciate their new schools, often referring to their school as a second family. For example:

Because some of the people that don't go to school, they have got personal reasons like trouble at home or school. And here, it's a second family to me; and I believe that if I believe it's a second family to me, it must be a second family to others as well. (Robyn)

The school's made me feel like I have got another family. Everyone is just so supporting and helpful. (Mitchell)

My studio is like my extended family, except I actually want to spend time with them! So much care and love which has helped me so much. (Knox)

My studio is a great, safe place. (Laura)

These analogies with family and community identified spaces that were considered as safe places. bell hooks (2008, p. 215) describes home as 'the safe place, the place where one could count on not being hurt. It was the place where wounds were attended to. Home was the place where the me of me mattered'. Such environments counteract the notions of waste and redundancy that were identified earlier in this chapter.

These relational spaces also focused on the social and emotional wellbeing of the individual. In its promotional material, Elysium stated that it 'bases its philosophy on establishing positive and respectful relationships between adults and students to maximise engagement, emotional wellbeing and academic achievement'. Robyn gives an example of how the material space of the studio enables the effectiveness of the relational space:

> A lot of our learning is kind of really personal learning, and you talk about your lives a lot. There are times where I know if I had been in a classroom with 10 guys and 10 girls I wouldn't have opened up as much. But when it's such a small classroom of all your girlfriends it's easier to express yourself.

The relational spaces are also characterised by inclusion and acceptance:

> To be a student at Elysium means being accepted by a group of people that actually like you and don't judge you and to actually be taught one-on-one by a group of amazing teachers and people. (Calvin)

> When I come to school each day, I feel accepted. I feel absolutely no stress to come here. It is so free-flowing and easy to do the work that I'm given. (Piper)

> It means I am always going to be included. There is no exclusion or any of that. (Davis)

The relationships with teachers and other workers were considered central to the young people's feelings of belonging and acceptance.

> The teaching is just really nurturing. They pay attention to you. They get deep into what is really troubling you, and they help you out and always treat you like one of us. It's really cool. (Davis)

Caring relationships are encouraged and practices within the relational space promote caring, tolerance and understanding:

> It is a lot easier to understand everyone. We normally sit down and have group discussions. If something is not right, we try to help each other. (Nora)

The young people feel supported by the school community, including their teachers and their peers:

> Just the support … family. Just, I know family will be there to back me up so I always have to prove [to] myself that I am worthy in the first place. I am glad to be doing hard work because at the end of the day I have a family to share that work with and for them to appreciate it, as much as I do. (Davis)

As with all social units, there are parameters that govern the space. Similarly, Mia points out that, at Elysium, the relationships guide behaviour and there is a sense of commitment to the group:

> To have a sense of belonging, equality, and that someone is just there to care about you. It's pretty chill, like casual, but still strict in the areas it needs to be. Yeah, it has good guidelines like family does; pretty much, all is good if you use your manners.

These socio-emotional elements of the relational space interact with the material space and enable productive learning in the pedagogical space.

Material Space

Space can be used to control individuals, for example, in traditional classrooms, the spatial arrangement of desks and other objects within a classroom are configured to regulate behaviour and confine the body within the educational space. However, alternative schools like Elysium College tend to utilise non-traditional spatial configurations for their learning spaces. Their learning spaces are described as 'studios' rather than classrooms as their composition and function is very different to that of a classroom. This excerpt from promotional material describes the material space:

> Studios—Our classrooms do not resemble traditional classrooms. There are no desks lined up facing the front. Elysium studios are spacious with lounges for discussions, computer workstations for autonomous study, a kitchen to prepare snacks and a group eating area. Elysium studios are your 'safe zone'.

Jordan, a student, shares his thoughts about the studios as being 'not like school', adding his association with the family home:

> Our learning space is like my home environment. We've got couches, we've got TV, we've got computers surrounding us, we've got a kitchen where we cook food, so I like that—no desks or a whiteboard and chalkboard.

Robyn describes these single-sex studios, explaining that the studios are a customisable space, able to better suit the needs of the individuals.

> There are two girls' classes and two boys' classes at our school and each one of them is so different. Just because, like, the way people gel together, so they can make those studios the way that they want it. You can put things that you like in there rather than having a plain classroom. My studio means a lot to me.

When spaces are treated as spaces of belonging akin to a 'home', individuals are able to modify the design of these environments to suit their individual preferences; which in turn can be associated with 'positive feelings' (McGregor 2003).

Food and sharing meals are often thought of as a utilitarian distraction within schools (Weaver-Hightower 2011). However, many alternative schools embrace the opportunities associated with this practice, often incorporating kitchens into their spaces (see, for example, McGregor et al. 2017). The students at Elysium associated sharing a meal at school with conceptions of family. Kelly explains:

> We have the convenience of lounges in our classroom instead of hard chairs and desks. When we have breakfast and lunch we sit around the table to make it a kind of family feel because some of us don't sit at the table with our family at home for dinner.

Within this discourse of 'family' there is a somewhat romantic notion of, most likely, a middle-class family that sits together to eat and share the day's events. Whilst family, like 'community' (Bauman 2001), is not a neutral term and does not necessarily provide a positive experience for all, here, its use in this way does imply that this space is one that creates a sense of belonging, as we discuss below. These elements of the material space facilitate and service the relational and pedagogical spaces, which are metaphoric spaces that can support feelings of belonging.

Pedagogical Space

Jan Nespor (2003, p. 98) suggests schooling moves people along spatial and temporal trajectories he identifies as 'curricula', where only 'certain meanings, identities, and lines of action can be easily sustained'. Alternative schools often seek to disrupt these trajectories, developing curricula and practices to better suit the young people rather than the systems that devise them. In their school documents, Elysium states their emphasis is on 'project-based learning, and individualised learning plans for each student'. Pedagogic spaces are small and intimate learning environments.

> Learning in small teams provides safety and security and encourages trusting relationships with both your team mates and your leader or advisor. The adults who work with you will understand your background and grow to know you well over time. This provides an added sense of knowing you are valued and respected at Elysium. Plus, it gives you every opportunity and the right support to learn and enjoy coming to school every day. (School documents)

Project-based learning (PBL) was frequently mentioned by the students as a meaningful way to learn that enabled choices at this school. Robyn shared her views:

> We get a lot of choices at Elysium, which I love. We do project-based learning, or just PBL. We have a folder and we are working towards one main goal which for this semester is an event that we are going to hold at the end of the year. It incorporates art, English, maths, creative learning. There are other things like visual learning and all that. You get all of your maths and English through the semester but you don't have to sit in the class. So you can do it with little activities. It's good because you don't just go from class to class. It's more up to the students. You have to push yourself to do it every day. It's a great motivational skill.

Ensuring that work is connected to young people's lives and is meaningful to them draws on integrated approaches to curriculum delivery and facilitates student input into decision making. This approach has long been argued as effective for engaging young people, especially those often deemed to be marginalised, in schoolwork (see, for example, Hayes et al. 2006; McGregor et al. 2015). This proved to be the case at Elysium. Jordan also enjoyed the school's learning approach as it supported his interests and preferences:

> PBL is project-based learning. You get tasks, and they are all colour coded and worth different points. So you try and work to get the points. I really like how we get to choose what we get to do. If I don't like the task I can pick another one I like. I eventually get through it all. A pretty good way of learning in my opinion.

The teaching approaches within this space were also exalted by the students. 'On my first day at Elysium, I felt a lot more comfortable coming into a more relaxed, laid-back learning environment' (Derek). Similarly, the teachers were considered a key part of the learning space.

> The style of teaching is more interactive, and it just gets you involved more. It actually makes you want to learn. (Derek)

> They're not like normal teachers. They'll actually sit with you one-on-one and explain what you need to do. And they don't just bug you about it. (Calvin)

Calvin goes on to describe these approaches as enabling his sense of identity and desire to work towards attaining his goals:

> When I was in mainstream schooling, I felt like I was left out and I was left behind. Just because they don't catch you up on the learning and when you get in trouble they send you away from the work instead of helping you with it. I felt that I wasn't really smart, I guess. I feel as though I am achieving something now, and that I can achieve my goals, and that I can actually be smart.

The pedagogic space also acted as a motivator for many students because it enabled them to work at their own pace, make decisions about their learning, and gain support from staff when required (Baroutsis et al. 2015, 2016). Johnny explains:

> When I got to Elysium, I settled down and started putting effort into schoolwork. It made me feel good. I don't need to stress anymore with work and stuff like that; I can just do it at my own pace and how I like it. I enjoy having a team leader and advisor as part of my studio because they help me with what I need help. I can ask them anything I want, if it's personal or to do with work, and they'll help me with that.

For some students at the school, their newfound 'success' worked to improve their lives and relationships beyond Elysium. For example, Jordan stated:

> Previously, I didn't really do well at school. I just sat around. Done nothing. But here, I've passed subjects and got 'B's and 'A's. That's motivated me to do better and see how far I can push myself. It feels amazing. My mum is proud of me. I haven't seen the look on her face of pride for a while and I was kind of ashamed of being like a 'drop-kick' because I got kicked out of school and didn't get good grades and now I'm getting 'B's. I'm happy with that.

Nira Yuval-Davis (2006) proposes that the stories people tell themselves are part of their individual identity narratives. In identifying himself as a 'drop-kick', a school drop-out that had not made it very far, Jordan used a spatially-based metaphor that denigrated himself to the bottom of the mainstream schooling system. However, Elysium worked to transform this metaphor into a situation where he now feels 'amazing' and 'happy'. Such spatial metaphors can thus be important indicators of ways of thinking (Paechter 2004; Thrift and Whatmore 2004).

Conclusion

This chapter explores the notion of spaces of belonging within spaces of learning. When listening to the young people's perspectives at Elysium, and other alternative school sites (cf. Baroutsis et al. 2015, 2016;

Mills et al. 2015; Loutzenheiser 2002), the spaces they most associate with belonging are those with schooling practices based on choice, mutual respect and support. The analysis identified three key spaces of belonging: relational, material, and pedagogical spaces. While addressed separately, these spaces intertwine and intersect to form the school space. The relational spaces were associated with those of a family that provided care, supportive relationships, and acceptance of the young people; enhancing their opportunities within the pedagogical spaces. The material spaces provided a safe environment for learning and development. It was identified as resembling a family home, rather than a school, with furniture such as couches and rooms such as a kitchen. The pedagogical spaces were characterised by environments that enabled young people to be supported and guided through meaningful learning experiences that were chosen by the individual student. Young people often identified themselves as active participants within this pedagogical space. Consequently, these spaces of belonging operate to include disengaged and marginalised young people in their education and schooling.

The material, relational and pedagogical spaces described in this chapter are not unique to this alternative school, nor are they spaces that cannot operate in mainstream schools. As such, working with the questions we posed earlier in the chapter, the challenge for education systems is to work towards creating a 'thirding' (Lefebvre 1991) or a 'thirdspace' (Soja 1996) that fragments or deconstructs the binary concepts of 'mainstream' and 'alternative' schooling to include a third option. While we do not have a name for this third option, the focus for this third possibility is to transform the 'categorical and closed logic of either/or to the dialectically open logic of both/and also' (Soja 1996, p. 60). That is, 'the creation of another mode of thinking about space that draws upon the material and mental spaces of the traditional dualism but extends well beyond them in scope, substance, and meaning' (Soja 1996, p. 11); thereby asserting that the practices of belonging to a learning community are educationally valuable and pedagogically effective for all modes of schooling.

Note

1. The notion of single sex classes can be problematic, see for example, Lingard et al. (2009), Martino et al. (2005) and Mills (2004). However, in this chapter we do not unpack these problematics.

References

Amin, A. (2002). Ethnicity and the multicultural city: Living with diversity. *Environment and Planning A, 34*(6), 959–980.

Antonsich, M. (2010). Searching for belonging: An analytical framework. *Geography Compass, 4*(6), 644–659.

Baroutsis, A., McGregor, G., & Mills, M. (2016). Pedagogic voice: Student voice in teaching and engagement pedagogies. *Pedagogy, Culture and Society, 24*(1), 123–140.

Baroutsis, A., Mills, M., McGregor, G., Te Riele, K., & Hayes, D. (2015). Student voice and the community forum: Finding ways of 'being heard' at an alternative school for disenfranchised young people. *British Educational Research Journal.* https://doi.org/10.1002/berj.3214.

Bauman, Z. (2000). *Liquid modernity.* Cambridge: Polity Press.

Bauman, Z. (2001). *Community: Seeking safety in an insecure world.* Cambridge: Polity.

Bauman, Z. (2004). *Wasted lives: Modernity and its outcasts.* Cambridge: Polity.

Boyatzis, R. E. (1998). *Transforming qualitative information: Thematic analysis and code development.* Thousand Oaks, CA: Sage.

Braun, V., & Clarke, V. (2006). Using thematic analysis in psychology. *Qualitative Research in Psychology, 3*(2), 77–101.

DET. (2015). *Reports and statistics: School disciplinary absences by region.* Retrieved August 11, 2016, from http://education.qld.gov.au/schools/statistics/pdf/sda-by-region.pdf.

Foucault, M. (1984). Space, knowledge and power (C. Hubert, Trans.). In P. Rabinow (ed.), *The Foucault reader: An introduction to Foucault's thought* (pp. 239–256). London: Penguin.

Foucault, M. (1986). Of other spaces. *Diacritics, 16*(1), 22–27.

Foucault, M. (1995). *Discipline and punish: The birth of the prison* (A. Sheridan, Trans., 2nd ed.). New York: Vintage Books.

Fraser, N. (2009). *Scales of justice: Reimagining political space in a globalizing world*. New York: Columbia University Press.

Green, B., & Letts, W. (2007). Space, equity, and rural education: A 'trialectical' account. In K. N. Gulson & C. Symes (Eds.), *Spatial theories of education: Policy and geography matters* (pp. 57–76). New York: Routledge.

Gulson, K. N., & Symes, C. (2007). Knowing one's place: Educational theory, policy, and the spatial turn. In K. N. Gulson & C. Symes (Eds.), *Spatial theories of education: Policy and geography matters* (pp. 1–16). New York: Routledge.

Hayes, D., Mills, M., Christie, P., & Lingard, B. (2006). *Teachers and schooling making a difference: Productive pedagogies, assessment and performance*. Sydney: Allen & Unwin.

hooks, b. (2008). *Belonging: A culture of place*. New York: Routledge.

Kraftl, P. (2013). *Geographies of alternative education: Diverse learning spaces for children and young people*. Bristol: Policy Press.

Lamb, S., Jackson, J., Walstab, A., & Huo, S. (2015). *Educational opportunity in Australia 2015: Who succeeds and who misses out*. Retrieved August 11, 2016, from http://www.mitchellinstitute.org.au/wp-content/uploads/2015/11/Educational-opportunity-in-Australia-2015-Who-succeeds-and-who-misses-out-19Nov15.pdf.

Lefebvre, H. (1991). *The production of space*. (D. Nicholson-Smith, Trans.) Oxford: Blackwell.

Lingard, B., Martino, W., & Mills, M. (2009). *Boys and schooling: Contexts, issues and practices*. Basingstoke: Palgrave Macmillan.

Loutzenheiser, L. W. (2002). Being seen and heard: Listening to young women in alternative schools. *Anthropology and Education Quarterly, 33*(4), 441–464.

Martino, W., Mills, M., & Lingard, B. (2005). Interrogating single-sex classes for addressing boys' educational and social needs. *Oxford Review of Education, 31*(2), 237–254.

Massey, D. (1993a). Politics and space/time. In M. Keith & S. Pile (Eds.), *Place and the politics of identity* (pp. 139–159). London: Routledge.

Massey, D. (1993b). Power-geometry and a progressive sense of place. In J. Bird, B. Curtis, T. Putnam, G. Robertson, & L. Tickner (Eds.), *Mapping the futures: Local cultures, global change* (pp. 60–70). London: Routledge.

Massey, D. (1994). *Space, place, and gender*. Minneapolis: University of Minnesota Press.

Massey, D. (2005). *For space*. London: Sage.

McGregor, J. (2003). Spatiality and teacher workplace cultures. In R. Edwards & R. Usher (Eds.), *Space, curriculum, and learning* (pp. 45–45). Greenwich, CT: Information Age Publishing.

McGregor, G., & Mills, M. (2012). Alternative education sites and marginalised young people: "I wish there were more schools like this one". *International Journal of Inclusive Education, 16*(8), 843–862.

McGregor, G., Mills, M., Te Riele, K., & Hayes, D. (2015). Excluded from school: Getting a second chance at a 'meaningful' education. *International Journal of Inclusive Education, 9*(6), 608–625.

McGregor, G., Mills, M., Te Riele, K., Hayes, D., & Baroutsis, A. (2017). *Reimagining schooling for education: Socially just alternatives.* Houndmills: Palgrave Macmillan.

Mills, M. (2004). The media, single sex schooling, the boys' debate and class politics. *Journal of Educational Policy, 19*(3), 335–352.

Mills, M., & McGregor, G. (2014). *Re-engaging young people in education: Learning from alternative schools.* Abingdon: Routledge.

Mills, M., Renshaw, P., & Zipin, L. (2013). Alternative education provision: A dumping ground for 'wasted lives' or a challenge to the mainstream? *Social Alternatives, 3*(2), 13–18.

Mills, M., McGregor, G., Baroutsis, A., Te Riele, K., & Hayes, D. (2015). Alternative education and social justice: Considering issues of affective and contributive justice. *Critical Studies in Education, 57*(1), 100–115.

Nespor, J. (2003). Undergraduate curricula as networks and trajectories. In R. Edwards & R. Usher (Eds.), *Space, curriculum, and learning* (pp. 93–108). Greenwich, CT: Information Age Publishing.

OECD. (2013). *PISA 2012 results: Ready to learn: Students' engagement, drive and self-beliefs (Volume III).* Paris: OECD Publishing.

Paechter, C. (2004). Metaphors of space in educational theory and practice. *Pedagogy, Culture & Society, 12*(3), 449–464.

Smyth, J., Down, B., & McInerney, P. (2010). *'Hanging in with kids' in tough times: Engagement in contexts of educational disadvantage in the relational school.* New York: Peter Lang.

Soja, E. W. (1996). *Thirdspace: Journeys to Los Angeles and other real-and-imagined places.* Cambridge, MA: Blackwell.

Soja, E. W. (2000). *Postmetropolis: Critical studies of cities and regions.* Oxford: Blackwell.

Soja, E. W. (2002). Interview with Edward W. Soja: Thirdspace, Postmetropolis, and social theory. *Distinktion: Journal of Social Theory, 3*(1), 113–120.

Te Riele, K. (2006). Schooling practices for marginalized students: Practice-with-hope. *International Journal of Inclusive Education, 10*(1), 59–74.

Thrift, N., & Whatmore, S. J. (2004). Introduction. In N. Thrift & S. J. Whatmore (Eds.), *Cultural geography: Critical concepts in the social sciences* (Vol. 1, pp. 1–17). London: Routledge.

Urry, J. (2000). *Sociology beyond societies*. London: Routledge.

Weaver-Hightower, M. B. (2011). Why education researchers should take school food seriously. *Educational Researcher, 40*(1), 15–21.

Wright, S. (2015). More-than-human, emergent belongings: A weak theory approach. *Progress in Human Geography, 39*(4), 391–411.

Yuval-Davis, N. (2006). Belonging and the politics of belonging. *Patterns of Prejudice, 40*(3), 197–214.

12

Reflecting on Belonging, Space, and Marginalised Young People

Kitty te Riele

Introduction

The complex nature of the concept of belonging is evident through this book, even within the specific scope of examining belonging in relation to the field of education. First, belonging is multi-dimensional: for example, relating to social elements such as sexuality, gender, rurality, race, culture, class, poverty—and, of course, the intersections of these. Second, belonging is multi-faceted: it can be examined through lenses such as space, time, agency and identity.

The chapters in this section examine the interplay of the book's core concept of belonging with the facet of space and the dimension of marginalisation. Each component of this triad is socially constructed and, therefore, subject to change and to contestation. As Mauro Giardiello and Hernan Cuervo point out in their chapter, belonging is not a fixed ontological attribute but a dynamic relation that is achieved through particular

K. te Riele (✉)
University of Tasmania, Hobart, TAS, Australia
e-mail: kitty.teriele@utas.edu.au

© The Author(s) 2018
C. Halse (ed.), *Interrogating Belonging for Young People in Schools*,
https://doi.org/10.1007/978-3-319-75217-4_12

practices and resources. Also, as Aspa Baroutsis and Martin Mills discuss, the concept of space goes beyond 'perceived' material or physical spaces to 'conceived' (imagined) and 'lived' (representational) spaces. Marginalisation, however, exists only in relationship—in what Stewart Riddle, Alison Black and Karen Trimmer (2015), in their book title, refer to as *Mainstreams, Margins and the Spaces In-Between*. For example, whether young people who leave school before completing upper secondary education (Year 12, in Australia) are 'marginal' depends on societal perceptions. Post World War II, 'early school leaving' was welcomed in Australia because both male and female[1] teenagers were needed in the labour market (Watson 1994). In the 1950s, in the context of discussions about raising the school leaving age, a commentator worried: 'Will the advantage to the community of providing more education for these adolescents offset the economic consequences of their withdrawal from the labour market?' (Spearritt 1958, p. 98, cited in Watson 1994, p. 400). Within decades, however, those 'at risk' of early leaving were considered vulnerable and problematic (Te Riele 2012a, 2015).

The particular nature of marginalisation differs in the two chapters in this section—both invoking as well as critiquing binary relationships. Baroutsis and Mills draw on their research with young people in an alternative school, in contrast with those in mainstream or conventional schooling. They outline young people's alienation in mainstream schools and experiences of 'a high degree of movement in, out, and across different schools'. They powerfully demonstrate how certain young people are excluded, and made to feel outcasts, from mainstream schooling—and how generating a sense of belonging is central to the work of the alternative school.

For Giardiello and Cuervo, the relationship is between young people in rural areas versus those in urban areas. They strongly object to common perceptions of rural areas as 'marginal, static, un-innovative' compared to cities but also describe the Italian and Australian rural settings of their research as 'characterised by uncertainty, fluidity and social fragmentation'. I would argue that such perceptions and conditions tend to generate the marginalisation of rural youth. In contrast, however, Giardiello and Cuervo argue that young people's sense of belonging in rural communities renders these settings significant and rich, countering perceived or experienced marginalisation.

Belonging can be both an outcome of the application of various resources and itself a resource for other outcomes or impacts. In this chapter, I focus mainly on the former, to examine the triad of belonging, space and marginalisation, reflecting on how belonging is generated by drawing on spatial lenses. In the discussion, however, I consider the impacts belonging can have. Throughout, the focus is on young people who are, in some way, marginalised. As an aside, while the chapters in this book pertain mainly to students' sense of belonging, it is useful to recognise that schools are affective spaces for teachers as well (Te Riele et al. 2017) and teachers do not always feel they belong, as Amanda Mooney and Chris Hickey show in their chapter in this collection. While the two previous chapters provide the springboard for my writing here, I also draw on my own research in alternative schools similar to the one discussed by Baroutsis and Mills and on the ideas and reflections from a wide range of students garnered in response to an invitation to write about '*The school that I'd like*'[2] (Burke and Grosvenor 2015).

Spatial Lenses on Resources for Generating Belonging

Spatial lenses can provide a useful tool for exploring how belonging may be generated, as demonstrated in the previous two chapters. Although space and place may be understood in different ways, and are recognised as complex concepts in the field of human geography (e.g., Kitchin and Tate 2013), I found the categories applied by Baroutsis and Mills useful as a starting point for this section: physical (material), pedagogical (educational) and relational space.

Physical Space

The physical or material is the most obvious form of space, easily 'perceived' (Lefebvre 1991) and often seen as somehow more 'real' than other forms (Soja 2002). As a resource for belonging, physical space can impact on how easy it is to 'meet the same people'—one of the items in the

Italian case study described by Giardiello and Cuervo. They also point out, based on their Australian case study, that a physical landscape itself can engender a sense of belonging. Place-based education approaches have particular resonance for Indigenous Australians—for example, William Fogarty and Robert Schwab (2012) recommend 'learning through country'. The Australian Curriculum, Assessment and Reporting Authority recognises 'Aboriginal and Torres Strait Islander histories and cultures' as a key cross-curriculum priority for all students. It positions 'Country/Place' prominently as the first of three key concepts, explaining that this: 'highlights the special connection to Country/Place by Aboriginal and Torres Strait Islander Peoples and celebrates the unique belief systems that connect people physically and spiritually to Country/Place' (ACARA 2016, n.p.).

In the context of alternative schools, as Baroutsis and Mills demonstrate, the material configuration of classrooms matters for belonging. Incorporating couches and kitchens means the perceived space (Lefebvre 1991) of alternative schools is more reminiscent of an (idealised) home than a school. This is a purposeful strategy to generate a welcoming space for young people who, on the whole, had not felt they belonged in traditional schools and who (too often) had experienced insecure or unsupportive housing arrangements (Mills and McGregor 2014; Te Riele 2014). Some such programmes go even further by using spaces that are explicitly 'not like school': for example, the SEDA programme uses sport as the hook to (re-)engage young people with upper secondary education, with local sports clubs used as sites of 'classrooms' (Te Riele et al. 2016).

Although the potency of physical space is perhaps more commonly recognised in alternative schools, it is equally applicable as a resource for belonging in more traditional schools. This is evident from many student responses about '*The school that I'd like*', such as:

My students would not sit on hard, cheap chairs; they would be allowed to sit on comfy beanbags. (Sophie, 12, in Burke and Grosveno, 2015, p. xvii)

The classrooms will be circular (so there won't be a naughty corner!). (Joe, 9, in Burke and Grosvenor 2015, p. 15)

Pedagogical Space

The physical space of classrooms highlights how schools and classrooms are 'meeting places where children and teachers are "thrown together" (Massey 2005) and must negotiate spaces of learning' (Comber 2016, p. 33). Barbara Comber goes on to connect such pedagogical space with 'pedagogies of belonging' (2016, p. 33), in particular in high poverty (i.e. marginalised) schools. In Baroutsis and Mills' alternative school, one resource for belonging provided through pedagogical space is related to size: keeping learning environments small and providing individual support. A student from my research in a similar school used spatial metaphors to contrast how his current teachers 'actually get in and help you' compared to previous schools where teachers would 'stand back and watch' (Te Riele 2012b, p. 78). Staff in such alternative schools acknowledge that smaller classes and schools facilitate a positive pedagogical space, which is harder to achieve in traditional, large high schools. A student writing about '*The school that I'd like*' suggested that, in a traditional school, smaller classes would also help:

> My dream school would [...] have smaller classes so that the teacher got to know you as a person, not just another pupil, and you would have more of their time and attention. (Sarah, 13, in Burke and Grosvenor 2015, 104)

As articulated so well by this young woman, an important benefit of small class size is that staff can get to know their students, which lays the foundation for strong staff-student relationships and strengths-based approaches to lesson planning. John Hattie (2005) argues, based on meta-analyses of effects of various factors on student learning, that the impact of reduced class size on learning is small but acknowledges that, for many staff and students, such as Sarah, the impact on the conditions in which they work is profound. The sense of belonging and improved wellbeing that smaller classes can generate are important building blocks for a positive disposition towards learning, so that students want to be at school, want to participate and want to learn.

In a different way, small size may also matter for rural young people moving to the city to go to university. Giardiello and Cuervo refer to a participant in the Australian study who explained how the residential college 'provided somewhat of a surrogate for that small-town feeling'.

A second resource for belonging evident in Baroutsis and Mills' discussion of pedagogical space is to do with choice and meaning in the curriculum. Enabling students to have input in what they learn and using students' experiences and knowledge to enhance the design of the curriculum to be more purposeful has the spin-off benefit of deepening the connection between student and school. Project-based learning is an effective medium for such work and can be used to integrate learning across various curriculum areas. This approach can be implemented at the level of individual students but, for belonging, is particularly powerful when shared. For young people in their Italian study, Giardiello and Cuervo show that the item 'to share the same interests beyond the place where you live' was important to their sense of belonging and community. Shared interest generates a common bond which, in an educational context, can facilitate peer, not just teacher, pedagogical support, as a staff member in an alternative programme explained: 'they work with each other ... it's like a pack mentality but for a positive thing' (Simon, in Te Riele et al. 2016, p. 59).

While in most schools, specific projects—and the groups of students they engage—change over time, some alternative education programmes are purposefully created around a common interest, such as sport, motor vehicles, or the experience of being a young mother. An example of the latter is Skills for Tomorrow, a programme set up as part of the Australian federal government's Helping Young Parents measure (Department of Social Services [DSS] 2013) which restricted access to welfare payments for young parents who had not completed upper secondary education. The sense of belonging in Skills for Tomorrow derived predominantly from the students' shared identity as young mothers, as illustrated by one student:

> It's just specific for younger mums, which I absolutely love. [...] It's good to get out and have conversations with younger mums, the same age as me, because we're all going through the same sort of thing. Whereas my other girlfriends that are the same age as me, that I went to school with, they don't have kids, they don't know what I'm going through. [...] They don't really get it, but these girls do. (Pippa, in Te Riele et al. 2016, pp. 58–59)

Relational Space

In terms of relational space, Baroutsis and Mills point to the powerful analogy of 'family' used by students to describe their alternative school. This is reflected across much research about such sites in Australia and elsewhere. One of the principles underpinning alternative learning programmes is that learning cannot be divorced from a young person's life (Te Riele 2014, p. 63). This leads to homely physical spaces (see above) as well as a family-like atmosphere. A student at the Melbourne Academy, a programme offered by Melbourne City Mission, explained her sense of the school as 'family' was reinforced when her mother died and her classmates and teacher all came to the funeral (Te Riele et al. 2015, p. 47). A staff member at the SEDA programme recalled how students used the Hawaiian word 'Ohana' for the programme: 'SEDA Ohana, they described it. It apparently means family. So that's how the students described it, because they felt really connected to each other' (Simon, in Te Riele 2014, p. 51). A different example is Tiwi College, a weekly residential school (students go home on weekends) for Indigenous students on the Tiwi Islands, off northern Australia, managed by the Tiwi Land Council. Students, teachers and residential home staff together form what they like to call 'the Picka Family', named after the school's location at Pickataramoor (Crump and Slee 2015, p. 24).

The centrality of relations in education is widely recognised, effectively summed up by the title of the book *No education without relation* (Bingham and Sidorkin 2004). Unsurprisingly, relations were a major topic of comment for students writing about '*The school that I'd like*':

> My perfect teachers would have a very big smile, rosy cheeks and be kind to children. (Ellis, 7, in Burke and Grosvenor 2015, p. 82)

> My ideal secondary school is a safe haven, not a prison. It shouldn't be somewhere you dread attending every morning, but somewhere you enjoy attending. (Angela, 15, in Burke and Grosvenor 2015, p. 115)

It is somewhat disconcerting that, in the experience of too many children and young people, teachers are not necessarily 'kind to children' and the spatial metaphor for school is 'prison'—a major contrast with the analogy of 'family' outlined above. Moreover, teachers most likely would also prefer to smile, to work with 'kind' people, and to enjoy school (see Kostogriz 2012). Making schools happier places for students, logically, should benefit teachers, too.

The spatial element of relations is also evident in what Giardiello and Cuervo refer to as 'secular rituals of caring' that provide 'individuals with an anchor in a particular social context'. In order to recognise the affective domain of life as a site of social practice, Kathleen Lynch (2012) advocates the notion of affective justice. For educational settings, affective justice is concerned with the quality of relationships, care and support available to students (and teachers). In this sense, belonging is also an issue of social justice—since for marginalised young people, too often that quality is not high, as outlined by Baroutsis and Mills in relation to the students' previous schooling experiences. Being a subject of care (Noddings 1992) in the context of learning is particularly empowering for students who previously have experienced a lack of care in their own lives at home, in school and/or with peers. Moreover, care in schools can be a two-way street—not just from staff to students but also in reverse (Te Riele et al. 2017). Reflecting on students' writing about teachers in '*The school that I'd like*', Burke and Grosvenor (2015, p. 80) comment that 'while children are teachers' most severe critics they are also their greatest advocates. [...] one can say that children care about their teachers'.

Re-thinking Belonging

In a regional Australian town, where the young people in the local alternative school were strongly connected to the local community through work placement, one of the employers in my research commented:

> Kids that you see on the street, I can't remember all their names. You see them around—"oh, g'day Mr [xx], I did work experience". Or, "I did this". But now they can communicate, whereas if they hadn't done that [...] they probably wouldn't even acknowledge my existence. (Te Riele 2011, pp. 225–226)

What is interesting here is that, presumably, this businessman would not have thought to say 'hello' to these young people either. Trust and reciprocity between marginalised young people and the broader community are central for generating strong social bonds and a sense of belonging. On the other hand, 'othering' relies, to a large extent, on ignorance (Douglas 1992). Schools can play a role in bringing people together to undermine such ignorance and create connectedness.

I move on to briefly considering the impact of belonging in the context of marginalised young people and education. I wonder: is belonging (part of) a 'solution' to the 'problem' of marginalisation? In the chapters by Giardiello and Cuervo and by Baroutsis and Mills, as well as in my own writing (Te Riele 2014; Te Riele et al. 2016), belonging is largely portrayed as positive and constructive. In particular, in education, belonging can have positive impacts on both wellbeing and academic outcomes—at the individual level for students as well as at the level of the community.

Without detracting from that productive potential of belonging, I want to unpack some of the conceivable counterproductive impacts of belonging. First, the feelings of wellbeing and safety generated by shared interests and a 'family-like' place of belonging may also be restrictive. Giardiello and Cuervo write about belonging being 'rooted in a specific place' and of 'the generative belonging of ties'. Such roots and ties not only enabled belonging, but also steered young people towards particular decisions while closing off other options. In relation to the Australian study, Giardiello and Cuervo indicate a kind of defensiveness among rural young people about 'their decisions to stay or return to their rural communities […] despite the apparent plethora of educational, work and lifestyle choices in urban areas'. They also describe how rural young people sought out other 'country kids' when moving to the city for university study. The desire to maintain one's belonging to a particular group can thus work to exclude oneself from other groups and life or work opportunities.

In her research in an Australian rural area, Ani Wierenga (2009, pp. 56–57) distinguished four ideal types of cultural orientation among young people. Two of those included an opening of doors beyond the local: 'exploring' and 'wandering'. In contrast, the two remaining orientations were inward-looking: 'settling' and 'retreating'. This is not to say that remaining in, or returning to, a particular locality or group cannot be rewarding. The extent to which the decision to remain is voluntary, however, may be limited. For example, a staff member in an alternative school (Te Riele et al. 2015, p. 23) referred to a student who was 'sabotaging' his achievement towards the end of the year and argued: 'I believe wholeheartedly that this was a fear of success rather than a fear of failure. [...] He even mentioned his concern at leaving the safety of our classroom'.

On the other hand, it may be families who are restricting young people's choices. A report from the Australian island state of Tasmania (Eslake 2015) refers to a culture in which parents 'have not been persuaded that their children need to complete Year 12' and may even fear losing their children to further study or employment on 'the mainland' if they do finish upper secondary education. People involved with Tiwi College (the Indigenous residential school mentioned earlier) similarly reflected on the tension between enhancing opportunities for young people on the Tiwi islands and enabling young people to explore opportunities 'off-island' (Crump and Slee 2015, pp. 61–62). Pertinent here is the reminder by Baroutsis and Mills of Zygmunt Bauman who 'cautions that communities can be spaces of constraint and conformity' as well as spaces of belonging.

A second possible counterproductive effect of belonging is that feelings of being an 'insider' at the micro level may work to maintain exclusion at the macro level. Baroutsis and Mills contrast belonging in alternative schools with students' previous 'feelings of alienation, marginalisation, and disengagement'. For these young people, the sense of being included in the smaller, specific spaces of alternative education certainly is a solution to their previous exclusion. In the bigger picture, however, the existence of alternative schools can let mainstream schools 'off the hook'. They do not need to be genuinely inclusive or comprehensive as long as special schools exist, for example, to cater for young people who are marginalised, have a disability, or are otherwise (as Slee 2011, puts it) 'irregular'.

This conundrum is recognised by Baroutsis and Mills: 'young people are being excluded from mainstream education by their very inclusion in the alternative school'. In other work, Mills and colleagues have critiqued increased authority for mainstream school principals to expel students and the concomitant increased use of alternative schools by mainstream schools 'as a 'dumping ground' for unwanted students' (Mills et al. 2013, p. 13;

also see Mills et al. 2015). There is a risk, therefore, that the separation of particular groups of young people into 'other' educational provision—however positive for those young people in the short term—may ultimately lead to further stigmatisation of those young people and also to diminished social justice and democracy for the community as a whole (Fielding and Moss 2011).

In their chapter, Baroutsis and Mills draw on Nancy Fraser's (2009) notion of parity of participation and Giardiello and Cuervo refer to broader social and civic solidarity. So—is belonging (part of) a 'solution' to the 'problem' of marginalisation? The short answer is that it can be. The challenges in education are to expand the sense of belonging from the micro level to the macro level—and to ensure that a sense of belonging works to open, not close, doors for all young people.

Notes

1. Watson (1994) also shows how the teenage labour market was more restricted for females than for males, and deteriorated significantly in the 1970s.
2. An initiative by *The Guardian* newspaper in the UK in 2001 and 2011, based on an earlier version by *The Observer* newspaper in 1967 and 1996.

References

ACARA. (2016). *Cross-curriculum priorities: Aboriginal and Torres Strait Islander histories and cultures*. Retrieved January 23, 2017, from http://www.acara.edu.au/curriculum/cross-curriculum-priorities.

Bingham, C., & Sidorkin, A. (Eds.). (2004). *No education without relation*. New York: Peter Lang.

Burke, C., & Grosvenor, I. (2015). *The school that I'd like: Revisited. Children and young people's reflections on an education for the future* (2nd ed.). London: Routledge.

Comber, B. (2016). *Literacy, place and pedagogies of possibility*. New York: Routledge.

Crump, S. J., & Slee, R. (2015). *Changing the rules of the game: The SEDA Program at Tiwi College*. Retrieved March 3, 2017, from https://www.vu.edu.au/sites/default/files/victoria-institute/pdfs/Changing%20the%20Rules%20of%20the%20Game--Final%28digital%20version2%29.pdf.

Department of Social Services (DSS). (2013). *Helping young parents measure participation requirements*. Retrieved May 20, 2015, from http://guides.dss.gov.au/guide-social-security-law/3/5/1/165.

Douglas, M. (1992). *Risk and blame: Essays in cultural theory*. London: Routledge.

Eslake, S. (2015). *TCCI Tasmania Report 2015*. Hobart: Tasmanian Chamber of Commerce and Industry.

Fielding, M., & Moss, P. (2011). *Radical education and the common school. A democratic alternative*. London: Routledge.

Fogarty, W., & Schwab, R. (2012). *Indigenous education: Experiential learning and learning through Country*. Canberra: ANU, Centre for Aboriginal Economic Policy Research (CAEPR).

Fraser, N. (2009). *Scales of justice: Reimagining political space in a globalizing world*. New York: Columbia University Press.

Hattie, J. (2005). The paradox of reducing class size and improving learning outcomes. *International Journal of Educational Research, 43*(6), 387–425.

Kitchin, R., & Tate, N. (2013). *Conducting research in human geography: Theory, methodology and practice*. London: Routledge.

Kostogriz, A. (2012). Accountability and the affective labour of teachers: A Marxist-Vygotskian perspective. *Australian Educational Researcher, 39*(4), 397–412.

Lefebvre, H. (1991). *The production of space*. Oxford: Blackwell.

Lynch, K. (2012). Affective equality as a key issue of justice: A comment on Fraser's 3-dimensiponal framework. *Social Justice Series, 12*(3), 45–64.

Massey, D. (2005). *For space*. London: Sage.

Mills, M., & McGregor, G. (2014). *Re-engaging young people in education: Learning from alternative schools*. London: Routledge.

Mills, M., Renshaw, P., & Zipin, L. (2013). Alternative education provision: A dumping ground for 'wasted lives' or a challenge to the mainstream? *Social Alternatives, 32*(2), 13–18.

Mills, M., McGregor, G., Hayes, D., & Te Riele, K. (2015). 'Schools are for us'. The importance of distribution, recognition and representation to creating socially just schools. In S. Riddle, A. Black, & K. Trimmer (Eds.), *Researching mainstreams, margins and the spaces in-between*. London: Routledge.

Noddings, N. (1992). *The challenge to care in schools: An alternative approach to education*. New York: Teachers College Press.

Riddle, S., Black, A., & Trimmer, K. (Eds.). (2015). *Researching mainstreams, margins and the spaces in-between*. London: Routledge.

Slee, R. (2011). *The irregular school. Exclusion, schooling and inclusive education*. London: Routledge.

Soja, E. (2002). Interview with Edward W Soja: Thirdspace, postmetropolis, and social theory. *Distinktion: Journal of Social Theory, 3*(1), 113–120.

Te Riele, K. (2011). Breaking down the sense of 'us and them'. In D. Bottrell & S. Goodwin (Eds.), *Schools, communities and social inclusion*. Melbourne: Palgrave.

Te Riele, K. (2012a). Challenging the logic behind government policies for school completion. *Journal of Educational Administration and History, 44*(3), 237–252.

Te Riele, K. (2012b). One size does not fit all – Belonging and marginalised youth. In N. Bagnall (Ed.), *Education and belonging*. New York: Nova Science Publishers.

Te Riele, K. (2014). *Putting the jigsaw together: Flexible learning programs in Australia*. Final Report. Melbourne: The Victoria Institute for Education, Diversity and Lifelong Learning. Retrieved March 3, 2017, from https://www.vu.edu.au/sites/default/files/victoria-institute/pdfs/27335_2%20VicInstitute_FinalReport%28LR%29.pdf.

Te Riele, K. (2015). Conundrums for youth policy and practice. In K. te Riele & R. Gorur (Eds.), *Interrogating conceptions of "vulnerable youth" in theory, policy and practice*. Rotterdam: Sense Publishers.

Te Riele, K., Davies, M., & Baker, A. (2015). *Passport to a positive future: Evaluation of the Melbourne Academy*. Retrieved March 3, 2017, from https://www.vu.edu.au/sites/default/files/victoria-institute/pdfs/Passport-to-a-Positive-Future-%28web%29.pdf.

Te Riele, K., Plows, V., & Bottrell, D. (2016). Interest, learning, and belonging in flexible learning programmes. *International Journal on School Disaffection, 12*(1), 45–63.

Te Riele, K., Mills, M., McGregor, M., & Baroutsis, A. (2017). Exploring the affective dimension of teachers' work in alternative school settings. *Teaching Education, 28*(1), 56–71.

Watson, I. (1994). Music while you work': Teenage women in the Australian labour market. *Australian Journal of Social Issues, 29*(4), 377–409.

Wierenga, A. (2009). *Young people making a life*. Basingstoke: Palgrave.

Part IV

Pedagogies of Belonging and Non-belonging

13

Pedagogies of Belonging in Literacy Classrooms and Beyond: What's Holding Us Back?

Barbara Comber and Annette Woods

Introduction

Going to school requires children to learn new institutional practices and ways of being. In classrooms, the routines and practices that require holding bodies in particular ways, regulating movement and speech, being one of a large group of children of around the same age, being captured in small indoor spaces and often the even smaller space of desk and chair, are new ways of being and thus need to be learnt. All of this is quite apart from the academic and social demands of being in school. Teachers discover, too, that orchestrating the material and social aspects of classroom life requires considerable thought and responses designed for that

B. Comber (✉)
Queensland University of Technology, Brisbane, QLD, Australia
e-mail: barbara.comber@qut.edu.au

University of South Australia, Adelaide, SA, Australia

A. Woods
Queensland University of Technology, Brisbane, QLD, Australia
e-mail: annette.woods@qut.edu.au

© The Author(s) 2018
C. Halse (ed.), *Interrogating Belonging for Young People in Schools*,
https://doi.org/10.1007/978-3-319-75217-4_13

particular cohort of children. Thus, 'belonging', in the context of school education, is not a simple matter of transition, induction or readiness; nor is it only a matter of facilitation on the part of teachers. What is required is explicit, specific and focused attention to creating socially just spaces where all children can learn to belong and then engage with belonging in diverse ways.

Marco Antonsich (2010) claims that belonging, as a concept, is 'vaguely defined and ill-theorised' (p. 644). We agree that the notion is often taken for granted, or romanticised, and believe that examining the actual work of belonging in a classroom space is helpful. Theorising schools as places (following Massey 2005) and classrooms as spaces, we foreground the negotiation required for belonging, in both a personal and political sense. In addition, we argue that belonging practices, in a broader sense, can become the focus of curriculum, thereby increasing the likelihood that children will come to understand the politics of different people negotiating being together in places.

To achieve this, we draw on recent research conducted with teachers and children across three schools in two states in Australia. In this chapter, we focus primarily on one classroom and the negotiations of belonging made available through the pedagogical and curriculum decisions made by one teacher (other stories from this research have been published by ourselves and our teacher colleagues elsewhere, see, for example, Comber et al. 2017). The *Imagination Project* is one attempt to consider the possibilities of teachers imagining and enacting curriculum together, with an explicit focus on creating socially just spaces of belonging in school.

Belonging in School

We contend, in line with Antonsich (2010) and Nira Yuval-Davis (2006, 2011a), that belonging is multidimensional—personal and political. Feeling attached, or 'at home', in a place is important for learning and engagement in any classroom space. However, the political dimensions of belonging are also important if we are to change broader patterns of inclusion and exclusion, access and denial, and citizenship and boundaries. A classroom space where all children have the opportunity to be 'successful' requires that everyone involved has the skills to 'read' the patterns of interaction and relationship, as well as the unfolding activities, in order to proceed. As such, belonging in the classroom requires sophisticated relations and an explicit focus on making visible the ways in which these are racialised, classed, aged, gendered, sexualised and situated in the space. Classrooms are never places of neutrality, or constancy, and access to these understandings is intricately enmeshed with enacting practices of belonging (Comber et al. 2017).

Achieving a sense of 'belonging' in a classroom space, then, requires everyone involved to understand and agree to routines, patterns of behaviour and interactional processes that are place conscious. By this, we mean routines, patterns of behaviour and interactional processes that take into account what is required now, in this space and with these people. The individual behaviours, movements of bodies, discourse, and social interaction in *this* space *now* become apparent when we consider belonging in this way. Hence, Doreen Massey's (2005) approach to place is important to our discussion of belonging as it foregrounds the politics of people in places and the micro-dynamics unavoidably associated with the negotiation of being 'thrown together'. An individual or personal sense of belonging in a place connects with the negotiation of boundaries, flows and relationships beyond the immediate here and now. Children's lives and histories beyond the school cannot be separated from their negotiation of learner identities and friendships within the school. This understanding is integral to the design and enactment of pedagogies of belonging.

> Place ... does change us ... not through some visceral belonging ... but through the *practising* of place, the negotiating of intersecting trajectories; place as an arena where negotiation is forced upon us. (Massey 2005, p. 154)

A classroom is always a space where people can be included or excluded, where a sense of belonging can be facilitated through negotiation, or blocked, and potentials can be opened or closed. Curriculum and pedagogy are implicated here, as well as the interactions and the discursive and organisational practices evident within the space. Of course, this potential engages the intent and behaviours of teachers *and* students—how places of belonging emerge is influenced by all who inhabit the classroom space.

However, having acknowledged the part that students individually and collectively take in this regard, we believe that there is a great deal that teachers can do to enhance the classroom as a democratic meeting place (Comber 2013) where all students are recognised and recognisable. That is, they are able to represent their best interests and able to receive a fair share of the available resources (following Fraser 2009, 2014). Nancy Fraser has suggested that any approach to socially just education needs to consider recognitive, redistributive and representational justice. That is to say, while it is important that children and young people can see themselves, and their families' and communities' values, languages, cultural practices and beliefs in the curriculum and institutional practices of the school, these recognitive moves will not be enough to ensure equitable access for those more vulnerable or marginalised student cohorts. Fraser (2003) first argued for acknowledgement that redistributive justice must work hand in hand with recognitive justice, so that there might always be a focus on ensuring equitable access to not only financial, but also to the social, languages, literacies and cultural capital valued by society. In her later work, Fraser (2009) has proposed a three-dimensional model that takes account of recognitive and redistributive justice but also provides a focus on students managing appropriate levels of representation in decision making about what is included and not included in the school curriculum and practices. While we are cognisant of the problems of considering identity politics and distribution in a dichotomist fashion (see, for example, Yuval-Davis 2011b) and the risk of conflating or, worse, homogenising identity claims, there is value in drawing on Fraser's heuristic when considering the weaknesses of schooling as an institution in providing socially just places in which children and their teachers can belong.

If, as we contend, belonging in recognitive, redistributive and representational ways is important, then the extension of this is that a lack of explicit attention to belonging on the part of teachers can result in students being left out of, or excluded from, what is on offer within schools (Comber and Kerkham 2016; Compton-Lilly 2011, 2016; Woods et al. 2014; Wortham 2006). In addition, as Allison Pugh (2009), following Anita Harris, put it, 'A child's goal is to become a successful child' (p. 81), and it is the school's responsibility to facilitate this for all children in socially just ways. School children may participate in a 'particular economy of dignity which can be intense and painful' (p. 80) or they may be educated in practices that make their worlds more just and humanising. Thus, we argue here not for a romanticised or tokenistic approach to belonging, but for an understanding of the academic, social and psychological long-term consequences of *not belonging* (Comber 2015; Rogers 2011; Woods and Henderson 2008) and the long-term consequences of exclusion (Dorling 2016).

The concept of belonging has a history in literacy education through the development of culturally and linguistically responsive pedagogy. Within the bounds of pedagogy, as Mary Kalantzis and Bill Cope (2008, p. 43) point out, 'a sense of belonging' is not just a romantic ideal:

> In order to learn, the learner has to feel that learning is for them. The learner has to feel a sense of belonging in the content, and that they belong to the community, or learning setting; they have to feel at home with that kind of learning, or way of getting to know the world.... The learning has to include them, and if they are learning in a formal educational setting such as a school, they also have to feel a sense of belonging in that social and institutional context. The more a learner 'belongs' in all these senses, the more they are likely to learn.

Learning then, is contingent on students having a sense of belonging in terms of the setting, ways of knowing, ways of relating to each other and to teachers, and also towards the objects of study. Teachers do not control all aspects of any classroom setting, of course. For example, they often do not control which children are assigned to a class, the actual classroom space and its location in the school, the other learning spaces available for use, and they frequently have little say in what furniture and other material resources are available. In addition, students' relationships with their peers are continually negotiated both in and out of the classroom, and in and out of the school. These relationships can relate to more than individual likes and dislikes. They are often also based in family, social, cultural and community practices around the big social issues of race, gender, language and religion. These processes of relationship negotiation are becoming ever more complex in a world of superdiversity (Blommaert 2013). Children not only bring already developed repertoires of communication and participation from their families and communities, many also bring dynamic histories and networks from migration and transnational networks.

As Jan Blommaert (2013, p. 194) observed, these new forms of complexity create a problem 'of imagination' for researchers and, we would say, educators more generally. This is occurring simultaneously with 'new forms of public management' (Griffith and Smith 2014) that seek to standardise and to make all educational accomplishments subject to measurement and comparison. Yet, even given such apparently pre-determined policy and educational contexts, teachers can significantly influence how the norms of the micro-politics of life operate in the classroom and work to negotiate and establish practices of belonging. Such pedagogical work can infuse the curriculum when teachers have a deep understanding of, and commitment to, social justice. In the rest of this chapter, we provide an illustrative example of how one teacher educated her class in practices of respect and belonging through designing and enacting a place-conscious curriculum of the neighbourhood.

Imagining Places of Belonging

Our approach here, as in our other projects, has been to document, with teachers and children, alternatives to the current regime of accountability and high definition curriculum. We know from our work with teachers and children that the current fetish with standards and individual performances of often simple and defined skills in schools has impacted upon the teaching and learning of literacy, and on teachers' and children's ways of belonging in classrooms (Comber 2013; Comber and Woods 2016). As such, we claim that it is now vital to do much more than document classroom practice. Our drive has been to actively work with teachers and children to find ways to resist the logics of accountability as testing and the de-professionalisation of teachers and teaching. Our aim has been to facilitate a long institutional memory of how education might work for social justice and to highlight positive stories of teachers and children working to place their teaching and learning within community concerns and possibilities. These stories are vital for current and future teachers, but especially for new teachers joining the profession in an era of accountability. In the schools where we do much of our research work, we know that the teaching workforce is generally younger and less experienced than in other schools. This is not to say that these new teachers do not have much to offer their schools and the children and their families with whom they work—we know that they do. However, when there is such little diversity in the teaching population in any one school, it is more difficult to resist and take carriage of the curriculum locally— there is less memory of how schools might be other than they currently are.

The *Imagination Project* was a small curriculum project where, in 2015, we worked with four teacher-researchers in two states to explore the use of place and space as curriculum resources for socially just teaching and learning. Together, teachers and researchers considered how foregrounding place and space might enable teachers to work with their students to imagine and enact an inclusive and equitable curriculum. The point was for teachers and students to take the opportunity to imagine new worlds and new solutions of belonging in relevant and placed ways. We worked with our teacher colleagues to collaboratively plan a unit of work. The teachers then negotiated and implemented the planned curriculum with their students and, as part of that process, collected artefacts produced by both themselves and their students. The teachers and researchers then reflected on and analysed what had been produced and achieved. Illustrative accounts are in the process of being produced and each teacher has also continued to work with their students to move into new phases of the project.

Drawing on feminist theory of social justice (Fraser 2014), space and place (Massey 2005) and critical multiliteracies (Kalantzis and Cope 2008; The New London Group 1996; Rogers and Wetzel 2013), we examine teachers' and students' work in terms of the extent to which the enacted curriculum attended to creating spaces of belonging. In this chapter, we pay particular attention to how one teacher, Marg, and her Year 5 students interpreted our invitation to be involved in this research. Of particular interest, in the current context of an over-crowded curriculum and over testing, is how Marg and her students made the space and the time to go about their inquiries. Her approach was to open out the curriculum, to step outside the bounds of the school, to explore how the built environment of the neighbourhood is organised and negotiated, and to then reimagine how it might be.

In what follows, we detail the approach taken by the teacher and her year five students. We are interested in the explicit ways in which a sense of belonging was achieved for the students who formed the class. The New London Group (1996) argued that the fundamental purpose of education 'is to ensure that all students benefit from learning in ways that allow them to participate fully in public, community, and economic life' (p. 60)—to be good citizens who belong in ways that carry benefit but also responsibility. This case provides the opportunity to consider belonging and how this notion is explicitly organised in the classroom through negotiations between Marg and her primary-aged, culturally diverse students. The resultant placed-based pedagogy and curriculum supported the children to consider their neighbourhood and local communities and their place within these spaces.

Belonging at School and in the Neighbourhood

Marg begins each year by explicitly working with her class on matters of belonging because she believes that academic learning is contingent upon addressing and negotiating the social relationships and the ways in which they will be together as a class. These processes have been detailed elsewhere (Comber 2013, 2016; Comber et al. 2001; Wells and Trimboli 2014). In addition, each year she also works out the approach to the curriculum most likely to engage that particular class of children and the potential of neighbourhood activity and change to become the object of study. Her continual questions consider, 'What's happening in the neighbourhood?' and 'What are the potential affordances for children's collective inquiries and action?'.

The school property is located in an area of long-term urban renewal and associated demographic change. In 2015, the school had approximately 600 students of which 11% identified as Indigenous and 67%

spoke a language or dialect other than English as their first language. Children spoke a variety of languages as first languages, including Vietnamese, Indian, Serbian, Chinese and a number of African languages. Many students were bilingual. The school's cultural and linguistic diversity is ever-changing, along with wider immigration and refugee patterns. The school reports in 2015 indicate there were 40 cultural/linguistic groups and 12% 'special needs' students. According to the *My School* website, approximately half the students come from low-income families, however school data suggests that there were 60% School Card (an indicator of poverty in the State system) recipients. In previous years, this percentage was even higher but it is gradually changing as new home-buyers enter the neighbourhood and there are fewer Housing Trust cheap rentals available.

In 2015, the potential of the geography curriculum captured Marg's imagination. This was not surprising as she had previously become very engaged in place-conscious pedagogies and participated in projects concerning architecture and the built environment. Ultimately, designing and enacting a pedagogy of belonging incorporated aspects of a range of subjects—geography, design and technology, art, English and literacy. One point to note here, and as we go onto to demonstrate, is that through these subjects and, indeed, beyond-school knowledges (e.g., architecture), Marg offered students alternative discourses for understanding and naming the material world and built environments in particular. While this work drew from her previous experience and practices about belonging, the impetus of geography as a specific curriculum area, combined with our invitation to weave in imagination, led Marg to plan a new ambitious two-term project which culminated in building a model of their preferred dwellings and neighbourhood.

The unit of work was designed around student tasks, some to be done individually, some in groups and some as a whole class. The overall research question they would explore concerned 'Which features of houses are a response to the environment?' that is, 'What is it that makes it comfortable for the people who live in it?' In order to carry out this investigation, Marg designed the tasks to cumulatively build knowledge of the relationship between house design and the environment and to consider questions around sustainable housing. For example, in the first term, they viewed a teacher-made video and photos of the local area including a range of housing, streets, traffic and so on; experimented with interactive websites of sustainable housing; analysed two aerial photographs of the neighbourhood taken five years apart (which showed empty blocks created by the incomplete urban renewal project); and planned a field trip to study the neighbourhood. The range of 'reading practices' here is significant in its own right. As documented elsewhere (Comber 2016), the approach was to induct students into research practices— observing, noticing, questioning, analysing and reading multiple texts. The teacher's questions which framed this work also indicated the kinds of thinking and discussion Marg sought to provoke. For example, in reviewing the video that Marg had prepared, they discussed:

- What accommodation was available?
- What was the most common housing?
- What is a feature?
- What features are common to all housing?
- What are important features?
- What are decorative features?

These initial questions were designed to build knowledge and a common language. The tasks were designed to gradually have students assemble relevant vocabularies and concepts, such as differences in the incline of roofs in relation to climate and building materials in relation to resources. Later, they would explore more critical questions. There is not the space here to describe all of the moves the teacher made, however, over a term, she worked with the students to build new understandings of neighbourhoods and buildings—to understand that the built environment is constructed and that it could have been made differently and, indeed, that it is in the process of being remade. The students realised that places are put together.

Preparing for, and participating in the field trip was particularly significant. Examining the aerial photos, the students noticed many differences. Marg explained:

I had chosen the area opposite our school as a good place to focus our research. The housing was mostly [Public Housing] maisonettes and many had been knocked down over the last three years with the vacant land being fenced. No new building had happened in this area over the last three years and there was no sign that anything would be starting soon. I obtained an aerial photo of the area in 2010 when it was fully occupied and a more recent aerial photo, two years ago, showing the vacant blocks of land. Students looked at these photos, making comparisons and asking many questions. These questions were discussed and recorded and kept to be dealt with at a later stage, that is, after our local walk when we had gained more knowledge and understanding and when we could decide what to do about these questions. Where would be the best place to get answers to these questions?

We can see here the long-term inquiry approach that underpins this unit of work. The students completed a scaffolded report on the walk and took photographs and made sketches to record particular places of interest, including empty blocks of land. To return now to the question of what this work has to do with 'belonging', we briefly describe several key moves Marg made during the following school term to consider what makes a 'good neighbourhood'. The first involved imagining where they might want to live in the neighbourhood if they could choose. The task (in italics) and Marg's explanation follows. In this work, students began to play with the neighbourhood and dwellings imaginatively.

- *Imagine being able to choose where you could live.* Students used their Field Study booklet notes and maps to locate a vacant block of land that they would like to build a house on for themselves and their family—present day.
- *Imagine what it would be like to live in various places within the boundaries of the area studied and make the decisions.* Students also brought local knowledge to this task. Where do I want to be close to? What local facilities do I use? Where is it safe? What would my family prefer? Are there friends or relatives in this area? The blocks of land (A4 paper box lids) were laid out in a grid on the floor to represent the vacant land in the area of our walk.

When the students had successfully made a case for their preferred block, they were able to 'purchase' it. They took a lid and placed it on the grid. From there, they went on to design their ideal house for their family in a number of media—a floor plan and a design of front and back yards (with labels naming key features). They completed a table listing the important (must have), desirable (might have) and wish list (love to have) features of their imagined houses. Marg then shared the Jeannie Baker book *Belonging* (2004), once again to re-consider the concept of change over time in the built environment. Subsequently, they used the research they had already undertaken to draw three pictures depicting change in the area, focusing on their chosen block of land—what it had looked like six years earlier (maisonettes), now (empty block) and how it could look in the future (their imagined house). Hence, there were multiple opportunities for students to represent their understandings of the changing local neighbourhood. Marg asked them to consider 'how the houses that they were designing and constructing could have a positive influence on the neighbourhood'. At the same time, they pooled the questions which had arisen during their field trip and a group of students wrote a formal letter to the Public Housing authority. The letter included the following questions.

- Why did the houses get knocked down?
- Where did the people go who lived in these houses?
- Why has the land been vacant for so long?
- What are the plans for the blocks of land?
- Are you going to build on the land or sell it?
- Will the houses be for sale or be rental housing?
- What will happen next?
- When will something be built there?

Next, the students used their plans to construct a developed model of their future house. Starting with an empty milk carton, and using paint, cardboard, straws, match sticks, pop sticks, small boxes, paper, tissue, cardboard rolls, modelling clay and assorted junk materials, the students constructed their houses. The students were required to ensure that they had included all features of their plan and had designed a house that would accommodate all family members and pets. They wrote a descriptive piece imagining what a real version of their house would consist of in terms of materials and so on. Marg led them to think about a virtual tour of their house, introducing specific spatial language as needed. Eventually, the completed house models were placed on the neighbourhood grid which, despite the use of the same materials, looked very different. Four final tasks completed the term's work, including imagining living in the new house with their family and imagining living in this new neighbourhood. They considered questions such as those listed below and wrote captions in response to the following prompts (Table 13.1).

Final activities included a whole class discussion concerning the differences between 'houses' and 'homes' and the students then presented their work to the audience of the Primary School Assembly. We have provided a summary of the kinds of work that the students engaged in, albeit with many gaps. Aspects of any of the tasks could have been elaborated in considerably more detail. However, we wanted to give a sense of the scope of the work attempted which went across geography, design and technology, English and other areas of the curriculum. The activities also allowed students opportunities for affective responses, whilst equipping them with a range of new ways of knowing the everyday places that they inhabited.

Critical to the design and the implementation of the unit was that questions of belonging were made material, and a range of criteria were introduced for students to consider belonging in a neighbourhood in terms of sustainability, safety, climate, space and so on. In addition, the students were supported to think about what made a 'good' house, a good home

Table 13.1 Neighbourhood project prompts

Imagining living in the new house	Imagining living in the new neighbourhood
What family members will use what parts of the house and why?	What would it be like to live in this neighbourhood now?
Where would your bedroom be and why? Other family members?	How has it improved?
Who uses the garage (for example)? How? Why?	What has changed?
Who uses different parts of the yard? How? Why?	What do you like about it now?

and a 'good' neighbourhood. So, students necessarily thought about built environments as relational places where different people used spaces within houses and suburbs in different ways and where relationships are important to practices of inclusion. Ultimately, once all of the individual homes were combined in a large student designed and produced neighbourhood model, there was visible evidence of their learning and engagement in the curriculum over time, as individuals and as a class group.

Conclusions

Marg's interpretations of our shared *Imagination Project* drew on years of complex knowledge-building as a teacher-researcher, drawing on critical literacy, place-conscious pedagogies and critical multiliteracies. Marg and her students learned respect for each other and for themselves through the teaching/learning activities; this became the foundation of all that they did as they actively negotiated how each would belong within the teaching and learning in which they engaged. Marg took real joy in fostering the interests, needs and collective achievements of the children with whom she worked. The *Imagination Project* proved to be the latest vehicle for focusing her approach to both curriculum and pedagogy to ensure innovative, complex ways of learning and representational practices were made available within the classroom space. She respected the individuals but also knew that having the opportunity to work collectively and to learn from peers was vital. By studying the neighbourhood together, the teacher and students embarked literally on a shared learning journey as they learned to see what they may have previously taken for granted with new eyes and re-named it with expanded vocabularies and, at the same time, played together in reimagining their ideal dwellings and neighbourhoods. In this classroom, being thrown together, in Massey's terms, became a resource for negotiating something new, even as they learned to be together. Children typically worked together in pairs or threes, sometimes in bigger groupings. Even when completing tasks alone, there was a sense of collective endeavour, a bigger class-made project, to which their products and processes would contribute. Learning about the neighbourhood is undertaken as a collective discovery with many inquiries and iterations of observation and research accomplished together over an extended time. These opportunities for shared meaning-making and representation became part of the classroom memory and points of reference and increased the likelihood that all children could contribute from their own perspectives. In this classroom, learning is not a solitary pursuit!

Like Marg, other teachers involved in the *Imagination Project* designed and negotiated curriculum and pedagogy that fostered significant participation for students to accomplish something new together. Each teacher and their students took different approaches, highlighting the importance of locally designed, negotiated curriculum that respects the diversity of children. Not all children are the same, so the logics of standardising what all children experience within their classrooms is difficult to justify and short-changes children. While we are convinced this approach makes a long-term difference to the participants, only longitudinal and in-depth case studies would provide the kinds of evidence policy-makers value right now. However, the student-produced artefacts, products and events clearly indicated the quality of their participation and understandings. The fact that, years later, many of these young people return to visit Marg and her colleagues is testament to its significance in their lives and reflects the investment we have observed in their intense involvement and commitment in the learning activities at the time. Importantly, such artefacts and events often represented a collective accomplishment, rather than the individualised literacy products and performances associated with testing. Documenting such pedagogies, and the take-up by students, in the face of generational change in the teaching profession is crucial for keeping our collective educational imaginations alive. Pedagogies of belonging bring content, activities and social interactions into coherent tasks which build both a sense of positive learner identity and collective classroom learning identity (Comber 2016).

The contemporary education context is problematic for socially just education and we know that, when education systems fail to provide high quality and high equity curriculum, the effects are most dramatic for those students already disadvantaged through their social positioning—for example, those children who are growing up in communities of high poverty. We have argued that this is particularly important in literacy education because of our understandings of the importance of learning

literacy as a collective practice. Marg's approach to teaching in a culturally diverse community of high poverty provided a re-envisioned model
of quality planning, teaching and assessment to improve learning outcomes for *all* students. The example detailed in this chapter provides evidence that, when it is foregrounded, social justice creates spaces of
belonging in classrooms where high learning expectations are held for all
without defaulting to solutions that ignore the diversity of teachers, children and communities. While we acknowledge that there is a great deal
of pressure to narrow curriculum and to standardise our teaching
responses, we firmly believe that there are still spaces for working in other
ways. Locally configured and place-conscious education, where teachers
and students imagine explicit places of belonging, are still possible.
Activist approaches, such as those described here, can ensure all students
develop a sense of belonging and recognition in classrooms that enables
them to participate and to assemble ways of representing themselves and
developing collective agency that counts.

> We cannot remake the world through schooling but we can instantiate a
> vision through pedagogy that creates in microcosm a transformed set of
> relationships and possibilities for social futures; a vision that is lived in
> schools. (Cope and Kalantzis 2000, p. 19)

We agree. In this chapter, we have described how one teacher worked
in a community, with her students, to transform not only how the classroom space might become one of negotiation but also a space where
children might find a place of belonging in which they could reimagine
their present and future worlds. We have focused on what was done in
the curriculum and pedagogy to achieve a just space of belonging for all
within the classroom space. This is important as it helps us to move
beyond an individual, personal notion of belonging and what it means to
belong in a place to reconstitute belonging practices as relational and as
accomplished through everyday interactions between people in particular
places. A focus on place and local relevance can foreground the integral,
but sometimes invisible, relationship between 'belonging' and learning.
A focus on place and what is going on in the neighbourhood repositions
the 'classroom' as a site of participation and negotiation in shared research.

It makes sense to make place the object of study in schools and classrooms because participants have no choice but to be there. However, their experience of 'being there' and feeling as though they can belong there, that they are included and have agency, is contingent upon the relationships they can accomplish therein. In classrooms of increased diversity, demystifying this complex social work can in part be done by making place curricular. Given increasingly unpredictable global instability, negotiating classrooms where children learn to learn about, and with, each other and to learn together is urgent work towards a better world, where people's equal rights to belong is the most important lesson.

Acknowledgments We wish to acknowledge the work of Marg, Helen, Brendan and Ruth who worked with us on this project, and the children and young people who meet with them in classroom spaces. Their insights are ever challenging and work to insist on our rearticulation of thoughts and theories based on their rigorous and contextualised version of 'evidence-based' practice. Special thanks to Marg and her students for allowing us access to decisions made and lessons learnt as they reimagined their work together.

References

Antonsich, M. (2010). Searching for belonging – An analytic framework. *Geography Compass, 4*(6), 644–659.

Baker, J. (2004). *Belonging*. London: Walker Books.

Blommaert, J. (2013). Citizenship, language, and superdiversity: Towards complexity. *Journal of Language, Identity & Education, 12*(3), 193–196. https://doi.org/10.1080/15348458.2013.797276.

Comber, B. (2013). Schools as meeting places: Critical and inclusive literacies in changing school environments. *Language Arts, 90*(5), 361–371.

Comber, B. (2015). School literate repertoires: That was then, this is now. In J. Rowsell & J. Sefton-Green (Eds.), *Revisiting learning lives – Longitudinal perspectives on researching learning and literacy* (pp. 16–31). London and New York: Routledge.

Comber, B. (2016). *Literacy, place and pedagogies of possibility*. New York and London: Routledge.

Comber, B., & Kerkham, L. (2016). Gus: I cannot write anything. Case Study in Chapter 2, A. H. Dyson (Ed.), *Child cultures, schooling and literacy: Global perspectives on children composing their lives* (pp. 53–64). New York and London: Routledge.

Comber, B., & Woods, A. (2016). Literacy teacher research in high poverty schools: Why it matters. In J. Lampert & B. Burnett (Eds.), *Teacher education for high poverty schools* (pp. 193–201). New York: Springer.

Comber, B., Thompson, P., & Wells, M. (2001). Critical literacy finds a place: Writing and social action in a low-income Australian 2/3 classroom. *The Elementary School Journal, 101*(4), 451–464.

Comber, B., Woods, A., & Grant, H. (2017). Literacy and imagination: Finding space in a crowded curriculum. *The Reading Teacher, 71*(1), 115–120.

Compton-Lilly, C. (2011). Literacy and schooling in one family across time. *Research in the Teaching of English, 45*(3), 224–251.

Compton-Lilly, C. (2016, in press). *Reading trajectories: Literacy learning across a decade in an urban community.* New York: Routledge.

Cope, B., & Kalantzis, M. (Eds.). (2000). *Multiliteracies: Literacy learning and the design of social futures.* Melbourne: Macmillan.

Dorling, D. (2016). *A better politics: How government can make us happier.* London: London Publishing Partnership.

Fraser, N. (2003). Social justice in the age of identity politics redistribution, recognition and participation. In N. Fraser & A. Honneth (Eds.), *Redistribution or recognition? A political-philosophical exchange* (pp. 7–109). New York: Verso.

Fraser, N. (2009). *Scales of justice: Reimagining political space in a globalizing world.* New York: Columbia University Press.

Fraser, N. (2014). *Transnationalizing the public sphere.* Cambridge: Polity.

Griffith, A., & Smith, D. E. (2014). *New public management: Institutional ethnographies of changing front-line work.* Toronto: University of Toronto Press.

Kalantzis, M., & Cope, B. (2008). *New learning: Elements of a science of learning.* Cambridge: Cambridge University Press.

Massey, D. (2005). *For space.* London: Sage.

New London Group. (1996). A pedagogy of multiliteracies: Designing social futures. *Harvard Educational Review, 66*(1), 60–92.

Pugh, A. (2009). *Longing and belonging: Parents, children, and consumer culture.* Berkeley: University of California Press.

Rogers, R. (2011). The sounds of silence in educational tracking: A longitudinal, ethnographic case study. *Critical Discourse Studies, 8*(4), 239–252.

Rogers, R., & Wetzel, M. M. (2013). Studying agency in literacy teacher education: A layered approach to positive discourse analysis. *Critical Inquiry in Language Studies, 10*(1), 62–92.

Wells, M., & Trimboli, R. (2014). Place-conscious literacy pedagogies. In A. Morgan, B. Comber, H. Nixon, et al. (Eds.), *Literacy in the middle years: Learning from classroom design experiments* (pp. 15–34). Newtown, NSW: Primary English Teaching Association Australia.

Woods, A., & Henderson, R. (2008). The early intervention solution: Enabling or constraining literacy learning. *Journal of Early Childhood Literacy, 8*(3), 268–276.

Woods, A., Dooley, K., Luke, A., & Exley, B. (2014). School leadership, literacy and social justice: The place of local school curriculum planning and reform. In I. Bogotch & C. Shields (Eds.), *International handbook of school leadership and social (in)justice* (pp. 509–520). New York: Springer Publishing.

Wortham, S. (2006). *Learning identity: The joint emergence of social identification and academic learning.* Cambridge and New York: Cambridge University Press.

Yuval-Davis, N. (2006). Belonging and the politics of belonging. *Patterns of Prejudice, 40*(3), 197–214.

Yuval-Davis, N. (2011a). *The politics of belonging: Intersectional contestations.* Thousand Oaks: Sage.

Yuval-Davis, N. (2011b). Beyond the recognition and re-distribution dichotomy: Intersectionality and stratification. In H. Lutz, V. Herrera, & L. Supik (Eds.), *Framing intersectionality. Debates on a multi-facetted concept in gender studies* (pp. 159–169). Farnham: Ashgate.

14

'The battle in belonging': Pedagogies, Practice and Hypermasculinity in Boys' Physical Education

Amanda Mooney and Chris Hickey

Introduction

Over ten years ago, Wayne Martino and Maria Pallotta-Chiarolli (2005, p. x) concluded, from their work with Australian adolescents in schools, that 'being normal is the only way to be'. Through the writings of their participants, these authors constructed 'specific knowledge about what it means to be a boy and a girl at school, what it means to be "cool" and "normal", and the effect of these social constructions on learning and relationships' (p. xi). This work suggests that dominant gendered narratives of specific school sites (places) were central in shaping identities and students' feelings of belonging. Inherent in individual aspirations to be 'normal' is a circumscribed, normative identity position, that is, a position from which individuals judge whether they are 'normal' or not. It is this judgement that becomes important in considering the place-based

A. Mooney (✉) • C. Hickey
Deakin University, Geelong, VIC, Australia
e-mail: amanda.mooney@deakin.edu.au; chris.hickey@deakin.edu.au

© The Author(s) 2018   **283**
C. Halse (ed.), *Interrogating Belonging for Young People in Schools*,
https://doi.org/10.1007/978-3-319-75217-4_14

and affective dimensions of belonging—why is being normal desirable, and how, when and where is this achieved?

Marco Antonsich (2010) argues that belonging to groups, cultures and places can be considered an 'inescapable condition of humanity' (p. 651), a sentiment that appears resonant for Martino and Pallotta-Chiarolli's (2005) participants. As others have observed, 'belonging itself is often considered self-explanatory' (Wright 2015, p. 391) and is frequently used 'as a synonym of identity' (Antonsich 2010, p. 644), but, as both these authors point out, it is a term that is far more ambiguous and almost always is prefaced with reference to space, place or practice.

Despite a growing body of work that explores belonging and specific theoretical constructs useful for making sense of this term (Yuval-Davis 2006, 2011), we still lack nuanced accounts of the ways in which place, practices and affective dimensions of schooling coalesce to produce normative identities with 'bounded meanings within and beyond schools' (Youdell 2010, p. 8). Further, there is a scarcity of literature that makes visible the politics of belonging (Yuval-Davis 2006) or, in John Crowley's (1999) words, 'the dirty work of boundary maintenance' that demarcates 'us' and 'them' (30).

In response, this chapter offers a micro-level analysis of the ways in which particular pedagogies privilege and cultivate hypermasculine identities that affect the belonging/non-belonging of young males and their female teacher in an all-boys' Physical Education (PE) class. Specifically, we discuss a pedagogic encounter of 'battle-ball' (also known as 'war ball', 'bombardment' and 'dodge ball') to illustrate the ways in which dominant gendered narratives are (re)produced in a particular place by specific practices and consider the implications of this in creating a sense of belonging for two specific participants: the female teacher (Rachel) and one of the students (Sebastian). This is because pedagogies of belonging/non-belonging are constructed and experienced by both teachers and students and the geographical and socio-spatial contexts in which these are enacted. After Richard Tinning (2010), we understand pedagogy as 'concerned with processes of knowledge (re)production and … of values, attitudes, dispositions, subjectivities and identities' (p. 17) but that pedagogical work involves both the intended and unintended consequence of pedagogy. As Tinning (2010) cautions, 'the pedagogical work done may not be that which was intended' (p. 18). Our discussion of the experiences and performances of belonging and non-belonging for Rachel and her student, Sebastian, we propose, illustrate these dynamics at work.

For the uninitiated, battle-ball is a game that regularly features in the everyday practices of PE in many schools. It involves two teams at opposite sides of a court and a 'battle' involving the throwing of balls at the opposing team with the intent of hitting and, thereby, eliminating players. The ultimate goal of battle-ball is to eliminate all players on the opposing team and then knock down the team's battlements defended, usually, by a last remaining player. In this chapter, we analyse the minutiae of this common practice in boys' PE to make visible the ways that pedagogies are implicated in framing and constraining 'who' both a female teacher and student 'can be' (following Youdell 2010), and how these operate as significant practices of 'belonging'. Conversely, matters of 'who' a student or teacher might be also involves questions of who they cannot be in a particular time and context. As Sarah Wright (2015) argues, 'the opposite of belonging may be exclusion; it may also be isolation, alienation, loneliness, dis-placement, uprootedness, disconnection, dis-enfranchisement or marginalisation' (p. 395). Consequently, our analysis of the pedagogies of belonging also attend to the nuanced ways in which the operation of place, cultural practices and specific pedagogies produce experiences of non-belonging.

Theoretical Background

Theories of Belonging

In this chapter, we draw particularly on theoretical work on belonging by Nira Yuval-Davis (2006, 2011), Wright (2015) and Antonsich (2010). It is the politics of belonging (Yuval-Davis 2011) that make it possible for individuals to belong/not belong even though 'people can "belong" [or not belong] in many different ways' (Yuval-Davis 2011, p. 12). Yuval-Davis' analytic frame for exploring the ways in which belonging is constructed comprises three intersecting 'facets' or strands. These are: the *social locations* and the positions that individuals and groups occupy within social groupings and through which identity markers and power relations are constructed; the *emotional attachments* individuals have to specific collectivities or groups; and the *ethical and political values* people draw upon to make judgements about who does or does not belong. In contrast, Eva Youkhana (2015) attends to the operation of the politics of belonging at a personal level. She argues that the experience of belonging and not belonging can range from 'a personal feeling, the sense of belonging to a certain group, place, or social location, to the understanding of belonging as a resource that can be used to draw social demarcations' (p. 11). For Wright (2015), this means that 'belonging resonates in people's lives in their practices of knowing, being and making sense of their world' (p. 404) but involves taking into account issues of feelings or affect in order to theorise belonging in a way that 'does not shut down its contradictions, its inconsistencies' (ibid., p. 392). Thus, Wright (2015) calls for approaches that interrogate 'the texture of how it is felt, used, practised and lived' (ibid., p. 392):

> Attending to belonging as an affective act tends to draw attention to the everyday, to the ways belonging is experienced, performed and practised … [this] avoids any need to solve the riddle of what it means to belong and instead focuses on the multiple ways that belonging is enacted. Such approaches emphasise the active and ongoing ways people behave to make their own place in the world. (Wright 2015, p. 400)

Yet, in considering the multiple ways that belonging is enacted in the context of an all-boys' PE lesson, a broader focus is required. Such an examination also calls for a focus on *place* as a socio-spatial concept, on the ways that pedagogical *practices* legitimate identities that belong or do not belong in this social place of the PE class, and on the *emotional attachments* individuals have to the activity, class and broader school context.

Extending the work of Yuval-Davis (2006), Antonsich (2010) offers an analytic framework for theorising belonging that considers both performances in spaces and places, and their affective dimensions. Specifically, Antonsich (2010) suggests that two key analytical dimensions need to be considered: 'belonging as a personal, intimate, feeling of being "at home" in a place (place-belongingness) and belonging as a discursive resource which constructs, claims, justifies, or resists forms of socio-spatial inclusion/exclusion (politics of belonging)' (Antonsich 2010, p. 645). The first dimension, *place-belongingness*, refers to the places that someone can feel 'at home', not in the 'domestic(ated) material space ... [but] a symbolic space of familiarity, comfort, security and emotional attachment' (ibid., p. 646). Auto-biographical, relational and cultural factors, amongst others, are central in generating a sense of place-belongingness. The second dimension positions belonging as not just a personal concern, but also a social one: feelings of belonging can be inhibited if one does not feel welcome in a particular place or space:

> one's personal, intimate feeling of belonging to a place should always come to terms with discourses and practices of socio-spatial inclusion/exclusion at play in that very place and which inexorably conditions one's sense of place-belongingness. (Antonsich 2010, p. 648)

Collectively, these contributions from Yuval-Davis, Wright and Antonsich provide theoretical tools to interrogate the ways in which pedagogies are mobilised in discursively constructed ways to impact the experiences of belonging and not belonging for students and teachers in the context of an all-boys' PE lesson.

Masculinities, Identity Practices and Belonging in Physical Education

Historically, boys' PE and sport strongly feature as places where identity processes are intensified (Atkinson and Kehler 2012; Hickey 2010; Pringle and Hickey 2010) and can be a 'site of ritual masculinising practices through which boys learn, embrace and embody, or are damaged by particular codes of dominant masculinity' (Atkinson and Kehler 2012, p. 166). Notwithstanding the gendered construction of various sporting sites such as the football field, boxing ring and change/locker room as 'male bastions' (Messner 2005), the cultural practices associated with hypermasculine performances of excessive or problematic displays of stoicism, aggression, violence and competition in sport privilege the skilled and brave, whilst marginalising and excluding others. We consider masculine subjectivities as discursive constructions that intersect with other vectors of identity, such as class, race, ethnicity, sexuality and religion amongst others (Hopkins and Noble 2009). Building on the seminal work of Bob Connell's (1995) *multiple masculinities* in schools and Jane Kenway, Anna Kraack and Anna Hickey-Moody's (2006) *shades of masculinity* in their analyses of the different pleasure pursuits of young rural males, this chapter focuses on *relational masculinities* to add to understandings of the ways in which gendered identities/subjectivities are constructed in specific places.

Conceiving of gendered identities/subjectivities in this way has implications for the theorising of belonging in the context of boys' PE, particularly in Western cultures where privileged (hyper) masculinities are often constructed as 'us', and marginalised (effeminate) masculinities construed as 'them'. Thus, the belonging/non-belonging of individual boys and their teachers are invariably based on a perception by self and/or others of one's alignment to these identity positions. Therefore, 'which identity they "take-up" will dramatically affect their relationships with other students and shape the opportunities, rewards and recognition they enjoy [or not]' (Reichert et al. 2012, p. 56).

Compounding these dynamics is a wide range of mainstream social practices that actively reinforce dominant gender politics and perpetuate identity positions of privilege and marginalisation, particularly in the context of an all-boys' school. Pedagogies and performances of various identity positions with respect to gender, ability and sexuality amongst others are important foci in any analysis of belonging/non-belonging in the context of boys' PE with a female teacher. As Wright (2015) stresses, 'performance thus has the capacity to bring structural, personal/affective and collaborative aspects of belonging together' (p. 400). Performances of belonging/not-belonging are socially constructed within particular places and, therefore, influenced by the dominant discourses and power relations that permeate these contexts. That said, belonging/non-belonging is not fixed and stable but rather dynamic; it can and does change over time and often from moment to moment. Thus, as Antonsich (2010) contends, belonging can be increasingly thought about as a *process* (becoming) rather than as a *status* (being). In our analyses of the following pedagogic encounter, we explore and illustrate some of the ways in which pedagogical practices are implicated in the *processes* of belonging and non-belonging.

Methodology

The data reported here came from a larger ethnographic case study that explored the work of female teachers in one, Australian, all-boys' secondary school, particularly in the context of PE. In this chapter, we analyse data collected from the observations of, and follow up interviews with, a Year 8 basketball class where battle-ball was featured as the warm-up game. Data comprised field note observations; a video-stimulated reflection interview with the female teacher, Rachel; focus group interviews with eight of her students; and individual, semi-structured interviews with four students who had participated in the focus group interviews.

The data are collectively presented as a vignette of a 'pedagogic encounter'. A pedagogic encounter traces the ways in which students and their teacher come into being in multiple ways in their encounters with each other, their transformations through these encounters and in the places and spaces in which these encounters are enacted (Davies and Gannon 2009). Using the lens of a pedagogic encounter, our analyses centre on the experiences of one female teacher, Rachel, and one of her students, Sebastian. Specifically, we illustrate the ways in which concepts of identity, belonging/non-belonging and the politics and pedagogies that perpetuated these perceptions are constructed. In short, our goal is to illustrate how 'an emphasis on the doing of belonging [or not belonging] brings attention to the ways belonging is nurtured and performed in different contexts' (Wright 2015, p. 400).

The use of the interview data, as woven into the vignette, is an important dimension through which to explore the affective aspects of belonging. As Yuval-Davis (2011) points out, identities are told through people's narratives. A focus on what participants say about who they are and how they feel in this *place* and the *practices* they engage with provides insight into their conceptions of *place-belongingness*. However, in presenting these data we offer a caveat. Although individuals may feel confident and coherent in their understanding of self, as Anthony Giddens (1991) cautions, 'on the other side of what might appear to be quite trivial aspects of day-to-day action and discourse, chaos lurks' (p. 36). Richard Pringle and Chris Hickey (2010) interpret this chaos as a recognition that our identities are not grounded in essentialised bodies. Rather, they are formed through social constructions and power relations that are changeable, the fragility of which can be illustrated in social experiences that differ from one day to the next, or from one lesson to the next. This view has implications for how belonging/not-belonging is constructed and operates because our analysis and interpretations centre on one pedagogical moment: the experiences of belonging/not-belonging here are neither fixed, enduring nor illustrative of belonging/non-belonging outside of this moment or socio-spatial context.

Battle-Ball as a Pedagogic Encounter

Rachel has been at the school for six weeks and describes her Year 8 PE class as 'generally pretty good, there are a few rowdy boys in there but, well they're just 14 and full of testosterone'. The class begins with the routine changing room experience where the boys change for class whilst Rachel waits outside the door. If she needs to intervene for some reason, she 'just blows her whistle and enters after the designated three seconds'. Rachel starts her class by asking the boys to 'sit on the three-point basketball line' to form a semi-circle and make sure they face away from the other class congregating at the other end of the gym. She introduces the lesson on basketball by explaining that they will play a warm-up game that uses the skills of throwing and catching. One boy yells out, 'battle-ball'? Before Rachel can even answer, what appears to be her entire class break out in what can be likened to a war-cry, 'bat-tle-ball, bat-tle-ball'. Rachel responds, 'I don't even know what that is'. Before anyone could answer her, the other class at the end of the gym join in the chant. Amidst all the noise and fluster as Rachel attempts to regain some semblance of control of her class, Mr W (the teacher of the other class) saunters into the gym bouncing a basketball and asks, with effect, 'who is ready to 'bat-tle'? Mr W dribbles the ball towards the hoop and effortlessly slam-dunks the ball before addressing his class. What Rachel wouldn't give to be 200cm tall at this moment and able to do that! 'Well, who's ready to go?' asks Mr W, from the sidelines. I observe Mr W approach Rachel and ask if she wants to join his class for a warm up game of 'battle-ball'. She indicates that she doesn't really know what the game is, but agrees. Cheers erupts from around the gym.

The game commences with Rachel's class at one end of the gym and Mr W's class at the other. The basketball court is divided into thirds, the third in which each class commences is 'their' zone but the middle third is a 'free zone' that any team member can occupy. At the end of each team zone are three 'battlements', cones balanced on one another precariously that need to be knocked down in order to win. Mr W signals the start of the game by throwing three foam-filled balls into the middle zone. Immediately, students from both teams run into the middle zone as fast as they can to get the balls and take aim at an opponent. As Matt explains later, 'everyone loves this game, it is competitive but it is also a team game ... like even the ones that aren't that good at it, you could make them captain I suppose, if you participate you will get better ... I mean there is nothing better than hitting someone full pelt when they don't expect it'. Jimmy explains, 'basically when the game starts, the good kids would always target the bad kids, they'd aim for those not so good at sport and you would always see these kids hiding down the back, but that is still OK because someone has to protect the cones [battlements]'. From the sidelines, I notice Rachel's unease with the game. When I talk with her later she explains, 'safety's pretty important in PE, I mean anytime kids are trying to kill each other [sic] it seems a bit wrong ... When they asked for the game I had no idea what it was but they all seemed to know it, and Mr W seemed to support it. Then I thought, well it is using throwing and catching skills so I suppose it will be OK, but I didn't really like feeling like I hadn't any idea what was going on'.

The objective of the game is to throw the ball and hit members of the opposing team to eliminate them from the game. If the 'attacking' throw is caught by a 'defender', he continues in the game whilst the attacker is eliminated and the player who caught the ball is entitled to bring a previously eliminated player back into the game. As more players are eliminated there are less players left to protect the battlements on the baseline. This is important because, in order to win, a team must knock down their opponent's battlements.

Sebastian, describes himself as 'wanting to be involved in everything' but explains that, outside school, he is 'involved in performing arts, you know *dancing, singing and acting, that kind of thing, I'm not sure if you classify them as sport'. Sebastian is not particularly skilled in Physical Education and Sport and, in this game, appeared to nominate himself for the job of 'battlement protector'. Observing him from the sideline, he seemed enthusiastic and regularly shouted support for his teammates, as he explained later, 'I find team games more enjoyable, I'm not the best at PE in my class and I just find I can be better with people than by myself'. Sebastian says that he used to play football but he didn't really enjoy it, it was too rough, but he felt that 'battleball' was a good alternative because people of all abilities could be involved. He commented, 'I actually loved it, I wasn't chosen last which normally happens, I got to play the whole time and was still there at the end, it was awesome. For once PE was really fun'.*

As the game progresses, Rachel comments to me that 'they all seem to love this game which is absurd, look at how many of them are sitting out'. As the numbers dwindle, Sebastian becomes an integral game player given that, until this point, he has evaded much of the 'action' and is still 'in'. The noise of boys' excited 'encouragement' and 'cheering' is deafening, but as Rachel commented later, 'I don't think it is good when they are all ribbing Sebastian by saying, 'C'mon Sebastian, get the ball and belt 'em, you're not a girl'. With multiple balls in play, it is often a contentious decision to leave the battlement and attempt to retrieve a free ball because one of the other balls could be used to 'hit' the battlement or eliminate the player retrieving the free ball. For this reason, Sebastian seemed conflicted, should he leave the battlements unprotected to get the ball that was free and in his half of the gym (there were very few players on his team left) or should he leave it to someone else? Sebastian looks around much in the way that a deer in a headlight might, but the chants from his peers is overwhelming, 'You can do it Sebastian, take them bastards'! As he cautiously heads towards the free ball, two members of the opposing team, both with balls in their hand, march towards him—the first throw goes astray and also misses the unprotected battlements. The second ball lands square on his chest and, miraculously, he manages to close his arms around the ball and catch it 'on the full'. This act earns him cheers from around the gym—Sebastian can now nominate a team member to return to the game. He picks the most skilled student from his class who is instrumental in not only eliminating the remaining players from the opposing team but in knocking down the battlements! The noise from his teammates leave little doubt about the team that had 'won' the battle. Sebastian comments later, 'it was so good, normally they encourage me to just, well try a bit harder and that kind of thing, but this time they were all saying 'Go Sebastian', it was kind of weird but I liked it, but don't get me wrong, I don't care if I'm not that good at PE, there are other kids that are good at Maths and things ... I don't want to be that sort of boy anyway, that over-competitiveness isn't healthy'.

In a conversation with Rachel later, where we watched segments of the lesson back via a video-recording, she confided, 'it is really hard, the kids well they seem to like being connected to a boys' school, in fact most of them love it! I've only been here six weeks, I wasn't that bothered with the lesson, but that wasn't really what I had planned for the warm up, I guess when you have been here for as long as Mr W you just have a way that the students know. I am sure with time I'll get to know all the 'in' games'.

Discursive Constructions of Belonging in a Boys' Physical Education Class

The above pedagogic encounter characterises an incidental moment in the everyday pedagogical practices of an all-boys' PE class. What might be considered incidental to many is actually a site of profound influence on the female teacher and one of her students, Sebastian. The ubiquitous nature of the term 'belonging' suggests that the way in which it is taken up, experienced, resisted, negotiated and felt can vary across individuals and contexts. Our discussion of Rachel's and Sebastian's experiences and performances of belonging and non-belonging illustrate this phenomenon.

Rachel: Constructions of Non-belonging as a 'Gendered' Teacher

The vignette of the pedagogic encounter (above) commences with a discussion of the practices associated with the start of the class. While these may appear mundane, when viewed through the lens of belonging, they illuminate the ways that pedagogic work operates to position some individuals within the dominant and normative identity positions in this particular 'place' while simultaneously rendering others outside of it. For Rachel, as a female PE teacher in an all-boys' school, the pedagogic work that precedes the lesson provides powerful contributors and constant reminders that she is considered 'other' in the socio-spatial context of the boys' changing room. An important element here is the work of the institutional policies and regulations of the school that mobilise or constrain belonging (see Wright 2015). There are very few female PE teachers in the school and the policy of the school's PE Department dictates that Rachel must wait outside the change-room while the boys change into their PE uniform. If an incident arises or there is a need for Rachel to enter the change-rooms, she needs to blow her whistle to indicate she intends to enter and wait three seconds before actually going in to give students an opportunity to 'cover up'. Whilst we acknowledge that the instigation of this policy is inherently bound to (perceived) risk-management protocols and procedures, this policy does not extend to Rachel's male counterparts. Rather, it works to exclude Rachel from this 'male bastion' (Messner, 2005) and thereby does pedagogical work that influences her sense of belonging in two ways. It challenges both her official status *of being* the teacher and her personal sense of belonging as a teacher *with* status because it curtails her autonomy, capacity for professional decision-making and action, and her power relative to her male teacher counterparts.

Returning to the vignette, the move from the change-rooms to the gym and the commencement of the formal instructional part of the lesson further challenges Rachel's sense of belonging, and underlines the role of 'place-belongingness' (Antonsich 2010). As an analytic frame, Antonsich's (2010) notion of place-belongingness connects the emotional with the experiential or, as he puts it, belonging as an emotional feeling towards, and experience in, places. This thinking extends previous theoretical work on belonging by underlining that experiences of belonging in social places do not exist in a geographic vacuum (Antonsich 2010). Specifically, belonging as a sense of feeling 'at home' generates emotional attachments that are very much grounded in a place, and that the discourses, power relations and taken-for-granted norms that germinate in and circulate throughout places contribute to how one might feel in a particular place—their *place-belongingness* (Antonsich 2010). Rachel, as the teacher and deliverer of pedagogy, is theoretically positioned within power relations that should facilitate some sense of authority and power that enables her to be 'at home' in front of the class. Yet, teachers and students filter their experiences through different personal and professional lenses and construct and take away particular and different meanings, learnings and understandings from their pedagogical experiences (Halse 2004). The change-room procedure described above privileges males so that, for a female teacher new to the classroom, 'place' here is not imbued with an immediate sense of belonging or 'feeling at home'.

Despite these structural and institutional constraints, Rachel endeavours to draw on pedagogical approaches that will reassert her authority, control and work in this particular teaching context. She seeks to minimise the potential distractions caused by sharing this geographic space—the gym—with another class by instructing her class to 'sit on the three-point basketball line facing away from the other class'. This assertiveness might seduce observers into thinking that, once Rachel has moved beyond the change-room, her 'otherness' is rendered insignificant because she becomes 'the teacher' who takes up the sense of place and belonging that many teachers experience when they are in front of a class. Yet, the managerial pedagogies typical of newly socialised teachers (Tinning 2010) create a false sense of 'control' and 'order' that is undone, as quickly as it is established, by the cry from one of the students of 'battle-ball'.

Antonsich (2010) argues that one's past history and autobiographical experiences are key factors that contribute to generating a sense of belonging. For Rachel, battle-ball is a game she has not encountered before. Consequently, the student's cry immediately marks her pedagogical content knowledge as deficient and renders her incapable of responding or acting from a position of expertise, control, authority and belonging in this pedagogical encounter between student and teacher.

It is through such 'relational factors' that 'the personal and social ties that enrich the life of an individual in a given place' (Antonsich 2010, p. 647) are either constructed or undermined. For Rachel, her unfamiliarity and inexperience with battle-ball not only unsettles her planned approach for the lesson but also contributes to a sense of non-belonging. This status is reinforced by the cultural factors (Antonsich, 2010) at play in this pedagogical encounter. Here language is paramount because 'language stands for a particular way of constructing and conveying meaning, a certain way of interpreting and defining situations ... which can also take the form of tacit codes, signs, and gestures, not actually uttered, yet still understood by those who share the same semiotic universe' (p. 648). The fact that Rachel has no notion of the 'language' of this game further works to marginalise her and reinforce her sense of non-belonging. Sensing her vulnerability, her students immediately pick up on and reinforce her non-belonging by chanting in unison to play battle-ball.

If we return momentarily to the notion of performance, the actions of the male PE teacher, Mr W, are also significant here. Through his everyday practice of sauntering into the gym, slam-dunking a basketball, and his acquiescence to the students' war-cry chant for a game of battle-ball, he wittingly or unwittingly participates in what Crowley (1999) describes as the 'dirty work of boundary maintenance'. As a tall, physically skilled, male teacher, Mr W possesses the physical competence and attributes that align him with dominant and privileged masculinities so often celebrated in masculine sporting contexts. Further, Mr W's personal history has relevance to understanding his belongingness in this particular pedagogical space. His autobiography as a former student of this school is replete with experiences, relations and memories (Antonsich 2010) of the privilege associated with being a celebrated male athlete. In short, his autobiographical factors significantly contribute to a sense of place-belongingness for him in this school context.

Further, as someone who has been a teacher in the school for a number of years and gained the degree of comfortability Mr W appears to have in this place, it is plausible to assume that relational factors are also significant here. Antonsich (2010) explains that not all relations matter in the same way but, important to generating a sense of belonging, relations should be 'long-lasting, positive, stable and significant ... [and] they should "take place" through frequent physical interaction' (Antonsich 2010, p. 647). These factors are integral to Mr W's biography and identity. His history assigns him a position as an 'insider' thereby affording him opportunities to develop expertise in using verbal, non-verbal and tacit language that consolidates his cultural locatedness and pedagogical work that position him as belonging in this particular space of the classroom and school. Thus, his actions operate within the 'politics of belonging' by demarcating boundaries that position some boys and himself as 'us' and those who are not skilled or excited by the prospect of a game of battle-ball as 'them', as in the case for Rachel and Sebastian. Further, through the process of his intervention, Mr W reinforces the power relations that privilege his identity position as the teacher who is 'in charge' and also as the authoritative male, through his public demonstration of the 'slam-dunk' that emphasise his height and physical skill. In highlighting the exclusionary nature of this pedagogic work, we also can observe the way in which these actions promote attachments to and a sense of belonging for others. As Antonsich (2010) claims, there is also the potential to 'evoke a sense of community, the "warm sensation" to be among people who not only merely understand what you say, but also what you mean' (Antonsich 2010, p. 648). This goes some way to accounting for the ways in which the boys' responded both to Mr W's entrance into the gym, and his instigation of the battle-ball warm-up game.

Sebastian: Belonging as Happenstance

In this section, we contrast Sebastian's experience of this pedagogical encounter with that of Rachel described above. We do this to illustrate the various ways that pedagogies can also create moments of belonging in quite serendipitous, happenstance ways. As a caveat, we are not advocating the strengths of these pedagogical approaches but merely, after Yuval-Davis (2006), drawing on them to illustrate the ways in which the boundaries that demarcate 'us' and 'them' are permeable. We highlight that these boundaries are not fixed and stable but, rather, fluid and dynamic and the focus is on the pedagogic conditions that facilitated this boundary-crossing.

Antonsich's (2010) concept of 'place-belongingness' is a helpful starting point. Sebastian's autobiographical experiences as someone not particularly skilled in the physical pursuits of sport and games contribute to a history of non-belonging in the context of a boys' PE class. Discursive constructions of gendered activities also contribute here. Hypermasculine discourses legitimate games like battle-ball yet, at the same time, marginalise activities constructed as feminine in the context of an all-boys' school, such as performing arts. These gendered discourses perpetuate power relations that position those who are physically skilled and fearless as privileged and those who do not, or cannot, engage on this level as marginalised. As others have pointed out, there is a 'very fine line between narratives of bravery, valor, devotion to a cause and unquestioning loyalty … that represent many of the grand myths of … sporting achievements, compared to the abusive and damaging behaviour that often characterise the culture of masculinist entitlement associated with sport (Fitzclarence et al. 2007, p. 129).

Others have highlighted the negative experiences of marginalised boys in PE and sport settings (Campbell et al. 2016; Hickey 2010). Because Sebastian's autobiographical history has revealed his limited physical competence in PE, he is positioned by and in his social relations with his classmates as not belonging, in this context. Our vignette indicates Sebastian's sense that he is often the focus of his peer's negative attention and that this constrains his sense of place-belongingness. Paradoxically, however, cultural factors such as language and Sebastian's previous participation in activities such as battle-ball afford him an understanding of the game that Rachel, as a woman and newcomer to the school, does not have. As Antonsich (2010) underlines 'on the one hand, language can certainly be activated in the politics of belonging, demarcating 'we' from 'them', on the other hand it can also evoke a sense of community' (Antonsich 2010, p. 648). It is paradoxical that, through participation in an aggressive, combative and competitive game that inherently privileges masculine identities and despite Sebastian's usual identity position, he is able to permeate the boundaries of belonging/non-belonging to experience belonging while the same factors contribute to Rachel's sense of not belonging.

In drawing on Antonsich's (2010) connection of the personal affective dimension of belonging with place-based experience, this vignette reveals Sebastian's attempts to evade involvement in the game by nominating himself the battlement-protector. In the socio-spatial context of battle-ball, he (reluctantly) elects to participate by taking up a position that enables him to participate vicariously for the most of the game. This position also affords him a degree of emotional attachment to the game because he can 'encourage' his teammates from the safe vantage point of the baseline. The pedagogic nature of the game means that boys can participate in a way that aligns with their ability levels, albeit one that reinforces the hierarchical matrix of their gendered belongings/non-belongings. Yet, as more players are eliminated, Sebastian's strategy of evasion means he remains an active player in the game and forces him to make decisions about the degree of his involvement. By happenstance, Sebastian becomes a central player in this game when he manages to catch an opposition throw and facilitate the re-entry of a skilled player back into the game. From this serendipitous act, he receives accolades and support from his classmates as they bond together in the interests of 'winning'. This is perhaps best illustrated at his moment of indecision— will he leave the relative safety of the baseline to retrieve the wayward ball? Through the social relations articulated in the 'encouragement' from his peers—'*You can do it Sebastian, take them bastards*'—Sebastian's decision to become a more active player in the game is fortified.

However, there is no guarantee that the risks Sebastian takes will produce his team's desired outcome. The notion of desire warrants further discussion. Desire or 'longing' is an important dimension of belonging (Antonsich 2010; Probyn 1996). Elspeth Probyn (1996) describes it as be-longing or 'a desire for becoming-other, a longing for someone/something else' (Probyn 1996, p. 5). Inherent in Sebastian's comments is a desire to be-long and, in considering this happenstance occurrence of belonging, we observe Sebastian's affective response from being someone who normally attracts critique and retribution for his non-ability to someone who becomes a celebrated member of the team. In Sebastian's own words: '*it was kind of weird but I liked it*'. Perhaps a most unsettling aspect of this tale is Sebastian's recognition that his moment of belonging is incidental, momentary and provisional because his very next utterance sought to rationalise his general position of non-belonging: '*I don't care if I'm not that good at PE, there are other kids that are good at Maths and things … I don't want to be that sort of boy anyway, that over-competitiveness isn't healthy*'. These sentiments expose the extent to which belonging is conditional upon the discursive constraints in which it is constructed. As Antonsich (2010) argues, 'not every form of belonging is possible, as people are not free to choose their belongings outside of the bounds of power' (Antonsich 2010, p. 652).

Implications

This chapter has sought to explore the ways in which pedagogy is implicated in construction and politics of belonging/non-belonging in the context of a particular PE lesson in an all-boys' school. In locating this incidental moment of pedagogical practice within boys' PE, we attend to notions of belonging and non-belonging within a particular socio-spatial location and the positions assigned and taken up by Rachel and Sebastian at different points in time during this pedagogic moment.

Yuval-Davis (2011) argues that belonging is not just about social locations and the constructions of individual and collective identities and emotional attachments to these but it is also concerned 'with the ways these are assessed and valued by the self and others' (Yuval-Davis 2011, p. 18). This, she argued, can be taken up in many different ways by individuals *within* a group. Our micro-level analysis of one pedagogic encounter of a common and normative event in many boys' PE classes highlights how Rachel and Sebastian grapple with the binaries that play into belonging and not belonging in this pedagogic moment. They contend with being 'new' or familiar with the game of battle-ball and the school, female/male, and being a physically skilled/unskilled embodiment of idealised masculine subjectivities. At the same time, our analysis reveals that, in the micro-detail of any pedagogic moment, the experience of and positioning as belonging is not fixed but in a constant state of momentary shifts and changes.

Antonsich (2010) argues that membership to a group and ownership of a place are key factors in any conceptualisation of belonging. Yet, to focus only on the personal dimension risks positioning belonging within an individualistic frame that is problematic. This is because if belonging is considered 'independent from the social context within which it is immersed; to focus only on the social dimension risks essentialising belonging as the exclusive product of social(ising) discourses and practices' (Antonsich 2010, p. 653). Our use of Antonsich's (2010) notion of *place-belongingness* reveals how the socio-spatial places associated with one all-boys' PE lesson, for example the change-rooms, gym, school policies, are places where pedagogic practices and institutional policies are discursively constructed in gendered ways that legitimate and privilege particular identities/subjectivities, whilst marginalising others. This privilege, we argue, contributes to a sense of belonging or feeling of being 'at home' (or not). Yet, feelings of belonging are invariably 'based on exclusionary ideas of sameness and uniformity' (Wright 2015, p. 397). Our focus on one specific pedagogical encounter has sought to illustrate how a sense of place-belongingness is generated through incidental, every-day and mundane practices and that the belonging/non-belonging effects of these practices either promote or restrict emotional attachments to a larger social collective.

We are mindful of Wright's (2015) critique that an inherent focus on place and place-making as the 'entry point' for understanding belonging may complicate ideas of belonging in unproblematic ways. Specifically, in her discussion of 'home', Wright (2015) cautions, 'in the home, diverse and sometimes conflicting subjectivities are brought together. "Home" is then a site where contradictions must co-exist and may be partially reconciled' (Wright 2015, p. 395). Yet, as Antonsich (2010) argues, when people reflect upon belonging, they often do this with reference to place—'I belong/do not belong at home, in the school, in the PE classroom'. This has affective implications. Probyn's (1996) work two decades ago sought to highlight emotional attachments and fluidity as central dimensions in belonging. For Probyn (1996), belonging can be thought about as a desire for:

Some sort of attachment, be it to other people, places, or modes of being, and the ways in which individuals are caught within wanting to belong, wanting to become, a process that is fuelled by yearning rather than the positing of identity as a stable state. (Probyn 1996, p. 19)

Yet, inherent in Probyn's (1996) notion of 'be-longing' is a sense of *wanting* to belong (desire) that presumes that a desire to belong is a precursor to actually achieving a sense of belonging. As we have argued in this chapter, belonging can be considered a relational state, albeit fluid and changeable, and not merely a matter of desire. Our illustration of the politics of belonging at play in the context of this particular boys' PE class highlight the ways in which constructions of belonging/non-belonging can also be shaped by discourse and power-relations.

Thinking about belonging as a *process* rather than as a *status* has allowed for a focus on the conditions through which desires and affect become embodied through practices. Belonging then, in this sense, can be thought about as a 'discursive resource' (Antonsich 2010) that 'constructs, claims, justifies or resists forms of socio-spatial inclusion/exclusion' (ibid., p. 645). Wittingly or unwittingly, the characters of this pedagogic encounter —Rachel, Mr W, Sebastian—and other boys in the class participate in politics of belonging (to varying degrees) which impact on the emotional attachments and place-belongingness individuals can or cannot have in this social place. In every circumstance of the politics of belonging there are two sides—a side that desires belonging and a side which by its discursive positioning has the power to grant belonging (Antonsich 2010). The place-based struggles and negotiations of Rachel and Sebastian in this pedagogic encounter illustrate this dynamic.

Whilst hypermasculine discourses and power relations act to position certain forms of belonging as a 'hegemonic construction' (Yuval-Davis et al. 2005, p. 528), these are not fixed and stable categories. The irony for Sebastian was that within a pedagogic game that by its nature seeks to exclude players by eliminating them, he experiences a sense of place-belongingness that is usually inaccessible for him in the context of boys' PE. The boundaries that demarcate his usual 'otherness' became permeable and are permeated in this happenstance way.

In contrasting the experiences of Rachel and Sebastian, we illustrate that not all feelings of belonging/non-belonging are agentially sought or controlled. Belonging/non-belonging can be 'done to you' by institutional policies and pedagogic practices. Yet, as our chapter highlights, these boundaries can be and become permeable in particular pedagogic moments for both teachers and students. In these ways, belonging/not belonging can best be understood as a dynamic *process* of desire and experience. While our chapter focusses specifically on a particular pedagogic moment in a particular PE class and school, we propose that this is an emblematic case and that the fluid processes of belonging are imbricated in the micro-details of any pedagogic moments of classroom practice.

References

Antonsich, M. (2010). Searching for belonging – An analytical framework. *Geography Compass, 4*(6), 644–659.

Atkinson, M., & Kehler, M. (2012). Boys, bullying and biopedagogies in physical education. *Thymos: Journal of Boyhood Studies, 6*(2), 166–185.

Campbell, D., Gray, S., Kelly, J., & MacIsaac, S. (2016). Inclusive and exclusive masculinities in physical education: A Scottish case study. *Sport, Education and Society,* 1–13.

Connell, R. W. (1995). *Masculinities.* St Leonards, Australia: Allen & Unwin.

Crowley, J. (1999). The politics of belonging: Some theoretical considerations. In A. Geddes & A. Fabell (Eds.), *The politics of belonging: Migrants and minorities in contemporary Europe* (pp. 15–41). Aldershot: Ashgate.

Davies, B., & Gannon, S. (2009). *Pedagogical encounters.* New York: Peter Lang.

Fitzclarence, L., Hickey, C., & Nyland, B. (2007). The thin line between pleasure and pain: Implications for educating young males involved in sport. In B. Frank & K. Davidson (Eds.), *Masculinities and schooling: International practices and perspectives* (pp. 129–152). London and Ontario: The Althouse Press.

Giddens, A. (1991). *Modernity and self-identity: Self and society in the late modern age.* Stanford, CA: Stanford University Press.

Halse, C. (2004). The identity of civics in teacher education. *Pacific Asian Education, 16*(1), 30–41.

Hickey, C. (2010). Hypermasculinity in schools: The good, the bad and the ugly. In M. O'Sullivan & A. MacPhail (Eds.), *Young people's voices in physical education and youth sport* (pp. 108–122). Abingdon: Routledge.

Hopkins, P., & Noble, G. (2009). Masculinities in place: Situated identities, relations and intersectionality. *Social & Cultural Geography, 10*(8), 811–819.

Kenway, J., Kraack, A., & Hickey-Moody, A. (2006). *Masculinity beyond the metropolis.* Basingstoke: Palgrave Macmillan.

Martino, W., & Pallotta-Chiarolli, M. (2005). *Being normal is the only way to be: Adolescent perspectives on gender and school.* Sydney: UNSW Press.

Messner, M. (2005). Still a man's world? Studying masculinities and sport. In M. Kimmel, J. Hearn, & R. Connell (Eds.), *Handbook of studies on men and masculinities* (pp. 313–325). Thousand Oaks: Sage.

Pringle, R., & Hickey, C. (2010). Negotiating masculinities via the moral problematization of sport. *Sociology of Sport Journal, 27*(2), 115–138.

Probyn, E. (1996). *Outside belonging.* London: Routledge.

Reichert, M., Nelson, J., Heed, J., Yang, R., & Benson, W. (2012). 'A place to be myself': The critical role of schools in boys' emotional development. *Thymos: Journal of Boyhood Studies, 6*(1/2), 55–75.

Tinning, R. (2010). *Pedagogy and human movement: Theory, practice, research.* London: Routledge.

Wright, S. (2015). More-than-human, emergent belongings: A weak theory approach. *Progress in Human Geography, 39*(4), 391–411.

Youdell, D. (2010). *School trouble: Identity, power and politics in education.* London: Routledge.

Youkhana, E. (2015). A conceptual shift in the studies of belonging and the politics of belonging. *Social Inclusion, 3*(4), 10–24.

Yuval-Davis, N. (2006). Belonging and the politics of belonging. *Patterns of Prejudice, 40*(3), 197–214.

Yuval-Davis, N. (2011). *The politics of belonging: Intersectional contestations.* London: Sage.

Yuval-Davis, N., Anthias, F., & Kofman, E. (2005). Secure borders and safe haven and the gendered politics of belonging: Beyond social cohesion. *Ethnic and Racial Studies, 28*(3), 513–535.

15

Belonging as Pedagogical, Practical and Political

Julie McLeod

Belonging is one of those terms with a life of its own. It circulates widely in social and political discourse, as a noun or a verb, often without an object. Questions about belonging where, to whom, and why appear subordinated to in-principle assertions of its value. It connotes a feeling, a political and cultural affiliation, a normative expectation, a position marked by its absence or precariousness, invoking exclusions and inclusions, attachments and estrangements. In these remarks, I reflect on the insights and arguments offered in the preceding two chapters, drawing out ideas they sparked for thinking about how belonging and associated notions of inclusion, voice or participation are mobilised in educational debates. Together, the chapters offer different angles on how feelings and processes of belonging and not belonging operate in the particular settings of schools and classrooms. On my reading, they show the everyday and profound ways in which pedagogical practices can facilitate, inhibit, make possible or impossible meaningful dimensions of, and dispositions

J. McLeod (✉)
The University of Melbourne, Melbourne, VIC, Australia
e-mail: j.mcleod@unimelb.edu.au

© The Author(s) 2018   **305**
C. Halse (ed.), *Interrogating Belonging for Young People in Schools*,
https://doi.org/10.1007/978-3-319-75217-4_15

towards, belonging—understood variously as a political category, a subjective experience and as orientation towards others.

In dialogue with these chapters, I highlight the practical ways in which pedagogies are implicated in the multifaceted work of belonging, which is represented as a dynamic and relational process rather than a relatively static attribute or state of being. As such, it is caught up in the politics of recognition, hospitality and power. Here, I interrogate belonging by looking at kindred concepts and argue for a reflexive and critical account of belonging that aims to do more than reiterate feel-good intentions and the promise of an inclusive cuddle. I do so by revisiting arguments from my own studies that have investigated topics of youth citizenship, wellbeing, voice and listening, with the aim of drawing together questions and approaches that could be helpful for reconsidering the claims and contradictions of belonging as an educational project and aspiration. 'Belonging' can be viewed as a keyword in contemporary social life, one that warrants attention as much for its aspirations as for its normative complications and erasures. Following an approach I developed with Katie Wright (McLeod and Wright 2016, p. 777) to interrogate another ubiquitous term, 'wellbeing', I outline a way of exploring belonging not simply in terms of what it means 'or how it can be measured, identified tracked, realised, hindered or enabled' but, rather, in terms of trying to understand what the discourse and promise of belonging *does*.

First, however, I turn to reflect on what the respective chapters offer for opening up fresh and productive ways of rethinking belonging as pedagogical, including the potential and practicalities of pedagogies in fostering a sense of social and subjective belonging.

Pedagogies of and for Belonging

In 'Pedagogies of belonging in literacy classrooms and beyond', Barbara Comber and Annette Woods draw out different registers of belonging, attending to belonging as a sense of connection to place and as a feeling of being included, valued and recognised. While these orientations are anchored to classroom interactions and pedagogies, the authors astutely show how their consequences resonate further afield. As they observe, 'feeling attached, or "at home", in a place is important for learning and engagement'. They remind us how creating a productive classroom environment 'requires sophisticated relations' and a commitment to making visible the diverse ways in which pupils are themselves 'racialised, classed, aged, gendered, sexualised and situated in the space'. Offering a refreshing insistence on the significance of the temporal and spatial specificity of classrooms, they position learning environments not as generic but as located in communities, with particular histories, politics and possibilities for enacting strategies of misrecognition and recognition. One of the many virtues of their discussion is how they gracefully move from the theoretical and larger political dimensions of belonging, to a close-up illumination of how pedagogies of belonging might be enacted.

Evocatively creating the scene of the classroom, Comber and Woods point to how wider socio-cultural factors impinge on classroom dynamics and are never properly external. In this way, a sense of belonging is examined as a powerful cross-over experience and response whose effects travel beyond and transcend classrooms. At the same time, they show how marginalisation or circumstances of exclusion can potentially be aggravated or alleviated in the classroom. How teachers respond to this dynamic is an important thread in the chapter: it offers a close-up view of the work of pedagogies and the creativity, persistence and investments of teachers in such practices. Belonging is, to be sure, a relational, provisional and, at times, uncertain process but, in this chapter, the dialogic aspects of belonging are also brought to the fore. Importantly, the hard work of teaching is not romanticised, nor are teachers chastised for falling short of the rhetorical claims for social justice agendas in schools. Rather, there is a respectful awareness of the complicated processes at play in trying to foster a sense of belonging as more than gestural, and as part of the collective orientation of the classroom as well as the identity processes and self-becomings of individual pupils. This marks an important analytical move from the rhetorical to the practical, attending to the enactment of ethical aspirations via pedagogies that are, on the one hand, everyday yet, on the other hand, far from ordinary.

A related attention to the dynamic effects of curricular and pedagogical processes is also evident in the chapter from Amanda Mooney and Chris Hickey: '"The Battle in Belonging": Pedagogies, practice and hypermasculinity in boys'. Here the unfolding of practices that produce feelings of un-belonging—of being out of place—are explored as they are intersect with and are mediated by gender relations, school cultures and curriculum histories. Either separately or in combination, such factors can render exclusion normalised. At the same time, the discussion prises open the possibility of more 'permeable and changeable' dynamics between students and teachers, illustrating the ways in which belonging and its shadow can be understood as a 'dynamic *process* of desire and experience'. As part of making 'visible the politics of belonging', they call for more school-based research that investigates the ways in which 'place, practices, and affective dimensions of schooling coalesce to produce normative identities'. Their 'micro-analysis' of pedagogies in action illuminates the value of such an approach. Focusing in on the pedagogical and inter-subjective dynamics in an all-boys' Physical Education class taught by a female teacher, Mooney and Hickey tease out how experiences of a rightful sense of belonging and non-belonging were constituted, relayed and replayed along alarmingly hyper-gendered axes. Emphasising the importance of attending to 'belonging as an affective act' allows them not only to identify moments of unease and discomfort but also to notice occasions when affiliations and investments could be challenged.

A welcome feature of the chapter is the extended ethnographic commentary that vividly conveys how the volatile positionings of student, teacher, male, female, are intensely played out in seemingly mundane ways. This is one reason why close attention to pedagogic encounters is valuable. It affords insight into how orientations, subjective investments and desires as well as the inheritance of social dynamics and structural asymmetries intersect in messy and compelling ways—sometimes predictably and other times with uncertainty. Like the chapter from Comber and Woods, this discussion brings to the surface the significance of place, framed as both the socio-spatial location of a school and the space—materiality, time, activity, practice—of pedagogical interactions, understood as either deliberate or incidental, or in an older language as formal and informal curriculum.

Citizenship, Hospitality and Dividing Practices

My own attention to the claims of belonging as an idea and an ideal, and arguably a keyword, has arisen in relation to studies of youth citizenship and voice (McLeod 2011, 2012). Here, I raise a number of questions and provocations for thinking with and against the concept of belonging and of bringing to the surface its 'double gestures' (Popkewitz 2011; Popkewitz and Lindblad 2000). Margaret Somers' (2008) argument that citizenship has become one of the central categories of public life offers parallel insights into the rise of the idea of belonging in educational and social discourse. This has been especially evident in relation to addressing groups and individuals constituted as vulnerable, disadvantaged or 'at-risk'. Somewhat paradoxically for such groups, citizenship is represented in the warm language of belonging—to local, national and imagined global communities—and, allied to this, problems of social disadvantage and inequality are frequently re-articulated through the language of social exclusion and inclusion.

The prominence of these related categories accompanies a changing view of citizenship itself, away from being principally or only about political rights or political socialisation to encompass a broader view of citizenship as also denoting a way of being and feeling. Citizenship can be 'an identity; a set of rights, privileges and duties; an elevated and exclusionary political status; a set of practices that can unify—or divide—the members of a political community; and an ideal of political agency' (Friedman 2005, p. 3). Thus, citizenship is widely understood as 'having three essential and complementary dimensions: it is a status, a feeling and a practice' (Osler and Starkey 2005, p. 11). There is, as well, a growing interest in knowing 'what it feels like to be a citizen and what the emotional aspects of belonging and not-belonging within the civic community are' (Arnot 2009, p. 7). In turn, this has led to a strong focus on citizenship as 'less a status and more of an identity and a set of social relations' (Donald 1996 cited in Arnot 2009, p. 12). There are resonances here with deliberations upon the experience and prospect of belonging. This is so in reference to the affective dimensions of being and becoming and to the ways in which experiences of belonging—like citizenship—cut across registers of legal identity, feelings and social practices. Parallels can also be drawn between the shadow sides of the two constructs of citizenship and belonging, as I consider below.

In his genealogies of citizenship, Engin Isin turns critical attention to the question: 'Under what conditions do subjects act as citizens?' (Isin and Nielsen 2007, p. 18). He argues that such acts, such 'habits of the everyday through which subjects become citizens' (ibid., p. 17) are relational practices in which the claiming and 'enactment of citizenship instantiates other subjects' (ibid., p. 19), across a spectrum of intensity, of 'strangers, but also outsiders and aliens' (ibid., p. 37). He sees constructs of citizenship constituted as binaries, invoking their other at the same time as asserting their categorical claims for inclusion, belonging, citizenship, and so forth. A decisive element is the insistence on acts and practices, and the technical and everyday ways in which citizenship or belonging is claimed. Popkewitz's (2008, 2011) analyses of the 'dividing practices' of educational reforms that promise salvation, or inclusion or cosmopolitan reason similarly underscore the ways in which such categories of subjectivity and social division are formed, remade, challenged and enacted in specific historical contexts and via social practices and pedagogies. Practices of belonging and non-belonging are also shifting and multiple, reflecting allegiance and connection to some communities, and estrangement from others.

In interviews with American school students following the events of 9/11, Katharyne Mitchell and Walter Parker (2008) found that youthful citizens-in-formation 'expressed a historicized affinity—constructed, contingent and impermanent … imagining and producing allegiances that were multiple, flexible, and relational' (Mitchell and Parker 2008, p. 775, 799). They argued that globalisation has led to 'an increased spatial and temporal flexibility of multiple allegiances rather than an essentially static and unidirectional movement of affinity from an inner concentric circle [the nation, the local] to outer [global, transnational]' (ibid., p. 279). The common binary of national/cosmopolitan or local/ global does not convey the multiplicity, fluidity and movement of citizenship allegiance. Moreover, this spatial binary creates an inner and outer model of citizenship belonging that does not accurately reflect the affiliations and worlds young people inhabit. It thus serves to inscribe a false stability on the scales and spaces of citizenship. By extension, related arguments and cautions can apply to the uses of the belonging/not-belonging binary.

I am not arguing that aspirations for 'belonging' can be directly substituted here, but there are suggestive resonances in focusing on the effectivity of practices and interrogating the micro, shifting and properly situated nature of claims, possibilities for and experiences of belonging. In other words, this requires framing belonging not simply as a political or rhetorical ideal or indeed as a subjective feeling, but as arising from specific practices that involve the making of those who belong and those do not belong, those who are recognised and welcomed as belonging and those who are not noticed or are misrecognised. In fact, some of the slipperiness and invented-ness of the term 'belonging' becomes very apparent in these discussions. One can too easily fall into normative pronouncements or saccharine statements about the self-evidently damaging effects of not belonging; and confusion abounds as to what sort of analytic or political category 'belonging' is.

While the lineage of its currency is no doubt multifaceted, I see the growing discursive and political mobilisation of belonging—as problem and solution—as implicated in the changing conceptions of citizenship noted above: the claims of identity politics and increasing interest in emotions in public life. Alongside this are the immediately pressing consequences of greater mobility, including the forced migration of people, which bring sharply into unavoidable view questions of borders, belonging, boundaries and hospitality. On the one hand, a sense of estrangement, of not being part of an inner circle, might generate powerful perspectives onto social norms and be part of how individuals and groups seek to mark themselves out. On the other hand, the clarity and angle afforded by an outsider's perspective is clearly not the same as that arising from imposed and enforced exclusion or by the micro-practices that recognise some and not see, hear or notice others.

Voice, Listening and (Not) Noticing

The issue of voice—variously as giving, claiming, acknowledging, acting upon—is a prominent theme in discussions of youth citizenship and student participation in schooling. Yet, for all the persuasive critiques of voice as a political and ethical project, an often neglected option is to turn the tables to examine who is, in fact, listening. This is to argue for the value of focusing not simply on who has 'voice' or what is voiced but to attend, also, to the relational and dynamic character of voice. Most notably, this requires attention to how 'voice' is listened to and heard and the circumstances that might permit recognition and action. Elsewhere, I have argued that:

> to focus only on voice as expression—or as code for agency, perspective, difference—is to ignore the significance of listening, and to skate over voice as a dimension of communicative practice that invokes self/speaker and others/listeners. This somewhat paradoxically constructs voice as non-dialogical, as disconnected from the contexts in which it is heard, and in which it is recognized as mattering or not. (McLeod 2011, p. 185)

Writing from the perspective of media studies, Nick Couldry (2009, 2010) argues that a rethinking of listening and speaking is required and that this is fundamentally linked to democratic projects, with the goal of fostering meaningful communication across difference. Voice—as both speaking and listening—matters because it concerns 'citizens listening and speaking together with the aim of engaging each other's perspectives, even when discord marks this joint interaction and requires participants to change of modify their communicative practice' (O'Donnell et al. 2009, p. 429).

For Couldry, the politics of voice also evokes the human capacity to 'give an account of their lives' (Couldry 2009, p. 580, 2010, pp. 120–123, cf Butler 2005). This should set in train a 'process of mutually recognising our claims on each other as reflexive human agents, each with an account to give, an account of our lives that needs to be registered and heard, our stories endlessly entangled in each other's stories' (2009, p. 580). I am wanting to draw parallels here between these analyses of voice and listening and claims for belonging and ethical obligations for welcoming and hospitality. In this framing, the responsibility is firmly on the 'host' to acknowledge and make welcome, to make belonging possible and practical. This does not remove questions of power, of the bestowing and withdrawal of hospitality, for example. It does, however, insist on the relational dynamic of belonging and the importance of recognising the 'objects' of belonging—where, how, with whom. This orientation encourages one to look critically not only towards the binary of non-belonging and belonging, or welcome and unwelcome, but, importantly, to acknowledge the contexts—embodied, spatial, geopolitical, historical—that make belonging realisable and practical.

The chapters that provoked my thinking on these matters both explored the situated, place-based, affective and practical ways in which belonging, as a pedagogical project with wider reach and resonance, might be brought to life. They each drew out the significance of educational settings for either fostering or undermining feelings of connection to communities. In this way, they showed how the experience of belonging is a dynamic, affective and relational practice and they pointed to the powerful and constitutive role of everyday encounters and pedagogies. For the teacher in Mooney and Hickey's chapter, this was mediated by intersections of gender and traditions of exclusion that spilled into the informal spaces of school. This showed the shadow side of belonging and the damaging effects of feeling estranged from dominant norms: here, belonging is chimerical. In Comber and Wood's chapter, teacher and pupil interactions are paramount, evident in the careful attentiveness to building confidence in a sense of belonging in and to a place. This evoked a feeling of being at home in an immediate or literal way, and in a larger meaning of mutual cultural recognition: here, belonging encompasses questions of hospitality and a welcome openness to others.

In my opening remarks, I suggested that it could be helpful to consider 'belonging' as a keyword in contemporary social and political discourse, one that has a particularly tight hold in educational debates. This led me to propose that we interrogate not only what constitutes feelings or experiences of belonging and non-belonging, but to ask as well what this keyword *does*. This involves an attempt to 'defamiliarise the epistemic authority' (McLeod and Wright 2016, p. 777) of the term and to analyse what the construct of belonging does 'in framing educational and social practices and in normalising particular conceptions and calibrations of' (in this case) of those who do and do not belong (McLeod and Wright 2016, p. 777). The chapters discussed here shed light on how the notion of belonging moves, animating pedagogical strategies and opening up fresh thinking about the affective dimensions of exclusion and inclusion across school spaces. Both studies also prompted me to reflect on the importance of attending to the dividing practices of belonging as part of claims for its dynamic and relational character. This requires, as I have suggested, fostering active, deliberate practices of listening, recognition and hospitality, not only interrogating experiences of belonging or not belonging.

References

Arnot, M. (2009). *Educating the gendered citizen: Sociological engagements with national and global agendas*. London: Routledge.

Couldry, N. (2009). Rethinking the politics of voice. *Continuum: Journal of Media and Cultural Studies, 23*(4), 579–582.

Couldry, N. (2010). *Why voice matters: Culture and politics after neoliberalism*. London: Sage.

Friedman, M. (2005). Introduction. In *Women and citizenship* (pp. 3–11). Oxford: Oxford University Press.

Isin, E. F., & Nielsen, G. M. (2007). *Acts of citizenship*. London: Zed Books.

McLeod, J. (2011). Student voice and the politics of listening in higher education. *Critical Studies in Education, 52*(2), 179–189.

McLeod, J. (2012). Vulnerability and the neo-liberal youth citizen: A view from Australia. *Comparative Education, 48*(1), 11–26.

McLeod, J., & Wright, K. (2016). What does wellbeing do? An approach to defamiliarize keywords in Youth Studies. *Journal of Youth Studies, 19*(6), 776–792. https://doi.org/10.1080/13676261.2015.1112887.

Mitchell, K., & Parker, W. C. (2008). I Pledge allegiance to … flexible citizenship and shifting scales of belonging. *Teachers College Record, 10*, 775–804.

O'Donnell, P., Lloyd, J., & Dreher, T. (2009). Listening, pathbuilding and continuations: A research agenda for the analysis of listening. *Continuum: Journal of Media and Cultural Studies, 23*(4), 423–439.

Osler, A., & Starkey, H. (2005). *Changing citizenship: Democracy and inclusion in education*. Maidenhead: Open University Press.

Popkewitz, T. S. (2008). *Cosmopolitanism and the age of school reform*. New York: Palgrave.

Popkewitz, T. S. (2011). Curriculum history, school and the history of the present. *History of Education, 40*, 1–19.

Popkewitz, T. S., & Lindblad, S. (2000). Educational governance and social inclusion and exclusion: Some conceptual difficulties and problematics in policy and research. *Discourse: Studies in the Cultural Politics of Education, 21*(1), 6–44.

Somers, M. (2008). *Geneaologies of citizenship: Markets, statelessness, and right to have rights*. New York: Cambridge University Press.

Part V

Afterword

16

The Trouble with Belonging…

Peter Kelly

My sense is that it is not my job in this chapter to summarise or to paraphrase, to agree or to confirm, to disagree or to dispute with and between the chapters that comprise this collection. Rather, I want to take the opportunity to articulate where it was that I was taken when I read these chapters, to sketch some of the *lines of flight*—to borrow a metaphor—that were provoked by the sorts of discussion and arguments that are presented in this collection. And there were many such lines of flight. So, in this limited space I want to follow just a small number of them.

My sense of the positive dimensions and possibilities of belonging, and of the negative dimensions and possibilities of *not* belonging is fundamentally ambiguous and ambivalent. Following Zygmunt Bauman (1989, 1991), I am not sure that I want to, or can, 'exterminate' that ambivalence. So, what I will do is unapologetically ambiguous and ambivalent. My aim is to 'trouble' belonging, to engage in some 'untimely thinking', about the concept of belonging.

P. Kelly (✉)
RMIT University, Melbourne, VIC, Australia
e-mail: peter.kelly@rmit.edu.au

© The Author(s) 2018
C. Halse (ed.), *Interrogating Belonging for Young People in Schools*,
https://doi.org/10.1007/978-3-319-75217-4_16

319

Troubling Belonging

In several places (Kelly 2011a, 2013), I have referenced a 2009 special issue of *Theory, Culture & Society* that presented a number of commentaries framed by the twenty-fifth anniversary of Michel Foucault's death in 1984, and by a new wave of scholarship related to Foucault's work as a consequence of the publication in English of his lecture courses at the College de France. Paul Rabinow (2009), a colleague and collaborator with Foucault at UC Berkeley (with Hubert Dreyfus) in the late 1970s, early 1980s, was a contributor to the special issue.

In a *Prelude* in his essay, Rabinow (2009, pp. 27–28) touches on Friedrich Nietzsche's *Untimely meditations* [*Unzeitgemässe Betrachtungen*] as a means to introduce a discussion of the 'problem of what *mode* is appropriate for giving form to thinking'. Part of the way Rabinow frames this discussion is by suggesting that the *intent* and the *affect* of the English and French translations of *Unzeitgemässe Betrachtungen* is captured best by the French term *l'intempestif*. For Rabinow, the 'semantic range' of the term covers not only 'untimely', but 'ill-timed', 'unreasonable', or 'inopportune'. In this sense, the term 'captures a striving to bring something forth, something that could be actual but does not yet exist'. Importantly, for the ways in which Rabinow wants to position his later discussion of the struggles that he claims characterised Foucault's mode of thinking, such a reading 'does not mean that there is something waiting around to come to fruition but only that, taken up in a distinctive way, the things of the actual and existing world can be made into something appropriate as well as inopportune' (Rabinow 2009, p. 27). The *inopportune*, as a mode of thinking, 'operates adjacently' to any relatively straightforward historical contextualisation, in a 'space of becoming where the old and the new are available if one approaches them in a mode of vigorous contemplation of the about-to-be-actual' (ibid., p. 28).

Rabinow (2009, pp. 28–29) argues that Foucault 'took up and experimented with the challenge of critical thought' in a variety of ways throughout his intellectual life. Indeed, for Rabinow, the majority of Foucault's work can be understood as 'an inopportune and vigorous contemplation'—a Nietzschean *untimely meditation*—'a critical contestation perpetually in search of new forms of criticism and invention' (Rabinow 2009, p. 28). Rabinow suggests that, like Nietzsche, Foucault 'almost always in an uneasy and restless fashion ... strove to invent and practice a form of asceticism' (ibid., p. 29). For Foucault, this asceticism took the form of 'an active attention to work on the self, on those he worked with and the material he was considering' (ibid.).

A central element of the discussion that Rabinow develops relates to the ways in which this asceticism did not take the form of a renunciation. Instead, it took the form of a positive engagement with the limits and possibilities of thinking, of the forms that thinking could take, where thinking could take place, the uses to which thinking could be put. Rabinow (2009, pp. 31–32) illustrates these claims through a reference to a conversation from 1981 between Foucault and Didier Eribon in which they address the concerns of the then newly-elected French Socialist government that French intellectuals should publically support the government's *reform* programs.[1] The reference, and the one that follows, is important in so much as Foucault makes a case for the space that should be given to thinking about thinking, and of thinking in its *untimely* mode:

> To begin from the outset by accepting the question of what reforms I will introduce is not, I believe, the objective that an intellectual should entertain. His role, since he works in the register of thought, is to see just how far thought can be freed so as to make certain transformations seem urgent enough so that others will attempt to bring their own into effect, and difficult enough so that if they are brought about they will be deeply inscribed in the real. (Foucault 1991 (1981), p. 33 cited in Rabinow 2009, p. 31)

What is more:

> We must free ourselves (*s'affranchir*) from the sacralization of the social as the unique instance of the real and stop diminishing that essential aspect of human life and human relations, thinking. Thought exists well beyond the systems and edifices of discourse. It is something that is often hidden but always animates ordinary human action. There is always some pinch of thought in the stupidest of institutions. There is always some thought in the most silent of habits. (Foucault 1994, p. 180 cited in Rabinow 2009, p. 32)

In leaving aside the particularities/peculiarities of post-1968 French politics and intellectual life, we can imagine, usefully, that thinking that is untimely is thinking that finds, tests, and possibly troubles the conditions and possibilities in which thinking occurs, and those who engage these limits and possibilities. Untimely thinking is an activity that can change the object of thought. Understandings—of education, of transitions, of sexuality, of risk, or work, of the self, of young people, of belonging—are rendered problematic by thought that is untimely. Untimely thinking can also transform those who do the thinking and those they conduct relations with. It is this mode of thinking that I want to employ here in thinking about, in troubling, the concept of belonging (see also Kelly 2011a).

Where Does 'Belonging' Come From, and Why Is It Important Now?

At the beginning, I need to acknowledge that, from my location in the field of Youth Studies, I have long been uneasy about the conceptual or theoretical or political limits and possibilities of the idea of 'belonging'. In this field, researchers from backgrounds in sociology, psychology, cultural and education studies have variously mobilised the concept of belonging in the conduct of research with, about and for young people. Why, we might ask, has there been the emergence of an interest in 'belonging' at this moment in the thinking that shapes these disciplines, this field?

Elsewhere (Kelly 2011a), I indicated that what struck me most about the issues, agendas, *problematiques* (Foucault 2000, p. 256) that shape Youth Studies at the start of the twenty-first century was a sense of a significant movement in the field from concerns—during the 1970s to the early 1990s under the influence of the Birmingham (UK) Centre for Contemporary Cultural Studies [CCCS]—with ideas such as *resistance*, *rituals*, *styles*, and *subculture*. The key texts here included books such as *Resistance through rituals* (Hall and Jefferson 1976), *Learning to labour* (Willis 1977), *Subculture: the meaning of style* (Hebdige 1979), *Louts and legends* (Walker 1988). This movement has seen the emergence of a pre-occupation, at the start of the twenty-first century, with ideas of: risk, transition, evidence-based best practice, and, more recently, generation (X&Y), adolescent brain development and belonging. A quick look at the contents of the second edition of the late Andy Furlong's (2017) edited collection *Handbook of youth and young adulthood* provides some evidence of these trends.

In my uneasiness, it is not my intent to romanticise, nostalgically, the overwhelmingly masculinist sub-cultural sociologies of resistance, ritual and style. Valerie Walkerdine (1997) and Angela McRobbie (1978, 1980, 1982, and, with Mica Nava 1984), among others, did a pretty good job of critiquing much of this work at the end of the 1980s and the start of the 1990s. See, also, the collection edited by Rob White (1993) for a flavour of some of these debates in Australia at the time.

But the nature of the problems that trouble those who do work in this field has certainly changed in that time. Why? 'Belonging', as a concept, as a referent for an intellectual politics, seems a long way from the concept or the politics of 'resistance', for example. Whether that 'resistance' is through 'rituals' or 'style' or 'subculture'. How is it that, at the start of the twenty-first century, we have come to imagine, to think about, a whole array of youth issues through the concept of belonging? What does a focus on belonging produce? What does a focus on belonging divert us from? Is there a need for a genealogy of belonging in which we might explore how it is that we have become who it is that we are when we concern ourselves with belonging?

Belonging and a Political Economy of Youth

I want to situate this troubling in the context of a recent debate in the *Journal of Youth Studies* about what a political economy of youth might look like at the start of the twenty-first century. I do not have the space to re-cover the ground covered by James Côté (2014, 2016) and Alan France and Steven Threadgold (2016) in their instalments. Instead, I want to pick up on a number of points raised by Mayssoun Sukarieh and Stuart Tannock (2016) in their response and only gesture at what a political economy of youth might look like, might do in the early decades of the twenty-first century. At the start of the twenty-first century, capitalism is globalising, is largely neoliberal, and is being reconfigured in profound ways by the Anthropocene, climate change, bio-genetics, Artificial Intelligence (AI), and the Internet of Things (IoT).

A political economy of twenty-first century capitalism, let alone a political economy of young people or of schooling, must be able to account for a capitalism that in many ways looks like the capitalism of the First Industrial Revolution (the capitalism of Marx and Weber) but which is, at the same time, profoundly different as it enters what is variously described as the Third Industrial Revolution or the Second Machine Age (Lanchester 2015; Rifkin 2015).

And it is these profound emergences that pose the greatest challenges for engaging with a political economy of youth. Indeed, the practice of youth research, and the field of Youth Studies as it has emerged in the last four decades, must be central to the thinking *about* a political economy of youth. In this, I am very much in agreement with key aspects of Sukarieh and Tannock's (2016) recent contribution to this discussion. The argument they present leads to a provocative critique of the theoretical and methodological orthodoxies that shape the current direction of the *Journal of Youth Studies,* and the field of youth studies more generally. A critique grounded, in part, in an analysis of the papers published in the journal in the past five years. They suggest that in:

> Reading over the five-year set of Journal of Youth Studies articles, one is struck by the narrow range of social actors that are the focus of youth research. On the evidence of these articles, one would conclude that being a youth researcher means interviewing, surveying and/or observing young people. Only rarely … are the activities, interests and agendas of elite social actors … the focus of research, despite the fact that few would dispute the enormous influence such actors have in shaping young people's lives. (Sukarieh and Tannock 2016, p. 1284)

A political economy of youth, or a political economy of schooling, might include some interest, some understanding of *belonging*, but it would also try to so much more. As Sukarieh and Tannock (2016) suggest, in a reference to their earlier work, a political economy of youth should:

look well beyond youth and young people in and of themselves. This is not just because of the wide range of social and political actors involved in shaping the meaning and salience of youth, but also because … [i]nvocations about youth are often made in the context of social struggles and political agendas whose central concerns may only be symbolically or indirectly connected to the lives of individual young people. (Sukarieh and Tannock 2016, p. 1283)

The Normalising Trajectory of Belonging

My being troubled in this space is also associated with a sense that 'to belong' is not an un-alloyed 'good'. That is, belonging invokes, for me, at different times and in different ways, a sense of the need to negotiate the complex, often difficult, often deeply emotional, embodied and cognitive effects and affects of the rules, the norms, the institutionalised practices and processes, the play of power relations, that shape the diverse spaces and relations of belonging.

This need, this demand to belong, particularly in the institutionalised spaces of schooling, tends, also, to make individuals responsible for the more or less successful carriage of these relationships. It tends to reduce, by and large, this hard labour to a set of positive psychological feelings, or, in their absence, toxic psychological effects that are imagined to echo in young people's immediate and longer term futures.

What happens, I wonder, to the 'outsiders', the 'out-riders', the 'non-joiners', the 'misfits', the 'fringe dwellers', the 'loners', if we valourise 'belonging', if we essentialise 'belonging'?

In a 2011 article (Kelly 2011b), I used Tim Winton's award winning novel *Breath* to unsettle what I called the governmentalisation of social science, to think about what a re-enchantment of a sociological imagination might mean. I suggested there that *Breath* could be read as an allegorical tale about the terror, for some young people, of *being ordinary*, and the ways in which surfing, sex and drugs provide the means for the story's main characters, Pikelet, Loonie, Sando and Eva, to identify, confront and challenge the limits shaped by this terror—sometimes with damaging consequences.

In Winton's narrative, a middle-aged Bruce Pike (Pikelet) explores his memories of a time in his life when he became entangled in a range of highly consequential behaviours and practices through a complex (damaging) series of relationships with the older, ex-champion surfer Sando and his (damaged) partner Eva. In these recollections, risk, danger and harm—to be found, possibly, in increasingly reckless surfing adventures, drug use and sexual experimentation—are far from being things to be rationally calculated or prudently managed with a wary eye to future consequences. Rather, they *breathe* energy, excitement, meaning and purpose into life-worlds that, for Pikelet and Loonie, are dominated by the imagined institutionalised ordinariness of family, school, and work in the relative isolation of the small, rural, working class town of Sawyer on the southern coast of Western Australia. I argued that there is much in this tale that can move us towards the limits and possibilities of thinking about the roles that 'risk' plays in making some sense of what it is to *be* young.

Just possibly, *Breath* is also an allegory of anti-belonging, a tale of rejecting—with some costs, but also with some benefits—the norms of belonging in these particular times, places and spaces.

It is in these ways that I am troubled by the sense that there is a normative, moral dimension to belonging that is about conforming to existing practices and relations, rather than disrupting or unsettling them. This is a theme taken up by a number of contributors to this collection. For example, Emma Charlton, Leanne Coll, Lyn Harrison and Debbie Ollis provide an account of a moment in a drama class in which the terms of belonging are set, and made explicit, through the interactions of teacher, young people and the materiality of the 'drama space'—including a key role played by a large gym mat. In their discussion, they raise a number of concerns about the hetero-normative dimensions of belonging in this space and the ways in which this moment can be imagined in terms of the 'chain of signifiers' that shape a 'politics of who or what "belongs" in the spaces of school, and, most significantly, the precarious nature of belonging otherwise and who is authorised to resist'.

What these and a number of other authors in the collection suggest is that we pay attention to the material, the symbolic, the discursive, the gendered, and the sexual character of the relationships, practices and processes, and power relations that shape the terms on which belonging, and not belonging, is possible in institutionalised spaces such as schooling.

Schooling and the Moral Economy of Belonging

Belonging, then, can be understood, as a number of contributors submit, as a normalising state, a normalising process, a normalising assemblage of relations and practices in which some 'shoulds', and some 'oughts', take some precedence over other 'shoulds', other 'oughts'.

Spaces, and the regulation and management of spaces, as Jo Pike and I have argued in *The moral geographies of children, young people and food* (Pike and Kelly 2014), and in a new collection titled *Neoliberalism and austerity: the moral economies of young people's health and well-being* (Kelly and Pike 2017), are always moral. In *The Moral Geographies of Children, Young People and Food*, Foucault's (1978, 1985, 1986, 1991) work on governmentality and the care and practices of the self enabled us to examine the ways in which young people are cajoled, directed, encouraged, rewarded to behave in ways that are considered healthy and civilised in school dining spaces and in other spaces—for example, around the family dinner table—that are joined to school dining rooms by particular ideas of health and civility (Pike and Kelly 2014). We highlighted the particular kinds of 'technologies' that are used, and the strategies that are employed, in order to achieve these ends. In this sense, government is always a moral project that is articulated in what we might understand as substantial, national, policy pronouncements about young people, health and well-being and public health crises; and in what might be called the more mundane, everyday project of feeding, say, 400 young people a nutritious, filling and appetising meal in a comprehensive school in South Yorkshire (Pike and Kelly 2014, p. 9).

Arts and practices of government are invested in, and with, an array of purposes and outcomes that the subjects of government 'should' be concerned with, and 'should' be concerned with in quite particular ways. Foucault's work, and the ways in which it has been taken up in governmentality studies over the last 20–30 years, points to a sense that neoliberal governmentalities invest in subjects who, ideally, should be capable of making choices and accepting responsibilities that align with the moral imperatives of government. From this perspective, the subjects of neoliberal government are imagined as being ethical beings, persons who have developed the capacity to make choices and recognise their responsibilities about such things as: the education of themselves and their children; the array of health services provided by the state, or for profit; housing; employment; and consumption (Pike and Kelly 2014, p. 9).

Understood in this way, we can identify and map the lines of force that shape particular spaces in ways that highlight their moral character, the choices made and not made, the demands to make certain choices, and those who benefit, those who pay some cost, for these 'oughts' and 'shoulds'. There is, in this sense, a particular crafting, a particular bundling, a particular gathering of relations, practices, processes and forces that shape belonging in spaces such as schools. So, how do we know schools and know schooling in order to think about 'belonging' in these spaces?

Schools, in their existing form, can be imagined as institutionalised, individualised, risk environments, primarily concerned with the shaping and distribution of life chances, life choices, life courses (Montero and Kelly 2016; Pike and Kelly 2014)—would that it were other…

Drawing on Ian Hunter's (1994) genealogy of mass compulsory schooling in *Rethinking the school*, and Nikolas Rose's (1999) *Powers of freedom*, schools can be imagined as governable spaces that have been made 'real' for an array of purposes and, always, in less than 'ideal' circumstances. Government is an activity that requires human experience to be subdivided, so to speak, by time and space. Government occurs across different 'time zones'. In schools, these 'zones' include the school day, week, term, year and out-of-school-hours. And in different 'spaces of government' such as the classroom, the staff room, the canteen, the playground. These 'time zones' and 'spaces of government' are not natural phenomena. They have to be thought about and brought into being, made real, as times and spaces appropriate to particular tasks of government. In this way, schools—with their timetables that break the day up into governable bits and the curriculum that divides knowledge up into knowable bits—have been built as governable spaces in which the making up of desirable behaviours and attitudes in young people might be readily accomplished (Montero and Kelly 2016, Pike and Kelly 2014).

Yet, as a consequence of this capacity for the abstracted ordering and regulation of the activities of large populations across time and space, social relations grounded in co-presence become re-embedded—as Anthony Giddens (1990) might say.

Classrooms, playgrounds, neighbourhoods and peer groups emerge as settings fundamentally structured by relations of co-presence. Such contexts and relations of co-presence become highly consequential in the identity work of young people in the labour (physical, mental and emotional) required to belong, to not belong. As Phillip Wexler (1992, p. 11) argued in his critical social-psychological account of *Becoming somebody*, these settings and relations constitute intense 'interactional economies' in which the identity work of 'becoming somebody' is the product of 'interactional labour' in concrete local settings. Such 'work' is very much 'action in the public sphere', and it is work in which belonging might be more or less important. It may even be, as a number of contributors suggest, 'dirty' work. For example, in their chapter, Christine Halse, Rosalyn Black and Claire Charles present an account of their research with young Australians in primary and secondary schools. The research they report on was concerned with exploring the ways in which young people imagined, and talked about, the thoroughly ambiguous figures of the 'refugee', the 'asylum seeker'. Halse and her colleagues consider the ways in which young people in schools, like all of us at different times and places, are caught up in a more or less intense, and differently consequential, 'politics of belonging' (Yuval-Davis 2006, 2011) that often involves the 'dirty work of boundary making' (Crowley 1999). The point I would make here is that a 'political economy of youth' would situate this 'dirty work' in wider entanglements of relations, practices, interests, and, possibly, class, gender and ethnic positions. These interests, positions and consequences—the politics of belonging—are fluid and uncertain, but can cohere around particular positions under particular circumstances. In the work Halse et al. discuss, this is at a time of heightened concerns about the figures of the 'refugee', is the 'asylum seeker', the 'stranger'.

Which brings me to my final line of flight and the idea that the work of belonging is work that also, always, excludes. Belonging, reflexively, works to include, and to exclude, not always in the same ways, or with the same consequences. But there are always those who belong, and as a consequence of those people being made to belong, being able to belong, others will not, others cannot. Again, this point has been picked up in a number of chapters and commentaries here, where it is acknowledged that the 'idea', and the 'practice' of belonging makes little sense without a reference to its Other.

This 'politics of belonging', the often 'dirty work' of boundary making and marking, the ambiguous, but often explicit dimensions of finding yourself—as an individual or as a member of a group—included or excluded, on the right side, or the other side of a wall (existing, yet to be built, metaphorical) are all things experienced by persons in particular spaces and settings. However, they are also always experiences that are shaped by the lines of force that give shape to a political economy of youth. My sense is that we can analyse these lines of force, and the assemblages that cohere around and along them, in different ways if we move to a more ambiguous, a more ambivalent sense of belonging, of what it means, of what and who and how it excludes, of what and who and how it includes.

Conclusion

What should education and studies of young people do with 'belonging'? How might 'belonging' become a part of a political economy of youth that is, at various times, interested in the ways in which young people make a life, but also with the relationships, practices, even 'structures', that shape the living of young people's lives that might, in the living of these lives, be obscured, strange, even alien, to these same young people.

How do we trace the patterns of belonging in ways that, for example, might extend far beyond the moment of a drama class or a gym mat, beyond the ways in which young people act, behave and think as they are required, in response to the directions of their teacher? Or in response to the questions put to them by youth studies/educational researchers? The point here is not that a focus on 'belonging' is flawed or wrong (headed). But, rather, what are the theoretical, methodological and empirical limits and possibilities we encounter in the mobilisation of these concepts?

How is it that we have become who we are when we concern ourselves with young people and belonging, and how might we move the 'boundaries of belonging'?

Note

1. From 'Est-il donc important de penser? (entretien avec D. Eribon)', first published in *Libération* (no. 15, 30–31 May 1981), then Foucault, Michel (1994b) *Dits et écrits*, vol. IV. Paris: Gallimard.

References

Bauman, Z. (1989). *Modernity and the holocaust*. Cambridge: Polity Press.

Bauman, Z. (1991). *Modernity and ambivalence*. Cambridge: Polity Press.

Côté, J. E. (2014). Towards a new political economy of youth. *Journal of Youth Studies, 17*(4), 527–543.

Côté, J. E. (2016). A new political economy of youth reprised: Rejoinder to France and Threadgold. *Journal of Youth Studies, 19*(6), 852–868.

Crowley, J. (1999). The politics of belonging: Some theoretical consideration. In A. Geddes & A. Favell (Eds.), *The politics of belonging: Migrants and minorities in contemporary Europe* (pp. 15–41). Aldershot: Ashgate.

Foucault, M. (1978). *The history of sexuality: Volume 1 an introduction*. London: Penguin.

Foucault, M. (1985). *The use of pleasure*. New York: Pantheon.

Foucault, M. (1986). *The care of the self*. New York: Pantheon.

Foucault, M. (1991). Governmentality. In G. Burchell, C. Gordon, & P. Miller (Eds.), *The Foucault effect: Studies in governmental rationality* (pp. 87–104). Hemel Hempstead: Harvester Wheatsheaf.

Foucault, M. (2000). On the genealogy of ethics: An overview of work in progress. In P. Rabinow (Ed.), *Michel Foucault ethics, subjectivity and truth* (pp. 253–280). London: Penguin.

France, A., & Threadgold, S. (2016). Youth and political economy: Towards a Bourdieusian approach. *Journal of Youth Studies, 19*(5), 612–628.

Furlong, A. (Ed.). (2017). *Routledge handbook of youth and young adulthood.* Abingdon: Routledge.

Giddens, A. (1990). *The consequences of modernity.* Stanford, CA: Stanford University Press.

Hall, S., & Jefferson, T. (Eds.). (1976). *Resistance through rituals.* London: Hutchinson.

Hebdige, D. (1979). *Subculture: The meaning of style.* London: Methuen.

Hunter, I. (1994). *Rethinking the school.* New York: St. Martins Press.

Kelly, P. (2011a). An untimely future for youth studies? *Youth Studies Australia, 30*(3), 47–53.

Kelly, P. (2011b). *Breath* and the truths of youth at-risk: Allegory and the social scientific imagination. *Journal of Youth Studies, 14*(4), 431–447.

Kelly, P. (2013). *The self as enterprise: Foucault and the "spirit" of 21st century capitalism.* Aldershot: Ashgate/Gower.

Kelly, P., & Pike, J. (Eds.). (2017). *Neo-liberalism and austerity: The moral economies of young people's health and well-being.* London: Palgrave.

Lanchester, J. (2015). The robots are coming. *London Review of Books, 37*(5). Retrieved March 29, 2015, from http://www.lrb.co.uk/v37/n05/john-lanchester/the-robots-are-coming.

McRobbie, A. (1978). Working-class girls and the culture of femininity. In Women's Studies Group (Ed.), *Women take issue* (pp. 96–108). London: Hutchinson.

McRobbie, A. (1980). Settling accounts with subcultures. A feminist critique. *Screen Education, 34*, 37–49.

McRobbie, A. (1982). Jackie: An ideology of adolescent femininity. In B. Waites, T. Bennett, & G. Martin (Eds.), *Popular culture: Past and present* (pp. 263–283). London: Open University Press.

McRobbie, A., & Nava, M. (Eds.). (1984). *Gender and generation.* Basingstoke: Macmillan.

Montero, K., & Kelly, P. (2016). *Young people and the aesthetics of health promotion: Beyond reason, rationality and risk.* London: Routledge.

Pike, J., & Kelly, P. (2014). *The moral geographies of children, young people and food: Beyond Jamie's School dinners.* London: Palgrave.

Rabinow, P. (2009). Foucault's untimely struggle: Toward a form of spirituality. *Theory, Culture & Society, 26*(6), 25–44.

Rifkin, J. (2015). *The third industrial revolution: How lateral power is transforming energy, the economy, and the world.* Retrieved March 29, 2015, from http://thethirdindustrialrevolution.com/.

Rose, N. (1999). *Powers of freedom: Reframing political thought.* Cambridge: Cambridge University Press.

Sukarieh, M., & Tannock, S. (2016). On the political economy of youth: A comment. *Journal of Youth Studies, 19*(9), 1281–1289.

Walker, J. (1988). *Louts and legends.* Sydney: Allen & Unwin.

Walkerdine, V. (1997). *Daddy's girl: Young girls and popular culture.* Basingstoke: Macmillan Press.

Wexler, P. (1992). *Becoming somebody.* London: The Falmer Press.

White, R. (Ed.). (1993). *Youth subcultures: Theory, history and the Australian experience.* Hobart: National Clearing House for Youth Studies.

Willis, P. (1977). *Learning to labour.* London: Saxon House.

Yuval-Davis, N. (2006). Belonging and the politics of belonging. *Patterns of Prejudice, 40*(3), 197–214.

Yuval-Davis, N. (2011). *The politics of belonging: Intersectional contestations.* London: Sage.

Index[1]

---

[1] Note: Page number followed by 'n' refers to notes.

© The Author(s) 2018
C. Halse (ed.), *Interrogating Belonging for Young People in Schools*,
https://doi.org/10.1007/978-3-319-75217-4

335

Printed by Printforce, the Netherlands